Australian Liberals and the Moral Middle Class
From Alfred Deakin to John Howard

When the Liberal Party of Australia was formed in 1945, it drew on political traditions which had been central to Australian politics since Federation. This book, by award-winning author and leading Australian political scientist, Judith Brett, is an exciting new political and social history of that tradition. It offers a rich and complex analysis of the shifting relationship between the experiences of the middle class and the Australian Liberal Party and its predecessors. It begins with Alfred Deakin facing the organised working class in parliament and ends with John Howard, electorally triumphant but alienated from key sections of middle class opinion. It challenges many settled assumptions about the Liberals, and about Australia's twentieth-century political history, and is destined to become the definitive account of the Liberal Party and its political forebears.

Judith Brett is the author of the highly acclaimed *Robert Menzies' Forgotten People*, winner of the Arthur Phillips award for Australian Studies, the Douglas Stewart award for non-fiction and the Ernest Scott prize. Formerly the editor of *Meanjin*, she has been teaching politics at La Trobe University since 1989.

Australian Liberals and the Moral Middle Class

From Alfred Deakin to John Howard

JUDITH BRETT

CAMBRIDGE UNIVERSITY PRESS
Cambridge, New York, Melbourne, Madrid, Cape Town,
Singapore, São Paulo, Delhi, Mexico City

Cambridge University Press
The Edinburgh Building, Cambridge CB2 8RU, UK

Published in the United States of America by Cambridge University Press, New York

www.cambridge.org
Information on this title: www.cambridge.org/9780521536349

© Judith Brett 2003

This publication is in copyright. Subject to statutory exception
and to the provisions of relevant collective licensing agreements,
no reproduction of any part may take place without the written
permission of Cambridge University Press.

First published 2003

A catalogue record for this publication is available from the British Library

Library of Congress Cataloguing in Publication Data

    Brett, Judith, 1949–.
    Australian Liberals and the moral middle class:
    from Alfred Deakin to John Howard
    Bibliography.
    Includes index.
    ISBN 0 521 53634 0.
    1. Liberal Party of Australia – History. 2. Middle class –
    Australia – Political activity. 3. Australia – Politics
    and government – 20th century. I. Title.
    324.29405

ISBN 978-0-521-53634-9 Paperback

Cambridge University Press has no responsibility for the persistence or
accuracy of URLs for external or third-party internet websites referred to in
this publication, and does not guarantee that any content on such websites is,
or will remain, accurate or appropriate. Information regarding prices, travel
timetables, and other factual information given in this work is correct at
the time of first printing but Cambridge University Press does not guarantee
the accuracy of such information thereafter.

In memory of my grandparents, Harry and Matilda Brett and Harry and Elsie Williams, none of whom ever voted Labor, and for their grandchildren, most of whom do.

Contents

Preface	*page*	ix
1 Australian Liberals		1
Names		1
The Moral Middle Class		7
2 Organisation and the Meaning of Fusion		13
Labor's Challenge		13
The Meaning of Fusion		20
The Liberals' Organisational Handicap		27
3 Protestants		35
Class, Religion and the Australian Party System		35
Fusion Again		40
Loyalty and World War I		44
Sectional Grievances		52
4 Good Citizens and Public Order		57
Service		57
Meetings		64
Order and Anarchy		69
Prime Minister Bruce		77
5 Honest Finance		86
War Bonds		86
Bonds of Honour		94
One Small Honest Man		100
The Menace of Inflation		108
The United Australia Party		112

6 From Menzies' Forgotten People to the Whitlam Generation — 116
Robert Menzies and the Formation of the Liberal Party — 116
Homes for Everyone — 120
Crown and Race — 125
The Decline of Protestantism — 128
From Duties to Rights — 132
Keynesianism, Affluence and the Expansion of Credit — 135
The New Middle Class — 139
Whitlam — 144

7 Fraser — 148
The Dismissal — 148
Shame Fraser Shame! — 152
Fraser in Government — 157

8 Neo-liberalism — 166
Economic Rationalism and the New Public Management — 168
From Citizens to Consumers — 172
From Independence to Choice — 176
John Hewson and the 1993 Election — 179

9 John Howard, Race and Nation — 183
For All of Us — 183
Pauline Hanson — 191
Asian Immigration and Multiculturalism — 194
Indigenous Politics and the Limits of Liberalism — 196
Claiming the Australian Legend — 202
Border Control — 206

Conclusion — 213

Notes — 218
Bibliography — 239
Index — 252

Preface

Midway through the twentieth century the Liberal Party published a little booklet called 'We Believe'. Comprising seventeen short paragraphs it was a creed for Liberal Party believers. Item 3 read 'We believe in the Individual. We stand positively for the free man, his initiative, individuality, and acceptance of responsibility'. In 1954 the party was less than a decade old, but its catechism of beliefs looked back to the formation of explicitly non-labour parties in the first decade of the century, and beyond to the nineteenth-century British liberalism the settlers brought with them to the new land of opportunity beneath the southern skies. It also looked forward, to the uncertain postwar future, confident that, whatever lay ahead, the party's fundamental beliefs would be sufficient guide.

The Liberal Party of Australia was formed in 1945, and although this marked a new beginning, a re-organisation after the low point of the 1943 federal election, it was also the continuation of a political tradition which has been central to Australian politics since Federation. This book is about that tradition. It begins with Alfred Deakin in the first decades of the century, and it concludes with John Winston Howard at the century's end. It is not a detailed history of the various party organisations, their periodic collapses and reformations; nor is it a history of these parties' fluctuating electoral success; nor of the various governments they have provided, though it will touch on such matters. Rather it is a history of the tradition of political thinking carried by these parties, and it takes as its primary material the words of those who subscribed to that tradition: the speeches of the party leaders, party policy statements and statements of philosophy, and material produced at elections to persuade voters to support the party. It seeks to understand the symbolic structure of that tradition: how the various beliefs and values hang together; how the contradictions among them are dealt with; the capacity of the tradition to respond to the challenges thrown up by other political traditions and ways of thinking; and the shifting relationship between the core values and beliefs and the lived experience and self-understandings of its supporters.

Statements such as 'We believe in the Individual' can be found right through the century, presented as enduring commitments, truths which never change, solid foundations on which to build a program of political action. But while the words may very well be the same, much in their meaning has changed. What was understood by the term 'individual' in 1910 is not the same as is understood at the century's end, after five decades of peace and postwar affluence and the rise of the identity-based social movements. A commitment to the individual has never been a sufficient basis for a political philosophy; also needed are ways of binding those individuals together into a political community. In 'We believe' the commitment to the individual came third, after expressions of belief in 'the Crown as the enduring embodiment of our national unity' and 'Australia, her courage, her capacity, her future, and her national sovereignty'. Today the relationship between the individual, the state and the social whole is thought about quite differently: the commitment to the Crown's capacity to embody national unity has not endured; statements about Australia's courage and capacities are challenged by the knowledge of the racism of Australia's history; postwar immigration has created a diverse society with fewer shared cultural norms; globalisation is changing the possibilities of national sovereignty.

Political conflict is in part a conflict over definitions, over how particular events, situations, and institutions are represented and the larger frameworks of meaning in which these are located. This struggle over meaning goes on at all levels of the political process: in the Cabinet and committees of the government, in the meetings and memoranda of the public service, whenever a politician addresses the public, in the media as people put forward differing interpretations and arguments, in the pressure and lobby groups as they decide how best to advance their case, and in the hearts and minds of people as they try to locate themselves and their interests in the ever-shifting political world. Political parties are key protagonists in this struggle over meaning, bringing order out of the chaos of competing issues, values and interests.

This book is about the stories Australia's Liberal Party, in its various manifestations since 1910, has told about the political world, in particular the stories it has told about itself and about its chief political enemy, the Australian Labor Party (ALP). In Australia's essentially two-party system, each party's story always involves a construction of the opposing party, and of why it would be foolish for the Australian people to entrust it with power. There is an interplay of virtue and vice in these constructions: the virtues the parties ascribe to themselves and the vices they see in their opponent. This is a particularly appropriate way to approach the Liberal Party which has always regarded the values it espouses as the basis of its political identity. As Robert Menzies said in his 1949 policy speech:

'We believe that politics is a high and real conflict of principles'. I explored this high and real conflict of interest in my earlier book, *Robert Menzies' Forgotten People*. This book is a sequel. It goes back to Deakin, Bruce and Lyons to explore the origins of Menzies' mid-century construction of the political world, and forward to Fraser and Howard to see what became of it. There are very few books about the Liberal Party, and even fewer ideas. The book the party commissioned for the Centenary of Federation, *Liberalism and the Australian Federation*, while containing some useful essays, fails to present a coherent and plausible account of the party's historical role. Yet without such an account, our understanding of the past hundred years of Australia's history is severely diminished. Labor has such histories. This is an attempt to present one for the other side of Australia's politics, with the century as its frame, in the belief that the deep patterns of politics reveal themselves best over longish stretches of time.

This book has taken a long time to write. The Australian Research Council gave me a generous grant for teaching relief at the very beginning when I needed space to think the project through. I would like to thank those of my colleagues at La Trobe whose unshakable commitments to teaching and research through difficult times have helped me sustain the effort for a long-haul project such as this; also colleagues in the Combined Departments of History at University College Dublin who made me welcome during my two-year stay. Various people read sections or all of the manuscript and I am grateful to them: Boris Schedvin, Stuart Macintyre, Janet McCalman, John Hirst, Bill Schwarz, Graeme Smith and the anonymous reviewers. At key points in my argument I have been helped immeasurably by the detailed research contained in PhD theses. Such research is the foundation on which later scholarship depends. I would also like to thank Humphrey McQueen who lent me his file on the debate in the 1950s on the introduction of hire purchase to Australia, and Susan Lever for her generous hospitality on my many trips to Canberra.

1
Australian Liberals

Names

What are we to call the political tradition which is the subject of this book? Liberal, conservative, anti-labour, non-labour? This is a fraught question, and there is no easy answer. The question is one that has exercised the party itself as it has re-formed throughout the century. In contrast to the Australian Labor Party (ALP) which has had a continuous organisation since 1901 and a coherent national structure from shortly after, the Liberals have re-formed four times: at Fusion in 1909 when Alfred Deakin's Victorian based Liberals and George Reid's New South Wales based free traders-turned-conservative and anti-socialist came together to form the first united non-labour party; in 1916 when Billy Hughes and other pro-conscriptionists left the Labor government to join with the Opposition and form the Nationalist government with a Nationalist Party quickly following; in 1931 in the depth of the depression when the Nationalists remade themselves as the United Australia Party with Joe Lyons as leader; and in 1944 when the Liberal Party was formed, finally stabilising non-labour's party organisation. Is it liberalism or conservatism that holds this party tradition together? Or, as the term 'non-labour' suggests, is it the opposition to labour which provides the strongest glue?

John Howard has argued that the Liberal Party is the trustee of both the classical liberal and conservative traditions;[1] that it combines a liberal economic policy and a conservative social policy.[2] Under his leadership this has translated into support for market-based or neoliberal economic policies combined with support for families and traditional narratives of Australia's national achievements. Menzies at the time of the new party's formation, however, was keen to stress its commitment to a forward-looking liberalism and to scotch suspicions that it was a reactionary party. And Deakin would never have countenanced the description 'conservative', regarding it as the name for those who defended unwarranted and entrenched privilege. On the other hand, the interwar Prime Ministers

Joseph Lyons and Stanley Melbourne Bruce, facing what they saw as urgent threats to Australia's fundamental institutions and values, were easier with the term. In 1930 Hancock wrote, 'if a politician claims he is *liberal*, his audience will understand that he is by nature *conservative*'.³

Despite this common usage, it is misleading to compare Australian Liberals with the British Conservatives. British Conservatism has deep historical roots in the landed gentry and deferential traditions of rural life, in the service to the Crown of the professional army and navy, and in the established church, as well as a well-developed intellectual tradition sceptical of the excesses of the modern faith in progress. None of this, except the loyalty to the monarchy, pertained in Australia where the defence of privilege has always been simply that. Particularly in the nineteenth century, the wealthy who filled the colonial upper houses had no hallowed traditions to sanctify their wealth; for most it was simply a matter of early arrival and a bit of luck. So-called Australian Conservatives generally shared many Liberal beliefs, such as support for manhood suffrage and no property qualifications for members of the lower house. They also agreed that a young country needed a strong and active state and supported an open society in which people should have an equal opportunity to get ahead. As one observer wrote in 1876: 'the old fashioned terms Liberal and Conservative were … quite unsuited to our young middle class community, where we have no privileged classes, no ancient institutions demanding reform'.⁴ In these circumstances, conservatism became identified with a relatively unreflective support for the way things are, as expressed in the oft-repeated slogan 'If it ain't broke, don't fix it'. In the new world of Australia, to be called a conservative has more often been an accusation than a self-description, and the name Conservative Party has never been chosen. At the 1944 conference to discuss the formation of a new non-labour party, Menzies argued that non-labour 'had been put into the position of appearing to resist political and economic progress' and so had adopted the role 'of the man who says "No"'. Thus it was easy for it to be branded as reactionary. But, he argued, 'there is no room in Australia for a party of reaction. There is no useful place for a party of negation'.⁵

The argument that Australian non-labour draws extensively from British conservatism fails to acknowledge the creativity and distinctiveness of Australian Liberals. It reads the opposition between the British Labour and Conservative Parties back on to the Australian party system and sees Australian Liberals as reproducing in their own political life the dependence on Britain they are seen to perpetuate for Australia as a whole. To see Australian non-labour as derivative is a familiar part of the left's armoury, but it is wrong in crucial ways and depends for its plausibility on a lack of knowledge of British political history. When the British Conservatives still faced the Liberals as their chief political opponent and vice versa, Australian Liberals were already facing Labor in parliament as a potential party of government. In Britain the Labour Party made no electoral impact until 1906, and operated as an appendage of the Liberal Party until after World War I. By contrast, Australian Labor's electoral power was already apparent in colonial elections in the 1890s and was confirmed in the first Federal Parliament. By 1910 Labor had formed a majority national government. Australian Liberals thus had to develop arguments and strategies to combat Labor on their own, and while they drew on the resources of British political thought, contemporary British political experience was of little use. The strategies Australian Liberals developed were distinctive, shaped in response to the demands of a new, relatively open society, to Australian Labor's organisational innovativeness, and to the early alliance that developed between Labor and Australia's Catholics. The distinctive Australianness of Australia's Liberals has been largely unacknowledged and their political creativity overlooked by previous political historians.

Non-labour's federal party names have oscillated between those which refer to the nation as a whole (the Nationalists, the United Australia Party) and those which refer to a distinctive political tradition (the Liberal Party). This was in part the result of the continuing strength of the state-based political parties which clung stubbornly to their various distinctive names as part of their autonomy within a federation. The federal level of the organisation hence needed to stress its national reach. But it also reveals an uneasiness about the purposes of parties and party organisation which runs deep in the Liberal tradition. When political parties first began to form in the eighteenth century, their legitimacy was dubious. The unitary representation of the body politic in the person of the sovereign was being replaced by a system in which parts competed to govern on behalf of the whole. But how could the part lay claim to represent the whole? Wouldn't the part always be a part – a faction, a vested interest, a class, a clique? There is a paradox at the heart of parliamentary government in which a divisive, adversarial, system produces a government which, for a time at least, governs in the name of all. We can call this the paradox of party government.

The great eighteenth-century parliamentarian, Edmund Burke, produced a solution to this paradox which profoundly influenced Liberal thinking about parties. In 'Thoughts on the present discontents' he famously defined party as 'a body of men united in promoting by their joint endeavour the national interest upon some particular principle on which they are all agreed'.[6] Burke was concerned to distinguish parties as legitimate groupings of men within the parliament, both from the discredited jockeying for personal favour and advancement of the court and from the parish pump politics of local pressure groups with no sense of responsibility to the wider nation. For Burke the distinguishing characteristics of legitimate parties were that the basis of their unity was shared principle, and that they were committed to the national interest.

The extension of the franchise greatly raised the stakes of party conflict over claims to represent the whole, by introducing into the parliament voices and demands which were never heard in Burke's eighteenth-century chamber of gentlemen, in particular the rough voices of working men who challenged the governing elites' assumptions about the national interest with notions of class and inevitable conflicts of interest within the nation. The working class came into parliament unabashedly talking the language of the part, of labour. The Australian Labor Party wore its partisanship on its sleeve and rallied people to it with appeals to their class-based self-interest. The Liberals opposed with claims to represent not the part but the whole, not class interest but the national interest. The following examples from Australian Liberals span the century and represent perhaps the most enduring of its arguments with Labor:

> This is not a policy aimed at the interests of any class. It is a national policy addressing itself in a practical manner to the practical needs of the people of Australia today. (Alfred Deakin launching Commonwealth Liberal Party, Melbourne Town Hall, 25 May 1909)[7]

> The League is strictly National; it takes in all classes of women, rich and poor. It does not matter what their employment or what their denomination is, if they love Australia, and want to work for her prosperity and for freedom of thought and action, the League will welcome them as members. (Description of the Australian Women's National League inside the front cover of its monthly journal *The Woman* during the 1930s)

> The Liberal Party has never been a party of privilege or sectional interests or narrow prejudice ... Liberalism has focussed on national interests rather than sectional interests. (John Howard, 1996 Menzies Lecture)[8]

But there has always been a danger in claiming the unifying, national and consensual for oneself: it is that the party will lose its distinctiveness and become seen simply as a party of the status quo rather than a party offering a positive vision of the nation's future. In projecting all the conflict and divisiveness on to one's opponents, one may also be projecting all the energy and vision. In a new country committed to building a new future this was likely to prove an electoral liability. This danger was seen early by Liberal politicians. At the interstate conference of Liberal Organisations in 1911 where possible names for a Federal organisation were being discussed, Mr Grogan of New South Wales argued that 'If you cut out the word "Liberal" you cut out our existence all together. We must hold fast to that name to meet the name "Labour" with its ideals of government with the name "Liberal" with its ideals of government'.[9]

At the 1910 election, the first election fought with Labor as the chief political opponent, non-labour called itself the Liberal Party for the purposes of the federal election. And in 1944 when non-labour was regrouping to face a popular Labor Party in government the name Liberal was again chosen, to stress the distinctiveness of the political values animating the new party. 'We took the name Liberal because we were determined to be a progressive party, willing to make experiments, in no sense reactionary, but believing in the individual, his rights, and his enterprise, and rejecting the Socialist panacea'.[10] When called on to state the basis of its political identity, the main non-labour party has explicitly drawn on liberalism and this book follows its lead, calling the people who supported Australia's major non-labour party Liberals, as they have most often called themselves.

The anxiety that they would be seen as reactive to the clear goals and identity of Labor has, however, continued to haunt the Liberals. *The Liberal*, the monthly paper of the Commonwealth Liberal Party, insisted on referring to the ALP as 'the Illiberal Party'. 'A party which legislates in the interests of a class is neither a true Labour Party nor a true Liberal Party. It is the Illiberal Party and it masquerades in the name of Labour.'[11] But the name never caught on. While the negative 'non-labour' continues to be used to describe the Liberal Party and its predecessors, the Labor Party is never described as 'non-Liberal'. In 1956 the Federal President, W. H. Anderson, asked whether, despite holding office since 1949, the Liberal Party really had seized the initiative in Australian politics: 'The great challenge to the Liberal Party is to establish ourselves in the public mind as *the* national party ... to establish a permanent Liberal tradition'. The danger facing the party in the mid-1950s, as he saw it, was that the recent electoral success was the result of both Menzies' skill as a leader and the failure of the Socialists, rather than of widespread support for Liberalism's positive values.[12] There was always the fear that perhaps Labor lost elections rather than the Coalition won them, and there was continuing aggrieved puzzlement that Labor continued to command such loyalty from its supporters, despite its internal divisions and poor leadership.[13]

One of the puzzles of Australian political history is the contrast between the organisational weakness and discontinuity of the Liberals and the strength and durability of their electoral support. Despite its four reformations, until 1983 when Labor began its record-breaking term of office, Liberals had governed for fifty-six of the seventy-three years since Federation. Organisational weakness and discontinuity had clearly not prevented them from winning elections, most of the time with strong majorities. One of the arguments of the book is that it is liberalism, albeit broadly understood and with many internal contradictions, that has provided much of the basis of the party's enduring electoral appeal, that people have voted for the party not just because it has represented their interests but because it has accorded with what they believed. This is an argument which flies in the face of the class-based model which has dominated interpretations of the Australian party system.[14] According to this model, the parties are to be understood primarily as agents or representatives of economic, class or sectional interests, and the explanation for their varying strengths is to be sought in the strengths of the class interests they represent. On this view, as L. F. Crisp wrote: 'the Liberal and the Country Parties are first and foremost the instruments of the owners and controllers of private, productive and commercial capital, urban and rural'.[15]

To see non-labour primarily in terms of its supporting economic interests has considerable explanatory power. It works well for the Country Party (now National), formed to represent the economic interests of small farmers. And it explains many features of the Liberal Party and its predecessors: for example, their financial dependence on business and capital; the characteristic occupations of their members of parliament; the interests to which they are most responsive when in government. Sections of the Liberal Party's support have clearly been happy to accept an essentially class-based reading of their opposition to Labor. I do not want to argue that such a reading has nothing to offer. It does not, however, explain the strength and durability of the Liberals' electoral appeal. The economic interests of the majority of the people are simply insufficiently coincidental with those of big business or financial capital. To win in lower house elections Liberals have had to do more than appeal to people's economic interests, they have also needed to appeal to their values, and to succeed in telling them stories about politics in which they recognised themselves.

Liberal leaders and party propagandists have regularly disputed a description of their beliefs and actions primarily in terms of class-based economic or sectional interests, and have steadfastly insisted that they are based on principles and values, and on a sincere commitment to the good of the nation. That the class-based Labor Party sees its opponents in its own image is simply further evidence to Liberals of Labor's fallen moral state; because it is motivated by selfish, sectional class interests, Labor is unable to recognise that its opponents march to the beat of a quite different drum. As *The Liberal* complained in 1912:

> It [the Labor Party] treats the profession by other parties that their politics are inspired by more generous aims, and that what they seek ... is the good of the State as a whole ... as mere hypocrisy, or at best as obtuse and ineffective good intentions.[16]

The Moral Middle Class

Closely related to the deafness of political historians to the Liberals' persistent self-descriptions is the problem of how to understand the Australian middle class which provides the historic core of its electoral support. Australian historians have on the whole been uneasy with the middle class.[17] When the middle class does appear in Australian historians' narratives, it has more often been one of the many factors frustrating Labor's political goals than as an agent in its right. The middle class is not generally the major villain, for after all most of the middle class are ordinary people; but they enter from stage right as the dupes of larger interests who mobilise their fears and anxieties to block the progress of Labor's various reforms. How they understand their political actions is only just beginning to be investigated, for example in Marilyn Lake's work on middle-class feminist activists in the 1920s and 1930s,[18] and in Janet McCalman's *Journeyings: The Biography of a Middle-Class Generation*, the only full-scale study of the Australian middle class in its own terms.[19]

One of the reasons for Australian historians' difficulty with the middle class is the failure to resolve whether the term middle class is an analytical one, part of a schema of social classification Marxist or otherwise, or whether it is a term of self-description. Of course it is and can be both, but it is important in using it to know which is which. In this book I am interested in the middle class as a term people use to describe themselves and in understanding what it says to them about the basis of their political identifications. This is a continuation of the exploration in the first part of my book *Robert Menzies' Forgotten People*, in which I argued that the middle class is best understood as a projected moral community whose members are identified by their possession of particular moral qualities, political values and social skills.[20] Here is how Menzies described the middle class in his 1942 radio broadcast 'The Forgotten People':

> But if we are to talk of classes, then the time has come to say something of the forgotten class – The Middle Class – those people who are constantly in danger of being ground between the upper and nether millstones of the false class war; the middle class who, properly regarded, represent the backbone of this country.

'The backbone of this country' is the key phrase here, making the moral qualities of the individual the basis of the nation's identity. However, Menzies does give the middle class a social location: 'salary earners, shopkeepers, skilled artisans, professional men and women, farmers, and so on. They are, in the political and economic sense, the middle class'. And he locates these people firmly in homes they own themselves.

How many Australians did these descriptions fit in the first half of the century? The information on income and occupational distribution for Australia before World War II is scanty, but in 1928 the Commonwealth Statistician's Office produced a table which combined occupation and income to divide the Australian population into four categories. A little more than half the population, including all the occupational categories Menzies listed, were in the top three, and 46 per cent in the bottom category, labelled 'unskilled, unemployed and poor'.[21] The cut-off income for the last category was £400 per annum, just the level of annual income which Stuart Macintyre has estimated was the dividing line in the 1920s between those able to enjoy a comfortable life and those living in the more straitened and precarious circumstances of the inner suburbs.[22] The figures on home ownership present a similar divide. During the nineteenth century Australian rates of owner occupation were high by world standards – between 30 and 40 per cent – and included many working men.[23] For the first half of the century the national home ownership rate was about 52 per cent, although there was a significant variation between country and metropolitan areas.[24] These figures are rough, but they do point to approximately half of the population bearing one or other of the unmistakable markers of middle-class socio-economic status – non-manual occupation and home ownership. For Australians living in the comfortable middle class suburbs these went together, but there were plenty of working class home owners to whom Liberals could pitch their appeal. The electoral record shows that after the Labor Party split in 1916, the combined Liberal and Country Party vote was for the most part comfortably over the 50 per cent mark.[25] Here it appears is confirmation of the class-based model: the socio-economic attributes of more than 50 per cent of the population easily explains non-labour's electoral ascendancy. Why look further?

This answer may well suffice if all one is interested in is the socio-economic basis of electoral behaviour and party identification, but it is of little use if one is investigating the political self-understandings of people who continually deny that their political commitments are the result of their socio-economic status or class position. The heart of the understanding by the middle class of its political and social role is its moral worth. In its own self-understanding, the middle class is not a class in the Marxist sense at all; that is, it is not a class defined by its members' economic role, but a class of individuals whose membership of the middle class is the result of their individual attributes and moral qualities. Crucial to the political logic of the way the term operates is that people possess these virtues as individuals rather than as members of a class. The middle class is thus not a class opposed to or in conflict with some other class, as in the Marxist schema, or in the labour movement's and left historians' model of class conflict; rather it is a mode of social classification opposed to the very idea of economically based social identity and economically based social classification.[26]

It is individuals, not collectivities like classes, which bear moral qualities; and a class defined by its members' moral qualities rather than by their social and economic role is open to anyone who tries hard enough to walk the narrow and respectable path of virtue. Of course these desirable moral, political and social qualities are more likely to be found in some social and economic locations than others, and to be associated with some particular life experiences, but they may turn up in the humblest of cottages. From this perspective it is who you are not what work you do that matters, and to judge a person by their manner of earning their living is deeply offensive. Listen to Liberal MP Jennifer Cashmore describe her parents:

> My parents were firmly in support of Menzies and there was much criticism of Ben Chifley, but I never remember Ben Chifley being derided because he was an engine driver. It really galls me when I hear people deride Liberals because they are allegedly rich farmers. To my mind it's not what a person does it's what a person is that counts.[27]

Contemporary Liberals would describe the moral basis of their political beliefs in terms of values. This is an anachronistic weakening of the moral thinking inherent in their political tradition. It was on virtues rather than values that Australian Liberalism was based. The term values implies attitudes and opinions held by the self and detachable from it; 'virtues' are constitutive of the self, part of its character or very nature, and immune from the relativising morality inherent in the concept of value. As the historian of Victorian social thinking, Gertrude Himmelfarb, wrote: 'One cannot say of virtues, as one can of values, that anyone's virtues are as good as anyone else's, or that anyone has a right to his own virtues'.[28] Where values could be changed or abandoned, virtues abided. It was their virtues not their values which underpinned the prewar middle class's claim to political power, as well as the fierceness of their opposition to political organisations and individuals they saw as bearers of political vice. To describe the moral foundation of Liberals' political commitments as values fails to capture the strength of these underlying moral commitments and their connection with people's sense of identity, as well as the moral urgency of political conflict for many of its protagonists.

Janet McCalman has described the middle class as an aristocracy of virtue. Middle-class children were brought up to be good, responsible, virtuous members of society, able to put aside the interests of the self for the greater good. Their social privilege carried social responsibilities: 'from those to whom much is given much will be expected'. It was the middle class which thus had both the capacity and the responsibility for social leadership.[29] This self-ascribed moral virtue was the basis of the middle class's view of itself as the proper holder of political power. The Services and Citizens Party, one of the shortlived groups which sprang up between the electoral collapse of the United Australia Party (UAP) in 1943 and the formation of the Liberal Party a year or so later, described the middle class as 'that cross section of the community which is fundamentally sound and fit to govern'.[30] The argument that the virtues of the middle class particularly fitted it for a political role had its roots deep in the nineteenth century's understanding of the relationship between character and good government. For the middle class it was its members' proven capacity in the arts of self government which fitted them for the tasks of governing others,[31] and it was self-evident that it was their soundness of character which was the basis for the soundness of the State. As John Stuart Mill explained in *Considerations on Representative Government*:

> If we ask ourselves on what causes and conditions good government in all its senses, from the humblest to the most exalted, depends, we find that the principal of them, the one which transcends all others, is the qualities of the human beings composing the society over which the government is exercised.[32]

For Mill, 'the problem of character is the determining issue of the question of government' and the provision of the circumstances in which character could develop became for new liberals the prime moral purpose of the state.³³ For colonial liberals it was self-evident that the New World offered opportunities for moral and physical development beyond anything available to the stunted inhabitants of industrial Britain.

This view of the middle class as bearers of virtue has a long history. It draws on Protestantism's commitment to the morally independent individual and its hostility to Roman Catholicism, on the struggle of the middle class for political representation against an idle and unaccountable aristocracy, and on the economic experience of the small entrepreneur who depended on disciplined hard work and self-restraint to survive. Its formative opposites were the vices of the aristocracy above and the working class below. In Australia at the dawn of the twentieth century the aristocracy had been well and truly left behind in the nineteenth century and the Old World. But the middle class hold on political virtue was facing a new challenge from the organised working class determined to replace with its own kind in parliament the educated middle-class men who had hitherto looked after its interests. The middle class rallied round a conception of citizenship which combined civic duty with a personal ethic of selfless service to challenge the moral basis of Labor's claim to be a party of government.

Facing the organised working class in parliament Australian Liberals were on the defensive and they knew it. Their claim to be the progressive force in Australian politics was contested by a party which had moved from a minor irritant to a party of government in less than two decades. Their rather loose organisational form, based on an uneasy combination of commitment to the individual's independence of judgement and faith in the exceptional man to lead these independent individuals, was challenged by Labor's disciplined organisation; and their passionate but rather hazy belief in the possibility of a unified national interest was forced into bitter conflictual modes as they confronted an opponent who constructed the national interest in ways they regarded as illegitimate. Whether they liked it or not, Australian Liberals were forced into a form of class politics by a party determined to construct political conflict along class lines. This does not mean, however, that they were forced into a simple conflict of material class interests. Rather they were forced into a conflict between class-based world views: between the middle class's construction of the political world as based on individuals' principles and virtues and the working class's construction of it as based on classes' competing material interests.

This book reconstructs the Australian party system from the Liberal perspective. The first five chapters cover the relationship between Australian Liberals and the moral middle class as it was experienced and maintained for the first fifty years of the twentieth century. The remaining four describe the way social change has undermined the foundational values of Australian Liberalism. Much has been written about the impact of the social changes of the second half of the century on the traditional thinking and social base of the Labor Party. Australian Liberals have also experienced an undermining of their foundational social formations. The transformation of the prewar middle class, while less visible than the decline of the maual working class, is a story that needs to be told to understand the state of Australian Liberals at the beginning of the twenty-first century.

2
Organisation and the Meaning of Fusion

Labor's Challenge

For a political party based on commitment to independent individuals and their freedom of expression and action, political organisation is a constant problem. On the one hand it is necessary for effective political action; on the other, too much organisation risks destroying the very individuality and independence which the political action is attempting to defend. This was the Liberals' organisational dilemma as they confronted a tightly disciplined Labor Party attempting, as they saw it, to turn parliamentary politics into an arena for class warfare. One student of political parties has argued that modern political parties are distinguished far less by their program or the class of their membership than by the nature of their organisations.[1] In considering the way Australian Liberals have distinguished themselves from Labor, organisational issues have been crucial as they have tried to balance their distinctive organisational values with their recurring organisational weakness. They did not achieve organisational stability until the formation of the Liberal Party in 1945.

When Menzies was working to persuade Australian Liberals that a new and better organised party was needed, he had two competing models of party organisation in mind. The first was the Australian Labor Party. Menzies was keen that the new party should emulate some aspects of the ALP, in particular its strong branch structure and organisational coherence.

> The Labour [sic] Party, though its policy and administration are repugnant to us, is not something which exists under a different name and with a different set up in each State. It is the Australian Labour Party. Its membership depends upon common considerations all over the Continent. It has State branches and local branches ... The results of this unanimity and cohesion on the organisational side has been that the disunities which exist in Labour circles are usually below the surface, are not advertised ... When I consider

the structure of the Australian Labour Party and realise that the political warfare to which we have been committed for a long time past by no choice of our own is a struggle between political armies, I am driven to wonder how we could ever imagine that a concerted force under one command and with one staff is to be defeated by divided units under separate commands and with no general staff.[2]

But those aspects of the ALP which subordinated the parliamentary membership to the party organisation, such as the pledge, or the policy-making powers of state and federal conferences, were anathema. Here Menzies' model was the eighteenth- and nineteenth-century British parliamentary parties.

Menzies' library, which is on display in the University of Melbourne's Baillieu Library, contains a well-thumbed paperback selection of the writings of Edmund Burke. The selection includes Burke's 1779 'Thoughts on the present discontent' in which Burke defends the existence of political parties within the parliament. As was Menzies' habit, sections are marked in pencil, including the already discussed famous definition of party as 'a body of men united in promoting by their joint endeavour the national interest upon some particular principle on which they are all agreed'. The selection also includes Burke's address to the electors of Bristol in which he argues that the parliamentarian should not be bound by the views of those who elected him, but should be free to form his own judgements on matters that come before the parliament. It too has been carefully read. A scrap of newspaper used as a bookmark still lies at this point in Menzies' *Selected Burke*. It carries an advertisement for a band concert in the Adelaide Town Hall on 18 December 1942, and so allows us to date at least one occasion when Menzies turned to Burke for guidance. December 1942 was the lowest point in Menzies' political career, only months after he had resigned from the Prime Ministership, when he was contemplating his future and in particular whether he would stay in parliament. He decided he would and shortly after Menzies was involved in talks about the formation of the new non-labour party.

Burke was writing in England before the right to vote had begun to be extended, when electors for seats in the House of Commons were so few that there was little need for electoral organisation. Burke was championing the parliament as the seat of government on the one side against manipulation from the court, and on the other, as in his conflict with the Electors of Bristol, against pressures from locally-based groups who had no consideration for the broader national interest. Burke's parties were groupings of men within the parliament centred on powerful individuals who competed to command a sufficient majority within the Commons to form a ministry. Burke argued that such groupings were honourable associations when based on principles, in contrast to factions which were concerned with self-promotion and self-interest. In Burke's parliament majorities were inherently unstable, dependent on the skills and standing of the 'great men' who led them, and they lacked any permanent connection with an organisation outside parliament. After the 1832 Reform Act, when election to the House of Commons became a much more complicated business, the parties in parliament needed extra-parliamentary organisations to canvass for votes among the new electors. As the right to vote was extended, so such organisations became more necessary. But the extra-parliamentary organisation always remained subordinate to the parliamentary wing. Its purpose was to work for the election of the parliamentary candidates, and to leave the sorting out of matters of government to the parliament.

Mass-based parties began to develop in Britain after the 1867 Reform Act and the way was led by the British Liberal Party. In Australia electorates were small, so despite the far more democratic franchise, parties required less electoral organisation. In the colonial parliaments they were generally described as factions, and, as most members of parliament prided themselves on their 'independence', they had few overt connections with external political organisations. Factions could form around shared values, interests or experience, ranging from something as simple as friendship to a shared commitment to a particular region. In this, skilful parliamentary leaders were crucial, men who were able to weave the intricate webs of reciprocal obligation and shared interest necessary to ensure parliamentary majorities. Heads of other factions were generally included in ministries, the gift of ministerial office being one of a leader's crucial bargaining chips.[3] As in Britain's eighteenth-century parliamentary parties, it was the action in the parliament that was crucial, and political stability depended on the capacities of the parliamentary leaders.

In Britain the development of modern party organisations was precipitated by the extension of the franchise and clearly linked in people's minds with the coming of democracy. In Australia men had had the vote for nearly half a century before modern parties developed, and in the minds of Australian Liberals it was the class-based Labor Party that was the agent of change. In 1911 after the election of a federal Labor government, the Conference of Liberal Leagues of Australia described their situation thus:

> the Liberals had no class organisation to rest upon ... The individual Liberal representative stood on his own merits and appealed to Liberal thought in his electorate. These days are no more. The onslaught of a highly organised

party representing a section of the people bound together by ties of solidarity and loyalty has routed in many States the old men and the old methods.⁴

In the mid-1940s the task before the Australian Liberals was to produce an effective national organisation without sacrificing key elements of their organisational tradition, in particular the primacy of parliament and the freedom of its proceedings from the interference of any outside body. This meant that the parliamentary body remained responsible for policy (the party organisation could advise but never direct); and that the leader of the parliamentary party had the power to choose his ministry as well as having ultimate responsibility for policy. In both these features the Liberal Party's organisation was different from Labor's in which a body outside the parliament, the party conference, determined the party's policy, and where the leader's powers were constrained by both the parliamentary party and the extra-parliamentary organisations. The Labor Party organisation was the product of very different historical experiences from the organisational traditions on which the Australian Liberals drew. Where Liberals were heirs to parties whose essential function was to select the men who would form the government, Labor members had quite different priorities. As an early Labor parliamentarian put it: 'We have not come into this House to support governments or oppositions. We have come into this House to make and unmake social conditions.'⁵

Labour parties first appeared in Australia in the early 1890s. The trade union movement had grown rapidly during the late 1880s, particularly among itinerant rural workers such as shearers. In the early 1890s, in deteriorating economic conditions, it embarked on a series of strikes. Employers who had been willing to negotiate when times were good dug in their heels as world commodity prices fell. The colonial governments sided with the employers, using troops to protect non-union labour and the courts to prosecute the union leaders. The union movement decided that working men should use their vote to elect their own kind to parliament and committed itself to the development of a political wing.

Labour electoral organisations developed separately in all the colonies during the 1890s, with different degrees of success. In Queensland the brutal response of the government to the 1891 shearers' strike strengthened an already emerging conviction that the way ahead was through parliamentary representation rather than industrial action. In New South Wales labour made a spectacular entry in to parliamentary politics, winning 35 seats out of 140 at the 1891 election. It had captured 21.8 per cent of the vote and held the balance of power.⁶ Here was evidence that the working class could be successfully persuaded to shift its vote, but electoral support was not a sufficient basis for success in the parliament. Also needed were organisational strategies within the parliament.

Labour knew from its industrial experience that unity was strength, that with the resources of wealth and the law stacked against it, organisation and loyalty were all.[7] The speed with which its thirty-five representatives were reduced to seventeen by clever political opponents convinced labour that effective parliamentary action demanded similar principles to effective industrial action. The men elected were young, not well-educated, and only two had any previous parliamentary experience.[8] To their and everyone else's surprise they found themselves holding the balance of power, but their strategy of support in return for concessions would only work if their vote was rock-solid. One member, George Black, successfully moved that all Labor members sign a pledge 'to vote in the House as a majority of the Party sitting in Caucus has determined', but only nineteen signed.[9] Not only were Labor members divided over the tariff, with those who had promised their constituents to support protection worrying that a caucus vote would pledge them to free trade, but some felt it would undermine the relationship between the parliamentary representative and his electors.[10] Labor's opponents were quick to sense their disunity and to capitalise on it, forcing a vote on a fiscal issue which caused most of the protectionists to leave the Caucus. Supporters outside parliament were appalled that Labor's parliamentary strength should collapse so quickly.

The underlying question here was, who was the Labor member in parliament to represent? His constituents, or the labour movement? The answer of the electoral leagues was clear. He was there as a representative of the labour movement, and should act in parliament in the way that maximised the chances of legislation being passed which furthered the movement's aims. At the next election, nothing would be left to chance. A special conference of the Labor Electoral League determined that in the upcoming election candidates supported by the League would sign the pledge before they were elected, pledging themselves to vote with the majority on matters affecting the Labor Party, the fate of the ministry, or on matters which further entrenched the privileges of the privileged classes. This was weaker than initially proposed, but opposition to the pledge was considerable.[11] Even so it was too much for many. Joseph Cook, the leader of the parliamentary party, refused to sign, arguing not only that 'the pledge destroyed the representative character of a member and abrogated the electoral privileges of a constituency', but that it drove away from the League staunch supporters 'who were now called traitors because they refused to be slaves'.[12]

The outcome of the dispute was both the institution of the pledge and the strengthening of the organisational control of the Central Executive of the League over the local leagues; henceforth these could only select candidates willing to sign the pledge. Those who signed the pledge were called 'solidarities'. At the 1894 election, fifteen 'solidarities' were returned, and twelve men stood as independent labour candidates. Three of these soon joined the 'solidarities' and the others either faded away or joined the non-labour parties. Joseph Cook, who had led the Labor parliamentarians' opposition to the pledge, was given the portfolio of Postmaster-General by Premier George Reid, thus confirming the suspicion that independence of judgement was easily put to the service of self-interest. As historian V. G. Childe put it, the outcome of the 1894 election 'proved that the pledge was essential in order to maintain the individuality and identity of a Labour party in a middle-class Assembly. Without it the Labour [sic] Party would have gone the way of the "workingmen" candidates in the past and become mere hangers-on of one or other of the older parties'.[13] For Labor, organisation was a survival strategy.

By the time of the first federal parliament, the pledge was an accepted part of Labor organisation, as was the determination of party policy by the party's extra-parliamentary wing. The new federal parliamentarians included twenty-four members elected by state-based Labor organisations, sixteen in the House of Representatives where they held the balance of power between the Protectionists and the Free Traders, and eight in the Senate. They moved quickly to organise themselves and give Labor a national structure to match that of the new Commonwealth. At a meeting on 8 May 1901 the Federal Parliamentary Labor Party was inaugurated, and a committee established to consider its constitution and rules. The party would assert its independence by sitting on the cross benches. It would meet together weekly, and on all matters except the tariff members would vote as determined by majority vote in the party meeting, or Caucus as it became known.[14] Their strategy was support in return for concessions, though it was considerably weakened by allowing a free vote on trade policy, the divisive issue of the day.

It is perhaps hard for contemporary Australians, with their long experience of stable two-party politics, to grasp the role that parliament played in the first decade of the twentieth century in the making and unmaking of governments. For us it is elections which determine governments and a federal government has not been defeated on the floor of the house since 1941. The first decade of the twentieth century was very different. Although elections were held at about three-yearly intervals, there were seven changes of government: no ministry governed for a full term, and five governments lasted less than twelve months. Ministries were formed from coalitions held together by temporary deals and the brokering skills of the parliamentary leaders who had honed them in the shifting alliances of the colonial parliaments. It was not until 1910 that any party achieved a clear electoral majority, allowing it to govern without the conditional support of another parliamentary grouping. And the party that did it was the Labor Party which was also the first to run a full term. This was not how Australian Liberals envisaged the political future when they welcomed the new Federation and they couldn't really understand how it had happened.

Labor's vote rose dramatically in the first decade after Federation. It polled 19.24 per cent of the valid vote in 1901, 30.95 per cent in 1903, 36.64 per cent in 1906, and 49.97 per cent in the watershed election of 1910.[15] Labor's rapid gathering of electoral momentum led to a three-way contest in the federal parliament – Labor, Liberal Protectionist, and Free Trade/anti-socialist. The Liberal Protectionists led by Victorian Alfred Deakin were the middle party, but Deakin knew that given the structure of the Westminster system three must eventually become two. 'What kind of a game of cricket … could they play if they had three elevens instead of two, with one side playing sometimes with one side, sometimes with the other, and sometimes for itself?' Deakin asked in 1904. Constitutional government, he went on, required that the three parties should be resolved into two: 'Someone must give way for the benefit of the State, and which was to give way was the delicate issue'.[16] Deakin's hope was that it would be Labor, accepting that its future was in alliance with the Liberals. The new Labor Party shared many of the same legislative goals as the Liberal Protectionists. In the past they had fought together for the same things against the same enemies. This seemed the natural alliance.

But the resolution of the three elevens into two did not follow the contours of the natural alliance as it appeared in 1904. Instead in 1909 Deakin led his Liberal Protectionists into an alliance with their erstwhile bitter enemies, the conservative anti-socialists, to form the Fusion Party, a short-lived interregnum party in which the various parliamentary groupings standing together under the banner of non-labour tried to sort out the longer term meaning of their alliance. Why did Deakin do this? Why did the two-party division not follow what appeared to be the natural line of cleavage, with the radicalism of Labor and the Protectionists uniting them against the conservatives?[17] Was it, as has generally been argued, that the Free Traders and the Protectionists recognised their shared class allegiances; or were there other reasons?

The Meaning of Fusion

The generally accepted interpretation of Fusion is that the two middle-class parties, Deakin's Liberals and George Reid's anti-socialists, buried their differences in 1909 to unite and face the common enemy, the working-class-based Labor Party, thus laying the class basis of the Australian party system. This, indeed, was the spin George Reid put on the new party: 'The question that separates us is whether the development of Australia along lines of private enterprise is the right method of development, or whether industrial development of Australia along the lines of state control is proper'.[18] Historians have generally gone along with Reid's interpretation.[19] The problem with this interpretation is that it buries the intentions of Deakin's Liberals beneath the bulk of George Reid's triumphalism. If Reid was only too happy to see the new lines of division in terms of class, Deakin's Liberals most decidedly were not. It was, in fact, to protect Australia's national politics from what they regarded as the improper distortions of class-based, sectional politics that they took the step they did, and they continued to refuse descriptions of themselves and their motivations in terms of class interests. Sir William Lyne, who vehemently opposed Fusion had, however, predicted the triumph of Reid's view: 'The Party is being thrown into a boiling cauldron. We are asked to join men who will hoodwink us in the carrying out of our programme. If the party does the thing contemplated we will go down, down, down as conservatives.'[20] This interpretation suited Labor which ruthlessly exploited its old ally's about-face. Opposing Hume Cook in the inner Melbourne suburb of Brunswick at the 1910 election, Labor candidate Frank Anstey said he would not have become a candidate were it not for Fusion: the Liberals had now shown their true colours as conservatives. Cook, who had previously held the seat by a comfortable majority, was easily defeated after a bitter and rowdy campaign.[21] We must, however, be wary of reading this later trajectory of political development back on to the events that set it in motion, or accepting at face value either Labor's representation of its opponents or Reid's of his new allies.

If we approach Fusion from the side of Deakin's Liberals the lines of division do not look quite so obvious. For the first decade Deakin's Liberals were far closer to Labor than to Reid's Free Traders turned anti-socialist. The Liberal Protectionists' base was in Victoria where manufacturing industries had developed to absorb the gold-rush immigrants and the Victorian colonial governments had used tariffs to protect the fledgling industries, provide employment and put a floor under wages. Colonial liberalism posited a harmony of interests between the fair-minded employer and the honest artisan, working together for the progress of the new country.²² This was more plausible in the open society of the new colony where many employers were self made and had themselves begun as workers than it would have been amidst the smokestacks and entrenched class divisions of the Old World. Liberals saw themselves as the friends of the working class in an alliance against the interests of the squatters and merchants.²³ They had fought together during the 1860s and 1870s against the plutocratic interests in the undemocratic Legislative Council; and during the 1890s the new Labor Party was reliant on the Liberals to give legislative form to its various demands. At the high point of legislative achievement in the interests of the working class, the Factory Act of 1896, middle-class activists had taken the lead. The National Anti-Sweating League, formed in 1895 to agitate for reform, was a product of the middle-class Protestant conscience, its slogan, 'the union of all who love in the service of all who suffer'.²⁴ After Fusion, when Deakin's Liberals faced the Labor Party as an enemy, they went over and over the debts Labor owed to them for all they had achieved together: 'Every man and woman who is today enjoying good wages and shorter hours may thank Liberals for the boon'.²⁵

The alliance continued at the federal level when the Deakin-led governments of 1905–08 won the Labor Party over to the 'new protection' in which manufacturers were granted a protective tariff only if they provided fair and reasonable wages and working conditions for their employees. Linking the provision of tariffs to state support for higher wages committed Labor to protection and killed free trade as an issue until the 1970s. This was the period in which the assumptions of what has become known as 'the Australian Settlement' (sometimes called the 'Deakinite Settlement') were hammered out, with the state playing an active role in the development of the Australian economy and mediating conflicts between producer groups. Protection, arbitration and state paternalism won the day, to join White Australia and reliance on Imperial protection as the five settled assumptions of twentieth-century Australian political life.²⁶

For the first decade Labor seemed the Liberals' natural ally and Reid's Free Traders its chief opponent. As it became clear that free trade was a lost cause, George Reid, the parliamentary leader of the Free Traders, started to reposition the Free Traders as a more broadly based conservative party committed to private enterprise and opposed to the extension of the state's role in the economy. Opposition to government involvement with trade slid easily into opposition to government involvement with other economic activities. Anti-socialist organisations had been gathering strength, particularly in Victoria, since the Kyabram movement of 1902, with its call for reduction in government expenditure and anxiety about mounting state government debt. This movement had spread beyond its origins in a small town in northern Victoria to establish the National Citizens' Reform League.[27] In the main its members were farmers and rural businessmen, alarmed at the disruption to state finances caused by Federation and by the increase in government activity. Robert Menzies' father, James, who owned a general store in Jeparit and was Dimboola Shire president, was a member of the League's first Executive in 1902.[28] Reid, ever on the look out for opportunities to make life uncomfortable for the Victorian protectionists, attempted to build such organisations into a wider anti-socialist alliance.[29]

At the 1906 election when Reid first introduced the anti-socialist theme, Deakin was scathing. Reid's anti-socialism, he said, was nothing but a 'necklace of negatives – no tariff reform, no relief for injured industries, no assistance to rural producers, no protection in any circumstances for anybody'.[30] It might just as well be called 'anti-liberalism' in that it 'justifies its existence, not by proposing its own solutions to problems, but by politically blocking all proposals of a progressive character and putting the brakes on those it cannot block'.[31] Rather than relying on 'bogey breeding epithets' like socialism to condemn a proposal, Deakin committed his Liberals to the 'plain, practical, sympathetic scrutiny … of every proposal on its own merits apart from names or systems'. He refused 'to be a party to any condemnation of "socialism" as an "ism"'.[32] In his 1906 policy speech, when defining the differences among the three parties, it is Reid's party which he sees as the Liberals main opponent: 'While the Liberal Party stands for all classes of the community, the anti-Liberal Party stands for the privileged classes in defence of vested interests'.[33]

In contrast with his scorn for the anti-socialists, Deakin looked favourably on Labor:

> [it] is not distinguished from the Liberal Party in regard to its main principle of seeking social justice. It is not divided from the Liberals when we trust the people with the powers of self-government. It is not divided from us in our use of the powers of the State; but it has associated with it those who … go faster and further than we do, though the bulk of the party blends with our own.[34]

In 1906 Deakin saw his political enemy as the anti-socialists and his natural allies as the Labor Party. When the instability of the three-party contest in both parliament and the elections forced the resolution of three into two, why did it not follow the contours of the alliance as it appeared in 1906, with the radicalism of Labor and the Liberal Protectionists uniting them against the conservatives?[35] The crucial question here is why did the middle party jump the way it did? How did those closest to Labor, the Deakinite Liberals, understand their differences from Labor, and what was it about the Labor Party that made an alliance with Reid's conservative anti-socialists seem to them the lesser of two evils? The answer, in brief, as Deakin put it when launching the Commonwealth Liberal Party, was that to join with Labor, the Liberals would have to put aside the only thing which makes them men – their judgement and conscience.[36] The insurmountable barrier between the Deakinite Liberals and the Labor Party was not Labor's policies nor its attitude to the state, but the nature of the Labor Party's organisation: the demands which it made on its members to subordinate their own views and judgements to the collective will of the party and the implications this had for parliamentary government.

The problems Labor's organisation posed for the Liberals were particularly apparent in Labor's hostility to alliances. Labor simply refused to play the parliamentary game as it had hitherto been played, and parliamentary leaders found themselves stalled at every turn as they tried to put together workable majorities in the usual way. A frustrated Deakin wrote to Reid in 1904 that where the best option would be for all the parties to unite, so far as principles would allow for the business of carrying on the government, the Labor Party maintains such a control as 'to make it hopeless to approach its members upon any terms of equality, even under the present exceptional circumstances'.[37] The face-to-face, man-to-man way of building majorities from coalitions of like-minded individuals was no more and there is a sense here of personal rebuff and loss as well as of political frustration. If they couldn't approach members on terms of equality, how could they approach them? As Labor became more confident that the electoral tide was running its way, its rejection of alliances hardened. Alliances with the Liberals were of course the main target, as Labor Senator Findley of Victoria made clear at the 1908 Federal Conference:

> We have been fighting against the 'good-as-Labour' men, and any alliance formed inevitably helps that tattered brigade of shreds and patches to a new lease of life, which is spent insidiously trying to undermine Labour [sic] organisation ... Labour is an uncompromising organisation which came into operation because the workers were dissatisfied with the Liberals. Should they then compromise with those people whose very inactivity and insincerity led to the birth of the Labour Party?[38]

The discussions among Deakin's Liberals prior to Fusion were preoccupied with questions of Labor's organisation, not its policy. Senator Trenwith, a former Victorian Labor leader, spoke of his aggravation at

Labor's attitude to 'those who, in all but name, were members of that Party'. Sir Thomas Ewing added that candidates were being nominated in all Liberal constituencies and Liberals must therefore 'give place to other men or sign the party's pledge'. But if they were to do that, said another, they would be giving over their judgment to 'a secret and irresponsible Caucus'.[39] This was the sticking point. No matter how close they were to Labor's goals, no matter how much they shared its legislative aims, these men would not sign a pledge to follow the party platform; these men would not allow their actions in parliament to be determined by the deliberations of an outside body; these men would not give up the very attributes which made them men – their judgement and their conscience. This was the issue on which men like Joseph Cook had left the New South Wales Labor League in the 1890s, and it continued to be a defining difference for Liberals.

The concern with organisational differences was signalled in the platform of the Commonwealth Liberal Party. Drawn up by Deakin and a group of mostly Melbourne-based businessmen with manufacturing interests, the platform had eight planks. The first five asserted commitment to protection, to Federation combined with a recognition of Australia's Imperial responsibilities, electoral reform, to White Australia and to the development of Australia's defence capacities. These shared many similarities with Labor's platform, but the platform needed to differentiate itself clearly from Labor without alienating Liberal sympathisers in the process. Planks six and seven which dealt with financial matters – an equitable scheme for the Commonwealth taking over state debts, and a commitment to economy and efficiency in the Commonwealth public service – were directed against perceptions that Labor did not have the financial experience to deal with matters of public finance, and would be tempted into irresponsible extravagance. It was the last plank, number 8, that caused the most difficulty. Its original wording was 'To oppose the collective ownership by the National Government of the means of production, distribution and exchange'. Such wording, prefiguring Reid's interpretation of the meaning of the party divide, would indeed support a class-based interpretation of the line along which the Liberals split from Labor. But this wording was dropped and replaced with wording that shifted attention from Labor's policy to its method of organisation: 'to oppose the caucus methods and extreme aims of the Labor Party'. Deakin then suggested an amendment: 'To assert the principle that all representatives of the people should be directly and solely responsible to the people for their votes and actions'.[40]

In his speech to launch the new Commonwealth Liberal Party, the organisation which was to keep an independent base for Deakinite liberalism inside the new Fusion Party, Deakin spent some time explaining the significance of this eighth plank in drawing the distinction between Liberals and the Labor Party. The Labor Party, he said, 'has political methods which carry obligations and restrictions to extremes existing nowhere outside its own ranks'. Binding decisions were made by small committees acting 'outside the light of day', and from their 'misguided sense of loyalty tens of thousands of voters put themselves in the clutches of a machine'. Raising the spectre of oriental despotism, he claimed that you 'can live in Russia or Turkey and say more than you can as a member of the Australian Labour (sic) Party'. Although party loyalty was very desirable, 'when it comes to penalising your best friend if in the exercise of his honest judgement he dares to speak his mind about a candidate or to differ from the dictates of a caucus machine, then you are laying the axe to the root of Parliamentary democracy'.

Deakin spoke directly to 'my Labour fellow country men':

> whose party loyalty I admire, whose political energy I commend, and, as regards some of them, whose hard lot at times all sympathise with, what I ask of them is not to adopt the programme I am now supporting, or any other, expect so much of it as commends itself to their reason and judgement … Let them never subject either a voter or his representative to the indignity of putting aside the only thing which makes him a man – his judgement and his conscience.[41]

During the 1910 election Deakin continued to stress Labor's organisational deficiencies:

> In the Labour [sic] opposition there is not a natural and real, but a narrow, mechanical, compulsory uniformity enforced by constant knee drill in caucus. They stand all alike and all apart. The Liberal Party stands in a broad unity, but individualities remain. Independence is asserted for ourselves and our constituents … in this government and in this party no man has parted with his individual judgement or his responsibility to his constituents. We enjoy a proud sense of free union as free men in a free party.[42]

In his use of the term 'caucus' Deakin was not referring as in today's usage to the meeting of the party in parliament, but to the whole party organisation. The term originated in eighteenth century America to refer to closed meetings of men who settled electoral affairs before the vote actually took place, and it quickly developed connotations of secrecy, manipulation, corruption and the illegitimate intent to undermine people's democratic rights.[43] When the British Liberal Party developed coordinated organisation of the electorate in the wake of the 1867 Reform Act, the term crossed the Atlantic with all its ambivalence about the consequences of popular democracy for the role of reason and sound judgement in political life. Tory Prime Minister Disraeli flung the term at the new Liberal electoral organisation, and it at once passed into everyday usage as their descriptive epithet. British Liberals reluctantly accepted the term, hoping its negative connotations would fade as people accepted the benefits of an electorally-based party organisation.[44] The term continued to do descriptive service, but it never entirely lost the negative associations of its origins, which were intensified by its frequent couplings with the image of the machine, another ambivalently regarded agent of modernisation, which presented human organisation as impersonal and relentless. In Australia where political organisation was pioneered by Labor, Liberals continued to use it as a term of accusation. *The Woman*, the monthly magazine of the powerful Australian Women's National League, mocked the Labor government which resulted from the Fusion Party's surprise defeat in the 1910 election, 'The Caucus whip has been cracked over the Labor Socialist Government's head'.[45] A Liberal leaflet for the 1914 Senate election exhorted electors:

> **WORKERS!** Ask your Candidate if he has **Signed the Pledge**. IF SO, do not waste his time and yours asking his opinions, for **he has agreed** to vote on all questions affecting the Labour Platform, **not as he thinks right,** not as you send him to Parliament to vote for you, but as the **Caucus tells him**.[46]

In such attacks, 'caucus' has a sinister ring. Its deliberations are secret, 'outside the light of day', its powers are exaggerated, and its motivation never anything other than to exercise control. This meaning is amplified by the standard description of party organisation as a machine. Often this was a dead metaphor, but its metaphoric powers could be reawakened to evoke individualism's deeply felt ambivalence about society's increasingly complex organisations. An advertisement in the *Australian Women's Weekly* for the 1946 election campaign has a worried young couple saying 'We Want to Retain Our Freedom! We *Don't* Want to be COGS in a MACHINE!'[47] Again, the imagery is of individuals subjecting themselves to external control and thereby losing individuality and autonomy and thus life and humanity. Menzies' famous description of Labor's Federal Executive as 'the thirty-six faceless men' exploits the same image of secret and unaccountable decision-makers undermining democracy.

In contrast to Labor's tightly disciplined 'machine', the Commonwealth Liberal Party, Deakin told its inaugural meeting, was 'a free union of free members': 'We do not turn out our citizens as mere duplicates in politics. They remain free. We unite them upon a broad national programme, conserving their independence and political manhood.'⁴⁸ To Liberals the Labor Party's organisational methods robbed party members of their independence, their unique and various identities, and even their masculinity. The line in the sand which the Liberals would not cross in 1909 was Labor's demand that its members subordinate their freedom of judgement to a party organisation and in particular sign the pledge. For Deakin's Liberals, those who had to decide which way to jump, it was their commitment to their independence of judgement which explained their decision. To do otherwise was for them unthinkable. At its basis were deeply held convictions about the role of independence of conscience and judgement in the integrity of the personality. Yes, this was partly about class, in that men and women of means with autonomy in their day-to-day lives were more likely to experience themselves as independent, but it was not just about class and it did not present itself to such people as a matter of class or economic interest. Rather, in today's terms, it was an identity issue. For such people, to join the Labor Party and sign the pledge was to give up one of the things which made them human, their freedom of conscience and independence of judgement, and to compromise their control over their moral integrity and their character, which was for many their self's chief attribute and achievement.

The Liberals' Organisational Handicap

Having come down firmly on the side of individual independence of judgement, Liberals still had to tackle the question of how to build an effective political organisation. As Deakin acknowledged following his attack on Labor's organisational methods: 'Electoral organisation is required by all parties. A committee of selection is quite a reasonable thing. Party loyalty is very desirable.'⁴⁹ *The Liberal*, the monthly magazine of the Victorian-based Commonwealth Liberal Party, is full of frustrated reflections on this dilemma:

> Everyone knows that the success of the Labour [sic] Party is due not to the wisdom and justice of its platform ... but to their absolute unity under their complete organisation. No matter what violent dissension in their branches they invariably present an unbroken front and a unity of action in the interests of their party ... With the Liberals, however, the situation is entirely changed. Their forces, like those of the highland clans of old, melt away at harvest time or when their recruits become weary of continuing their march. Each man of them asserting his own individuality and independence yields only a temporary and conditional allegiance to his chief ... No

coercion is possible. Nothing approaching regimental unity can be maintained for more than a short time.⁵⁰

The belief that the individuality of non-labour's supporters makes them more difficult to organise was still powerful when Menzies addressed 'The Forgotten People' in 1942, describing them as 'not sufficiently lacking in individualism to be organised for what in these days we call "pressure politics"'.⁵¹

The Commonwealth Liberal Party failed to establish an effective political organisation. It never spread beyond Victoria, where it was rivalled by two other non-labour leagues, the conservative People's Party and the Australian Women's National League. It remained very much an amateurish, old-fashioned organisation, based on networks of family and friendship with Alfred Deakin at the centre. Its journal, *The Liberal*, was established, edited and financed by his son-in-law Herbert Brookes, and Deakin's wife Pattie chaired the women's section. The fate of the Commonwealth Liberal Party shows well the problems for a political party which seeks to rely only on voluntary self-recognition of like-mindedness, and eschews both appeals to political interests and hard-headed organisational tactics. On the other hand, the more effective its organisation, the more it risked alienating its supporters by being seen as dictatorial and bureaucratic, the very vices attributed to Labor.

The Liberals in New South Wales were much less squeamish about political organisation. The embodiment of Liberal machine politics was Archdale Parkhill, a short, pugnacious man, who began his long career as a political organiser in 1904 when he was appointed Secretary of the Liberal and Reform Association of New South Wales.⁵² A letter from Joe Carruthers advises the young Parkhill on the tactics for ensuring a successful public meeting: 'get every seat occupied by 7.45 by friends and have the doors lined with friends … tell Howe to have 2 or 3 here and there to lead off the applauding and to put down with cheers every hostile remark. He can well spend a fiver on the meeting.'⁵³ In 1910 Parkhill became secretary of the Federal Liberal League, and was a constant organising presence through the various re-formations of the 1910s and 1920s. Before he left organisational politics to contest a federal seat in 1927, he had directed nineteen federal and state election and referenda campaigns, winning praise for his success against the well-organised New South Wales Labor machine. But the cost of this success as a professional political organiser was to imitate Labor's tactics too closely for some, who accused him of setting up a 'dictatorship' with a coterie of bureaucrats.⁵⁴

Compounding the Liberals' sense of their organisational handicap in the conflict with Labor was their reluctant recognition that Labor's electoral strength was not simply the result of its rigid organisational methods but also of its camaraderie, idealism and sense of common purpose which the Liberals lacked: 'The main strength of the Labour movement in Australia is its spirit of unity created by the common interests of its members in their union ... the feeling of fellowship permeating the Labour ranks, healing differences and closing up its ranks at election time'. Worse still, Labor's strengths were seen as being at the Liberals' expense: 'Some of its ideals, and much of its enthusiasm, have been appropriated in the past years by the Labour movement'.[55] Liberal campaigners had been taken aback by the strength of support for Labor at the 1910 election,[56] and impressed by the energy and youth of its leaders. One worried Liberal wrote to Deakin that 'The youth of labour leaders is one of the most potent causes of that party's success'. The impression was that all the young men were on the government's side.[57]

The tide of political energy seemed to be running Labor's way in the years before the war and Liberals vainly sought for means to invigorate their own supporters. Herbert Brookes established *The Liberal* with the aim of reforging the spirit and ideals of liberalism, but it was more successful in its denunciation of Labor than in projecting a politically persuasive and revitalised liberalism.[58] Meetings of representatives of the different state-based Leagues were held to enable the 'leading spirits' to 'meet and know each other and feel that thrill of esprit de corps that springs from a common and righteous cause'.[59] In 1912 *The Liberal* announced a competition for a party rally song, to be set to some well-known martial air such as 'Men of Harlech'. Such a song would 'add more zest and enthusiasm' and 'create an atmosphere for good Liberal speakers to develop their arguments and to fire their audiences'.[60] Apparently the competition fizzed, as there was no subsequent announcement of a winner of the 2-guinea prize. There was also some attempt to establish club rooms as rallying points for Liberals, equivalent to the role Trades Halls played for the Labor Party.[61]

Labor in its early days displayed all the characteristics of a social movement. It was committed to fundamental social change, it called on people to identify themselves and their political interests in new ways, it unleashed a huge amount of reforming social energy and activity. Liberals could see this, and were frustrated by their inability to tap into similarly strong sources of political energy. It was a lament that recurred whenever Labor seemed to gain the upper hand. After Bruce was defeated in 1929 *The Woman* editorialised:

> We see the Labor party machine ruthlessly but efficiently crushing factions and oppositions and we lament the inadequacy of our own machinery. We imagine that stricter party discipline and greater efficiency of organisation

will restore our party to its pristine glory ... Effective machinery is only the outward and visible sign of the spirit that gives it birth ... Have we no clarion call? Are there no inspiring principles that would give us that exuberant vitality that ensures ultimate victory?[62]

For a brief moment between 1946 and 1949 Liberals again spoke confidently of 'the Liberal movement', but its energy soon dissipated in the paranoia of the Cold War. By 1957 Harold Holt was again voicing the familiar lament: 'We have never experienced the fervour and unquestioning loyalty which Labour [sic] could confidently expect for so many of its better years from a great mass of people'.[63] But in 1957 the Liberals had Menzies, and with such a leader the qualities of the organisation seemed scarcely relevant, although some party officials still worried if the party would be strong enough to survive his departure.[64]

Australian Liberals' ideal solution to resolving the tension between their commitment to independent individuals and the necessity for political organisation is the strong leader who can so inspire and unite his fellow party members that no discipline is necessary, whose political judgement is so acute that policy can be left in his hands without the need for formal votes, whose public personality is so vivid that people easily recognise him as bearing the qualities which fit him for high office. Deakin and Menzies were undoubtedly such leaders, both choosing the moment of their retirement. Announcing the election of Joseph Cook as leader on Deakin's retirement in 1913, *The Liberal* gives a clear account of Liberals' view of the role of the party leader. Whereas a Labor leader needs to be able to do nothing more than 'obey promptly without qualification and without hesitation whatever orders are issued to him', the Liberal leader faces 'a very different task and a much heavier burden':

> Consulting his Party and keeping in close touch with them, he is required to consider and appreciate many more or less conflicting suggestions ... Instead of his course being settled for him beforehand, it is chosen only after he has explored so far as he can all the possibilities of different lines of action.[65]

This view of leadership is still manifest in the power today's Liberal Party leader exercises over party policy. It gives priority to deliberations in the parliament, or at least the parliamentary party, and places its faith in the powers of one individual to rise above the ruck and resolve within himself the competing tendencies and values at play in any issue. Political mechanisms, such as obligatory consultation or binding votes, are eschewed in favour of the exercise of one man's deliberative judgement. This does indeed place a great burden on the individual leader, and the Liberal imagination is much exercised by the great men of history who have been able to rise to such challenges.

The fundamental purpose of the Liberal Party is to provide the right men in government, and the party's organisational traditions are much better suited to the needs of government than those of opposition. Electoral success legitimises the leader, quelling doubts about policy directions and keeping rivalries in check; and the Westminster convention of collective Cabinet responsibility provides the government with coherence. However, if the leader fails to deliver government, support and organisational coherence quickly evaporate, with the party's weak organisational structure leaving it floundering as it seeks to regain direction. Major party reorganisations followed within a few years of the election defeats of 1914, 1929 and 1943. After the election defeat of 1972 none of the party's parliamentarians had any experience of being a member of the Opposition, and senior members were lost without the public service support to which they had become accustomed.[66] Some attempt was made to rework the party's philosophy, the first reworking since 1944, and to involve the party's membership, but the mounting problems of the Whitlam government and the drama of the dismissal soon rendered any need for organisational reform redundant. Back in office after a mere three years in Opposition, the party reverted to its traditional organisational reliance on a strong leader who can win government.

The weaknesses inherent in the party's organisational traditions did not become a serious liability to the party again until the 1980s. The immediate trigger was not the absence of an electorally successful leader but the intrusion of radical ideas into a party hitherto based on consensual commonsense. The lack of an organisational structure to facilitate and resolve policy debate mattered little when the Liberal Party was the natural party of government, relying on a match between its general policy directions and the electorate's commonsense understandings. Appeals to pragmatism and some very generally expressed ideals were then enough to steer the party through the ebbs and flows of public opinion and resolve differences within the party. But by the early 1980s this was no longer the case, and the Liberal Party began to experience what has always been a feature of the ALP – a group of people committed to changing the party's policies on the basis of a set of well-worked out ideas. A revival of neoliberal economic ideas was underway in the western world, attacking the political assumptions of the postwar Keynesian welfare state and winning adherents within the Liberal Party, though not the support of Prime Minister Malcolm Fraser. After defeating Whitlam in 1975, he saw his main task as the restoration of good government and sound financial management after three years of impropriety and extravagance, and had no interest in challenging the settled assumptions of the government's role in the economy. The party's organisational traditions made it all but impossible for the new ideas to be openly debated. Without Fraser's support, even raising them could be taken as a sign of disloyalty. The party used to governing on the basis of pragmatic commonsense had no structures for debating radical or reforming ideas, and no experience with handling ideological differences. Neoliberal converts resorted to semi-clandestine meetings outside both parliament and the party organisation where they could explore policy alternatives with likeminded others from the universities, the media and the new right wing policy think-tanks. John Hyde described the importance of Crossroads, one of a number of such organisations: 'It gave us courage when we needed it because we were challenging the leadership of our own party'.[67]

Fraser's loss of the 1983 election and his immediate resignation cleared the way for neoliberal ideas, but without a leader quickly able to restore the party's electoral fortunes the party floundered, changing leader six times between 1983 and 1996: Andrew Peacock, John Howard, Andrew Peacock again, John Hewson, Alexander Downer and finally John Howard again. Because the development of policy is the ultimate responsibility of the leader, genuine differences over policy within the party cannot be openly debated and resolutions negotiated. What might have been a debate between the advocates of radical new ideas and the supporters of the party's traditional policies was instead fought out in the personal politics of struggles over the leadership, crippling the party's ability to develop coherent and electorally attractive policies. Examples abound throughout the 1980s of policy differences within the party sliding into leadership crises: Howard over immigration in 1988, Hewson over Fightback! and the goods and services tax (GST) at the 1993 election, and Downer in 1994 over the federal privacy legislation when he sacked John Hewson for disloyalty. With so much of the party's electoral credibility riding on perceptions of the leader's 'strength', those with different views are expected to keep quiet in the interests of party unity. When they don't they are accused of disloyalty, of not being good team players, and are likely to find themselves on the back bench.

After John Hewson lost the supposedly unlosable election to Keating in 1993, there were some moves to give more power to the party organisation. Hewson had been an adviser to John Howard when the latter was a frustrated Treasurer in Fraser's government. A relative newcomer to parliament and filled with reforming economic liberal zeal, he produced a comprehensive policy package called Fightback! which proposed to overhaul the Australian taxation system and introduce a consumption tax.

The problem was that, as Howard had done with his 1988 manifesto *Future Directions*, he produced it with no consultation with the extra-parliamentary party organisation and only minimal consultation with his parliamentary colleagues. The party loyally supported him through the election campaign, but when it lost the recriminations were swift and bitter. The media filled with disappointed and angry supporters saying that they had never been consulted on the GST. In the wake of defeat there was a revival of commitment to the policy partnership between the parliamentary and nonparliamentary wings of the party, with some other reforms mooted to strengthen the capacities of the national organisation.[68]

The Liberals' other long-standing organisational problem has been the weakness of the national organisation in a party which gives its state-based divisions virtual autonomy. Again the contrast is with the ALP. Both parties began the twentieth century with strong state-based organisations and weak national structures, but the ALP national organisation had a coherence which the Liberals lacked until the formation of the Liberal Party in 1944. In both the Nationalist Party and the United Australia Party the federal parliamentary parties were supported by a range of loosely coordinated state-based extra-parliamentary organisations. In a party which supported states' rights, the autonomy of the state-based organisations was fiercely guarded. As federal sentiment has faded among Australians, the ALP has strengthened the power of national structures while the Liberal Party has continued with its state-based organisational structure.[69] Organisational innovation in the parties is still led by the ALP with the Liberals slow and reluctant followers. Downer did manage to increase the power of the Federal Executive over the state divisions,[70] but there has been marked reluctance to use the new powers. And since the Liberals regained power in 1996 under John Howard's leadership, the urgency has gone. Once back in office the party's organisational difficulties are resolved in the way the Australian Liberals have always preferred them to be – by a strong leader able to win successive electoral victories.

The social fault-line along which the Liberals split from Labor was not the simple fault line of class interest. For those who had to decide which way to jump, Deakin's Liberals, it was not economic issues which were decisive but the organisational values of the Labor Party and the demands it made on its members to subordinate their independence of judgement to the political processes of the party. Differences of values were as important in the formation of the Australian two-party system as differences of interest.

The rise of the Labor Party challenged the Australian Liberals' organisational capacities and their ability to mobilise political supporters. The stronger and more disciplined the organisation became, the more effectively to fight Labor, the more it risked producing splinter groups which rejected the party machine in favour of non-party politics. And occasional successful moments of mobilisation notwithstanding, the Liberal troops continued to melt away between crises, needing to be rallied anew at each election. Despite Labor's greater organisational strength, however, until the 1980s the Liberals were far more electorally successful than the Labor Party. Between the 1910 and 1983 elections the Liberals held federal office for fifty-four years in comparison with eighteen for Labor. Clearly the Liberals' organisational handicap has not precluded electoral success.

In the early 1950s liberal intellectual and political activist Frederic Eggleston offered an explanation. Contrasting the tradition of the parties which represent vested interests (the ALP and the Country Party) with 'parties who entertain political ideas of the traditional type', he described these latter as residual. Having no single organised vested interest behind them, they become the home of all those smaller, less-organised interests excluded by the parties of vested interest. They band together less out of common material interest than out of desire to stop the more extreme demands of the parties of vested interests and to protect what he rather blandly describes as 'the pattern of Australian life'.[71] Fresh in Eggleston's mind when he wrote this was the Liberal Party's 1949 election victory and before that the defeat of Labor's attempts to nationalise the banks. Notwithstanding the obvious fact that Labor continued to enjoy loyal support, Eggleston pointed to the foundation of Liberal political support in the lived experience of a substantial number of Australians. For the Australian middle class as it entered the 1950s, the Liberal Party represented their commonsense understanding of the world. The Liberals could survive a relatively weak political organisation because its values were already deeply embedded in many people's daily lives and in the self-understandings they brought to their political choices. The next three chapters will discuss the formation of these values and self-understandings in the first half of the twentieth century, in terms of Protestantism, of liberal ideas of civic citizenship and public order, and of middle-class financial practices.

3
Protestants

Class, Religion and the Australian Party System

The great majority of Australian Liberals were Protestants, and, even when they were not, the virtues on which they based their claims to govern were Protestant virtues. Australian Liberals were independent, they were loyal, and they did not pursue group-based sectional claims. Roman Catholics were welcome in their parties, but only if they displayed and adhered to these virtues. But even when Catholics tried their hardest it was difficult for them ever to be entirely free of the suspicions which dogged their religion. When John Cramer won preselection for a winnable Liberal party seat at the 1949 election, he was aware that he 'was something of a freak, as it had seemed in the whole of Australia almost impossible for a Catholic to win preselection for a safe seat in the Liberal Party', as indeed had been the case in the United Australia Party (UAP) and the Nationalists before that. In a preselection marred by terrible sectarian bitterness, he had been asked by one member of the selection committee whether he owed allegiance to the Pope or the King. And after winning the seat he still felt branded. Whenever he entered the room Menzies would remark 'be careful boys, here comes the Papist': 'For some reason I cannot understand it always seemed uppermost in his mind that I was Catholic and therefore in some way different from the others'.[1] To Australian Protestants Catholics were different, and their responses to this difference had a far greater influence on the formation of the Australian party system than has hitherto been recognised.

The affinity between Australian Liberals and Protestantism and between Labor and Roman Catholicism has long been recognised. It was clearly evident in electoral support by the 1910 election[2] and still visible when full-scale voting and public opinion studies began after World War II. In Gallup Poll samples between 1946 and 1954 about 70 per cent of Catholics intended to vote for the ALP, compared with 40 per cent of other denominations.[3]

The religious affiliations of parliamentary representatives present an even starker picture. Until comparatively recently there were very few Catholics among non-labour parliamentarians, and most of these represented country electorates. Catholics have been well-represented among Labor parliamentarians, but they have had to share the party with Protestants and the small number of parliamentarians who gave no religion.[4] The same pattern of alignment is evident in the links between various religious organisations and the main parties, in particular the various Protestant pressure groups which have waxed and waned on the Liberal side around questions of imperial loyalty and the wowser issues of drinking and gambling. This alliance was at its height at the turn of the century when the party system was forming, and the alliance has long been seen as significant in pushing Catholics towards the new labour parties.[5]

Such evidence, however, has not been sufficient to dislodge the dominant class-based explanation of the formation of the party system. The parties' religious alignments have, on the whole, been pulled into line as overlapping cleavages, with both Protestantism and support for Liberal parties seen as expressing an underlying middle-class identification, and Roman Catholicism and support for Labor as expressing working-class identification. These class and religious identifications have then been overlaid by the complementary rival ethnic identifications of British and Irish. The predominant picture of the social base of the Australian party system for its first fifty years has been one of overlapping cleavages, in which class (middle class/working class), religion (Protestant/Roman Catholic) and ethnic (British imperial/Irish nationalist) identifications overlapped and reinforced each other.[6]

Of these two pairs of identification, far more ink has been spent pondering the meaning of Roman Catholic identification with Labor than Protestant identification with the Liberals, and in the main it has been seen as built on a solid foundation of Catholic overrepresentation in the working class. David Kemp, for example, hypothesises that Roman Catholic support for the ALP has mainly been a matter of class rather than religious status.[7] Don Aitkin, who gives a good overview of the standard historiography on the religious basis of the party alignment, sees social structure as the key in which 'on all accounts' Irish settlers were 'disproportionately concentrated in the working class'.[8] Celia Hamilton writes 'that though it is difficult to document, there is a very strong tradition that the Irish settlers tended to be concentrated amongst the landless unskilled labouring classes in the colonies', and she argues that their natural economic interest lay with a working-class party. The crucial development as far as her argument is concerned is that the Catholic hierarchy did not proscribe the new party and so block the expression of this natural class interest.⁹ Alan Gilbert sums up the general view: 'The bulk of the Catholic population was working class'.¹⁰ Only R. N. Spann sounds a note of caution: the Catholics, he writes, 'seem to have been more highly concentrated amongst the poor; at any rate, this was a widely-accepted stereotype'.¹¹

None of these confident assertions that Australian Roman Catholics were predominantly working class is supported by clear statistical evidence, and I have been unable to find any. The one piece of available evidence correlating religion and occupational status in the first half of the twentieth century, the 1933 Commonwealth census, does not show a sufficient over-identification of manual and unskilled occupations with Catholicism to support the interpretation that the massive over-identification of Catholics with Labor is based *primarily* on class interest. This interpretation is given in an article by Oliver MacDonagh in which he argues that, in sharp contrast to the experience of Irish Catholics emigrating to the United States and to Britain who were concentrated in particular areas of major cities and in the lowest paid and most manual occupations, Irish Catholic emigrants to Australia were spread relatively evenly geographically, socially and occupationally.¹² Although many entered as labourers and domestic servants their status rose slowly but surely during the second half of the nineteenth century.¹³ They settled on the land proportionate to their numbers, and there were rich, successful and influential Irish Catholics to be found in considerable numbers at the top of every tree except that of high finance. By the Australian Commonwealth census of 1933, Catholics who at this time were approximately 19 per cent of the total population were slightly underrepresented in the top income group at 15 per cent of male bread winners, and slightly overrepresented in the bottom at 20 per cent and among those with no income, presumably the unemployed, at 22 per cent.¹⁴ There is little here to support the class-based reading of Catholics' support for the Labor Party, except the underrepresentation at the very top where the Liberal powerbrokers were to be found. And the slight overrepresentation at the bottom contrasts starkly with the massive over-representation of Catholics among Labor parliamentarians. Shortly before this census was taken, Catholics made up more than half of Jim Scullin's Labor Cabinet, and for the period 1901 to 1980 made up 36 per cent of Labor parliamentarians.¹⁵

What is going on here? Why have political scientists and historians alike been so ready to push the majority of Catholics into the working class? The mixture of prejudice and myth which surrounds the role of Irish Catholics in Australian history suggests a number of possible explanations, as Spann hints when he refers to stereotypes. Let us begin with the stereotypes.

Perhaps Catholics are simply expected to be poor, or at least no one is very surprised when it is claimed that they are. Or perhaps in a society in which Catholicism was the main marker of minority status, poor Catholics were more visible to observers than the larger, more heterogeneous, non-Catholic poor, perhaps because of the strength of their locality-based family and friendship networks and the visibility of their religious institutions. Catholic doctor, H. Moran, described the position of Catholics in Australia in the early twentieth century as 'a breed apart, firebranded like travelling stock in a strange country so that all might know whence he came'.[16] Catholic churches surrounded by the school and the houses of the religious orders were an imposing presence in Australian suburbs and country towns, easily appearing to outweigh the scattered Protestant buildings.

Residential patterns are important here, and such evidence as exists suggests patterns of residential segregation between Protestants and Catholics which would contribute to the development of community class consciousness, particularly in pre-automobile times when people's social relations were more geographically bounded. Richard Broome's analysis of the religious residential patterns of Sydney in 1900 has shown that Catholics were overrepresented by about 10 per cent in the older inner city suburbs and underrepresented by about 15 per cent in the late Victorian and Edwardian suburbs of garden villas.[17] Spann shows the persistence of these patterns into mid-century, when 40 per cent of all Catholics in Sydney lived within seven inner city municipalities, but argues that this is the result of the cultural and social conservatism of close networks of social relations, economic-based family ties, common schooling and the parish church rather than of continued socio-economic deprivation.[18] Comparable material for Victoria shows some similarities with the Sydney data. Oliver MacDonagh has analysed the Victorian censuses from 1851 to 1891 and he finds a similar pattern in Melbourne to Broome's in Sydney, with Catholics constituting roughly one-third of the oldest inner urban wards and roughly one-sixth in the good eastern suburbs. The greatest concentration of Catholics, however, was found in small, mixed farming rural areas like Kilmore, Warrnambool and Port Fairy where Catholic concentration was of little relevance to ALP politics.[19]

Class consciousness is based on more than occupation, and it may be that mixed occupation, close-knit urban Catholic communities had strong working-class cultural characteristics. The crucial questions are about the relative contributions of simple socio-economic disadvantage versus religious-based community consciousness to the residential patterns and their role in forming and maintaining patterns of party identification. There is, too, abundant evidence that Australian Catholics suffered from lower status than Australian Protestants, particularly in the higher income groups, but this was in good part the result of their religion, rather than of the generally disadvantaged position of Catholics in terms of simple economic stratification.

As well as stereotypes, there is myth. Australian Catholics have themselves been complicit in the class based explanations of their support for Labor, and it is common to hear Labor supporters with Irish names citing their family's working-class Irish origins as the basis of their political commitment. To believe that the majority of Catholics are in the working class justifies not only an Irish Catholic sense of grievance at their minority status, but the pursuit of the remedy for that grievance in a predominantly class-based party. If Catholics were thought to be overwhelmingly working class it helped justify their obvious overreprestantion in a party in which class provided the main language of legitimation. It may well be that the New South Wales Labor Party has played a special role here, with the obvious power of Catholics within the party strengthening the need to project this as the legitimate expression of their class interest rather than the result of an ethnically or religiously based political machine.

Also at work in the hold of the class-based model on the politico-historical imagination has been a reluctance to take religious belief seriously. The preference is to see religion as an aspect of social structure and to ignore the role that religious belief itself may play in motivating political choices. For example Joan Rydon sums up a general view on the link between Protestantism and non-labour thus: 'These parties are seen as respectable and waspish ... As the parties of the status quo and the people who have "arrived", they have reflected the Protestant ascendancy'. The actual nature of Protestant religious belief is seen as having no role to play in explaining Protestants' preference for non-labour; the implication is that if some other religion had been 'ascendant', then it would have been the religion of the respectable people who had 'arrived' and nothing else would be different. Similarly Don Aitkin assures readers that 'it is important not to attach too much *religious* significance to the links between Catholics and the ALP'. There are some notable exceptions to this, for example Patrick O'Farrell's argument that the early Labor movement drew much of its energy from redirected sect type religious impulses, but most historians writing in the secular second half of the twentieth century have preferred to see religion as a somewhat awkward fellow traveller of class interests, rather than an agent in its own right, endowing people's political commitments with moral conviction.[20]

If Catholic alignment with the ALP is not as firmly based on economic class interest as has previously been assumed, what is its explanation? Three answers present themselves. The first keeps with social structure, but argues that it is status rather than class disadvantage from which Catholics suffered and for which they sought remedy in the only available party which challenged the prevailing social structure. They took their status grievances into the party based on class grievance, and for the reasons canvassed above were not too careful about keeping the two distinct. The second is that there was a sympathy between Catholic religious teaching and values and aspects of Labor thinking, in particular its greater commitment to ameliorating the harsh social consequences of market-based capitalism; that Catholic religious thinking drew Catholics to Labor, particularly in the wake of the Papal Encyclical *Rerum Novarum*. The third is that Catholics who might otherwise have supported the non-labour parties were prevented from doing so by the Protestant character of these parties. This book develops the third of these lines of argument – that it was the Protestantism of Australian Liberalism which pushed Irish Catholics away.

The links between Protestantism and Australian Liberalism are deep and enduring. Australian Liberalism was built on a Protestant foundation: the virtues which underpinned Australian Liberals' claims to political power were Protestant virtues, and the vices they perceived in their political enemies were based on the vices of Protestantism's historic enemy, the Roman Catholic Church. The militant Protestant organisations were only the tip of the iceberg; even when these were dormant or marginal, and there was no overt appeal to Protestant religious beliefs, Australian Liberals' central values and stories drew on Protestant values and stories such that in tracing the contours of the Australian Liberal political tradition one is tracing the contours of the Protestant world view. British Protestantism carried a baggage of anti-Catholicism which made Catholics inevitable objects of political suspicion and unwelcome in Liberal political organisations.

Fusion Again

In the previous chapter I argued that the demands the Labor Party made of its members explain why many Australian Liberals were unable to countenance joining with Labor. To sign the pledge was, in Deakin's words, to ask a man to give up what made him a man, 'his judgement and his conscience', and this they could not do. Deakin's definition of a man had its tap root deep in the complex intertwined history of liberalism and Protestantism in which the Protestant reformation's fight for freedom of religious conviction paved the way for its secularisation in liberalism's independence of political judgement. Chief among Australian Liberal virtues was that Liberals were independent, and whenever this claim was made religious meanings were brought into play. Conversely, chief among Liberal vices was the failure of individuals to value independence and exercise their own judgement, and when Liberals contemplated these vices in their political opponents they drew in their imagination on the vices of the followers of Rome.

The British Liberalism on which the Australian Liberals drew had a Protestant history. Unlike the secularist, anti-clerical European liberalism, it was not concerned with freedom *from* religion, but with freedom to follow the religion of one's conviction, and this meant dissenting Protestantism. In his study of the formation of the British Liberal Party, John Vincent has argued that the development of the party was fuelled less by the emerging industrial capitalism than by the energies of dissenting religion which created the community of sentiment on which the parliamentary party depended.[21] The religious dynamics were obviously different in Australia, where the early disestablishment of the Church of England deprived dissenting Protestants of the major focus of their struggle for religious freedom. However, the Roman Catholic Church was on hand as a potential threat to liberty, and this threat had the advantage of unifying all Protestants, such that by the early twentieth century the fundamental religious divide in Australia was between Protestants and Catholics.

Since its adoption in the early 1890s the pledge had posed a serious moral and political dilemma for Protestant Labor supporters. The men who left the New South Wales party over the pledge in 1894 were nearly all active Protestants who saw the pledge as a threat to their freedom of conscience: G. D. Clark 'refused to hand over to a caucus his religious convictions, his temperance principles, and his freedom of action on moral questions'; John Cotton asked if he were to go into fight for labour 'handcuffed, muzzled, useless for good and evil'; John Hindle said that the pledge 'took liberty from a man and made him a slave'. The Protestant press supported the parliamentarians for refusing 'to have their mouths muzzled, their thoughts tethered, their volitions vitiated, and their consciences concussed'.[22] Not only did these men directly cite their religious convictions as a reason for their decision, but a statement like Hindle's used imagery redolent of British Protestantism's view of its historic mission, as a defender first of religious and then of political liberties, and its commitment to keeping alert against the enemies of liberty. Many Protestants, of course, were able to reconcile their conscience with their commitment to majoritarian democracy, but many were not.

The pledge also posed an insurmountable obstacle for a man like Deakin for whom the independence of his intellectual and spiritual life was the bedrock of his personality. Deakin is a remarkable figure in Australian politics. The first native-born politician of any stature, he was a gifted orator, a skilled and charming politician, and a deeply though unconventionally spiritual man with a life-long interest in theology. He entered Victorian colonial politics when he was twenty-two, essentially as a radical liberal and a committed protectionist; and his attendance at the 1887 Imperial Conference provided the London political elites with their first experience of a native-born Australian politician unfamiliar with the rules of class and deference within which they operated. In his radical liberal heritage and his colonial self-assertion Deakin embodied the commitment to independence of judgement and belief which he regarded as man's defining virtues. Less visible is the religious dimension of this commitment. As we now know, chiefly through the work of Al Gabay, behind the charm and bonhomie of 'affable Alfred' was a deeply serious man with an intense religious life.[23]

Vincent comments that for many British Liberals politics was not an autonomous activity but one deriving, in a way we cannot now trace, from a religious centre.[24] In Deakin's case we can, for he left rich evidence of his life-long quest for spiritual affirmation of his political work. He approached religion not as a sceptic, but with an open and enquiring mind, seeking to embrace truth wherever he found it, and seeking always for direct knowledge of his Duty. For the most part he pursued his spiritual quest outside organised religion. He read widely in the world's religions and in his youth was an active Spiritualist, meeting his future wife Pattie when she was a teenage medium. He sought the guidance of spiritualists at various stages in his political career and in his work for Federation believed he was fulfilling a prophecy.[25] From the age of twenty-eight he kept a prayer diary which he maintained on and off till 1913. In these prayers, writes Al Gabay, we see a deeply religious man conversing with his God, struggling to do his will.[26] Despite the mysticism, the interest in spiritualism and the occult, and the wide reading in world religions, Deakin's religious imagination remained deeply Protestant. As a young man, he had received messages from beyond from John Bunyan, and had written 'The New Pilgrim's Progress' on Bunyan's dictation. And he reconciled himself to the 1910 election defeat with the words 'When Christian's pack fell from his back, he did not go upon his way more lightly or more rejoicing than I'.[27]

Freedom of judgement was the core conviction of both British liberalism and Protestantism, and its absence was the chief vice of the Labor Party in the eyes of Deakin's Liberals. It was also, of course, the chief vice of Protestantism's historic enemy, the Roman Catholic Church, and arguments about freedom of conscience and independence of judgement inevitably raised its spectre. Long before the Labor Party instituted the pledge,

Protestants had a model of an organisation with no place for individuals' freedom of conscience and independence of judgement, in which individuals simply followed orders rather than thought for themselves. Deakin was not consciously sectarian, but the images on which he drew in his description of Labor's organisational machine carried sectarian meanings for those who wished to hear them. The masses who once bowed their heads before the ecclesiastical whip now bowed their heads before the whip of the union boss, knees which would bend to no one were contrasted with the knee drill in Caucus, the secret Caucus room where decisions were made outside the light of day conjured up the secret recesses of the Vatican. It was thus very easy for slippage to occur between anti-Catholic and anti-Labor imagery, particularly once the alignment of Catholics with Labor became increasingly apparent. After all, it was only to be expected that those who had no commitment to freedom of religion would support a party with no tolerance of independence of judgement. And didn't the pledge, 'the powerhouse of the new political machine', have an Irish origin in Parnell's Home Rule Party?[28] In early twentieth-century Australia, Irish meant Catholic, the Protestant Irish having all but disappeared from public view.

Herbert Brookes shows the ease of the slippage. The son of a wealthy pastoralist, he eschewed luxury and ease for a life of dutiful and highminded good works, and in 1905 married Deakin's eldest daughter Ivy. Throughout his life he used his wealth and network of connections to support the Liberal cause. From 1911 to 1916 he financed *The Liberal* to provide a continuing voice for Deakinite Liberalism and wrote many of its articles and editorials.[29] This is how *The Liberal* describes the new Labor government's decision to establish a national bank: 'Mr Fisher obeys; and his caucus bound followers meekly bend their necks beneath the yoke of their political serfdom: the whips crack, the ponderous wheels of the parliamentary machine move swiftly – and Australia has a National Bank'.[30] Almost ten years later the very same imagery appears in *The Vigilant*, the organ of the Victorian (later Australian) Protestant Federation which he financed, to describe Roman Catholic opposition to Bible instruction in state schools: Mannix 'has cracked the ecclesiastical whip and declared that every representative of the people who will not become a tool of Rome must suffer political extinction'.[31] Like Deakin, Brookes' political commitments were underpinned with a sense of spiritual striving, though with a sharper, more belligerent edge from his Ulster Protestant mother. His political trajectory is indicative of the fate of moderate Deakinite Liberalism within the fused party. Entering World War I still committed to Deakin's vision of a harmonious national interest, he came out the other end a confirmed sectarian and swam easily in the divided political world of the 1920s and 1930s.

Militant Protestantism pushed the suspicions of Catholics' propensity to docile subservience to extremes which many Liberals were not prepared to follow, but nevertheless its presence provided continual reminders of the links between commitment to political and religious liberty and independence of judgement. Catholics had proved their lack of commitment to independence of judgement, otherwise they would not have been able to tolerate the strictures of their church, and this made them automatically suspect as holders of political power. If the right to govern others is based in one's proven capacities in self-government, it was axiomatic to the Protestant imagination that in their religious life Catholics were not self-governing; their claims to be responsible holders of political power were thus automatically dubious. As Irving Benson, a prominent Melbourne Methodist, put it in 1930, the difference between Roman Catholics and Protestantism is that 'one is a religion of authority and order, the other of freedom and faith'.[32] The logic behind this view of Catholicism is clear in a 1962 letter to the editor of the *Sydney Morning Herald* defending an employer's right to know a prospective employee's religion:

> Any business executive who is looking in a prospective employee for initiative, new ideas and the capacity to shoulder responsibilities, cannot find these qualities in a person whose religion indicates that he is content to let religious institutions control and mould his intellectual powers, within the limits prescribed by dogmatic theologians.[33]

This is a surprisingly late expression of anti-Catholic prejudice and its existence has long been recognised. The same anti-Catholic logic is embedded in the foundational beliefs of the Australian Liberal political tradition as it was shaped at Fusion, whether the anti-Catholicism was voiced or not. Is it any wonder that Catholics felt more comfortable in the Labor Party?

Loyalty and World War I

Fusion consolidated the Australian Liberals' commitment to the Protestant virtue of independence. World War I added loyalty, and the deeply Protestant imagery of British imperialism ensured that in this too Catholics were lacking. As has been well documented, World War I consolidated the alignment between Catholics and the Labor Party by amplifying Liberal suspicions of Catholic commitment to independence of judgement with the much more serious suspicion of their loyalty. The imperial loyalty which reached its height at the outbreak of World War I had been building since the beginning of the century. The minor stream of nineteenth-century republicanism was all but extinguished by the new Federation's growing sense of regional vulnerability which made Britain's defending arms seem all the more necessary. From 1905 Queen Victoria's Birthday on 24 May became a day for celebrating the British Empire. While never a public holiday, Empire Day was a focus for patriotic gatherings and an occasion for school children to be impressed with the manifold virtues of the British Empire, through songs, flag waving and inspirational addresses from public figures.[34]

This new phase of imperialism celebrated the racial superiority of the British evident in the empire on which the sun never set. In Australia this racial superiority was given particular expression in the universal commitment to unity of race as the essential basis for the new nation. White Australia was embraced by virtually all Australians. Both the indigenous Australians and the populous Asian countries of the region were seen as threatening, racially-defined others against whom the new white settlers defined their identity and interests. The resurgent imperial imagery, however, also carried within it another other from an earlier period of British nation formation, Roman Catholics. Linda Colley has argued that Protestantism is the basis of British nationalism; that England, Scotland and Wales were forged into the British nation by their shared Protestantism and its continuing struggle against Catholicism both at home and abroad. Catholics were the other against whom Britishness was formed, and ordinary Britons, whatever their income, regarded themselves as particularly blessed in their religious and political freedoms and in their economic wellbeing, all of which were interpreted as the consequences of living in a Protestant country.[35] Catholics' allegiance to the extraterritorial authority of the Pope, together with their suspected bonds of sympathy with their foreign coreligionists, made their loyalty suspect, and there was ample evidence in British history of Catholic traitors to the British throne. For the Catholic Irish, the disloyalty of their religion was overlaid by the disloyalty of their race, as Catholic Ireland continued to resist the English colonisers.

As Michael Hogan has argued, a sectarian strand runs through Australian colonial history. By the end of the nineteenth century, when Labor parties were being formed, sectarianism had been part of the currency of Australian politics at least since mid-century when Irish immigration in the wake of the famine brought both a significant Catholic population and the Catholic Church to Australia. The anti-Catholicism brought by the English immigrants to Australia as part of their cultural baggage was reworked, and arguments and images with their origins in Tudor England were given new relevance in the colonies. This anti-Catholicism provided Protestant politicians with easy weapons to attack opponents who happened to be Roman Catholic. Throughout the nineteenth century and during the first quarter of the twentieth, different issues hooked into different aspects of Protestant myths about Catholics: the Irish question into Catholics' doubtful loyalty; the maintenance of separate schools into Protestant fears of the institutional power of the Catholic Church; drink and gambling into the association between Catholicism, moral weakness and poverty; women's suffrage, even, into the fear that it would swell the ranks of gullible voters susceptible to persuasion by priests. But whatever the hook, each of these issues would draw up the whole, scarcely submerged, complex of Protestant beliefs about Catholics, and give them new currency in the politics of the day.

There is, argues Hogan, a marked imbalance in these disputes. Catholic political mobilisation always excited far superior Protestant mobilisation; and Catholics had nothing to match the scurrilousness of militant Protestantism's anti-Catholicism and its lurid imaginings of the sexual licentiousness of priests and nuns. The church hierarchy was thus cautious about appearing to support identifiably Catholic political initiatives, and any relaxation of this caution only proved its wisdom.[36] When Cardinal Moran put himself forward as a candidate for the 1897 Federal Convention with very moderate views, there was an immediate sectarian mobilisation against his candidature.[37] In the case of Moran, who was prone to triumphalist comments on the weakness of Protestant religious belief and practice, the question arises of whether or not the Catholics gave as good as they got in the sectarian wars of words. Michael Hogan argues, however, that despite occasional provocative remarks by prominent Catholic bishops, Catholic sectarianism was primarily defensive. Where attacking Catholics and Catholicism was central to Protestant sectarianism, Catholic sectarianism focused on Catholics' historic sense of injustice and grievance at their persecution, but had little that was specifically anti-Protestant.[38] Sectarianism forced Catholics defensively inwards while Protestants indulged themselves in the pleasures of projection.

Australian Catholics were well aware of the anti-Catholicism carried in British imperial imagery and the ease with which it could be turned against them. For example, from describing the Union Jack as the flag of liberty, as did His Excellency the Governor of New South Wales in his address to the school children of Woollahra, it was but a short step to the various enemies of liberty, including the Roman Catholic Church.[39] To take another example, consider the word 'slave'. It was because the pledge 'took liberty from a man and made him a slave' that John Hindle had left the New South Wales Labour Party in the early 1890s. 'Slave' was a powerful word in the

British Protestant lexicon, conjuring up those still kept from the light by the darkness of ignorance and religious superstition, the morally weak, 'slaves' to the lower passions and the temptations of drink, gambling and vice, and those real slaves whom Liberal Britain's trenchant opposition to the slave trade had so nobly helped to free. The campaign against slavery gave a mighty boost to nineteenth-century Britain's moral self-confidence, offering it 'irrefutable proof that British power was founded on religion, on freedom and on moral calibre'.[40] Slaves were the opposite of free, independent men, and as the stirring chorus line of 'Rule Britannia' repeatedly affirmed at Liberal political gatherings, they were the opposite of British:

> Rule Britannia!
> Britannia rule the waves.
> Britons never, never, never will be slaves.[41]

Catholics knew the anti-Catholic potential of this resurgent British imagery and so preferred to focus their loyalty on the new Australian nation rather than the British Empire. From 1911 Catholic schools celebrated Australia rather than Empire Day on 24 May.[42] Alan Gilbert describes this as provocative.[43] It is better described as defensive: through focusing their loyalties on the new nation they hoped to escape the anti-Catholicism implicit in British imperial imagery.

As the violent sectarian conflicts of World War I showed, however, this was a vain hope. The war shifted the focus of sectarianism from local and state issues such as gambling, drink and education, to the national level of politics where loyalty became the central issue. Already Catholics' stance on Empire Day had revived Protestants' doubts about Catholics' loyalty. In 1913 Thomas Henley, a New South Wales member of parliament, told a Protestant demonstration that 'The disloyalists of Australia are mostly Irish-Roman Catholics'.[44] When war finally arrived, Catholic priests urged their parishioners to do their patriotic duty,[45] and Catholic men volunteered in numbers almost proportionate to the Catholic share of the population (19.26 per cent of the first Australian Imperial Force was Catholic, in comparison with 22.3 per cent of the population).[46] The war seemed to provide the opportunity for Catholics to show their common membership of the nation. But despite the contribution of young Catholic lives to the war, Protestant attacks on Catholic loyalty continued and Australian Catholics became increasingly bitter. These attacks made it clear to Catholics that their hopes that participation in the common war effort would cement their national membership had been ill-founded and that they were not fully accepted as part of the national community.[47]

War broke out in August 1914 during a federal election campaign, following a double dissolution to resolve the deadlock between the House of Representatives and the Senate which had resulted from the 1913 election. The resolution of the deadlock did not turn out as Prime Minister Joseph Cook had planned. After only a year in government, the Liberals were again on the opposition benches facing a Labor ministry, and this time one responsible for leading the country at war. That the electors were prepared to vote in a Labor government at a time of national crisis was a great boost to Labor's claims that it was a party able to govern on behalf of the nation as a whole, and a vindication of the Fisher government's commitment to developing Australia's defence forces.[48]

By 1916 recruitment was falling, casualty rates high, and the war effort stalled. Prime Minister Billy Hughes, who had succeeded Andrew Fisher in 1915, was convinced of the need for complete mobilisation. The trade unions, however, were, on the whole, hostile to conscription, as well as being divided over the call to suspend all class-based demands till the war was over. Hughes knew that to attempt to introduce conscription through an Act of parliament would divide his party and bring down his government, so he called a referendum, hoping that victory would force the party to accept the people's will. As a Labor Prime Minister, Hughes put the national issue of winning the war ahead of the sectional concerns of the labour movement. The Liberals were solidly for conscription, and there was a great deal of overlap between the Liberal Party organisation and the pro-conscriptionists, with Liberal politicians among the most prominent proponents of a 'yes' vote.[49] The referendum, however, was lost narrowly, and the result split the party. Hughes and twenty-three pro-conscriptionist members of Federal Caucus (twenty of whom were Protestant) left the government to form an interim minority government while they negotiated with the Liberals. In early 1917 the Nationalist Party was formed, with Hughes retaining the leadership.

The defeat of the referendum intensified Protestant sectarianism. There were many factors contributing to the referendum's defeat, and with so close a result there was no way of determining which was decisive. Protestant public opinion, however, settled on Catholic disloyalty, and Protestant church papers became filled with virulent attacks on treacherous Irish Catholics. Pamphlets with titles such as 'Rome Rule in Australia' and 'Is the Papacy anti-British?' began to circulate, and Catholics realised how ill-founded had been their hopes at the outset of war that their patriotic participation would break down the barriers of suspicion and intolerance.[50]

An election was due in 1917, and although Hughes opposed it on the grounds that the divisiveness of elections was not appropriate during war, the Senate disagreed and the election was held. The new party fought on the issue of winning the war and won. Labor was presented as disloyal, using its well-tried Caucus methods to tie its members to party rather than national concerns. Answering the question 'Why were we expelled?' in his campaign opening policy speech, Hughes said: 'We were expelled because we dared to speak and act as our consciences dictated ... because in the gravest crisis in which the Commonwealth and the Empire have ever been involved we preferred to stand for national rather than party interests'.[51] Buoyed by the election victory, Hughes and the government decided to try again on conscription. This campaign consolidated the pattern of Protestant and Catholic political alignments which held till the Labor Party split again in the 1950s. During the conscription campaigns, anti-Catholic feeling among Protestants reached fever pitch, focusing on Daniel Mannix, the Catholic Archbishop of Melbourne, and on T. J. Ryan, the Catholic Labor Premier of Queensland. Ryan had been the only state premier to oppose the first conscription campaign and Hughes regarded his government as a disloyal Irish Catholic junta.[52] Protestant clergy were prominent among the pro-conscriptionists at loyalist rallies, and the Protestant press supported the cause, one editorial going so far as to claim that had Jesus been given the opportunity he would have voted 'yes'.[53]

Mannix, who had made only a couple of mildly critical remarks about conscription during the 1916 campaign, became conscription's most prominent and effective opponent. For Hughes he became the main target, replacing radical International Workers of the World (the Wobblies) and internal Labor Party enemies of the first campaign.[54] Hughes was joined in his anti-Catholic campaign by other prominent Australians, like the Governor-General, Sir Ronald Munro-Ferguson, who was convinced that 'the Catholic net is now being spread over Australia'.[55] For loyalist Australia, the second conscription campaign became a righteous crusade against the power of priests and the forces of Catholic disloyalty, and when it was again defeated, Protestant anti-Catholicism's belief in the sinister power of the Catholic Church seemed confirmed.

Australia emerged from the war bitterly divided along sectarian lines. The anti-conscription campaign had made Mannix a hero among working-class Catholics and strengthened Catholic self-confidence. Protestants retaliated with revitalised Protestant organisations. Loyalty Leagues were set up across Australia to confront Mannixism and Sinn Feinism, and both sides were alert for signs of disloyalty or insult. Sectarianism was played out in the symbolic politics of song, gesture and mass displays of communal strength. In Melbourne, Mannix's failure to lift his purple bonnet for the playing of 'God Save the King' and his leading of the 1918 St Patrick's Day march which included a float depicting the 'martyrs of the Easter rising' was met with a loyalist rally at the Town Hall and a march to Parliament House which was addressed by Hughes himself.[56] Such loyalist rallies stirred the crowds with musical items, 'The British Grenadiers', 'Scots Wha hae wi Wallace Bled', and 'The Red, White and Blue', with all joining heartily in the singing of the national anthem and 'Rule Britannia'.[57] On tour in Adelaide in 1920, the celebrated Irish tenor John McCormack omitted to sing the national anthem; when some members of the audience sang 'God Save the King' themselves he took this as a studied insult and cancelled the rest of his tour.[58]

Through flags, hymns, anthems and colours people displayed their political and religious loyalties to themselves and each other. Today's society, uneasy with ritual and regalia, its members' identities shaped by very different social forces, looks back on such past expressions of group solidarity with some bemusement. Its vestiges are generally described by the term 'tribalism', a commonplace in contemporary political commentary to describe political expressions of group-based identities. Although these political expressions have very little in common with the experiences of people living in face-to-face, kinship-based societies, they do differ significantly from the dominant forms of contemporary social experience in the depth of people's identification with their social position and in their experience of their social affiliations in terms of shared group identities. Far more than today, Australians before World War II valued opportunities to experience their shared group membership in rallies, meetings and marches, where the symbols and songs united the participants not just with each other but with past generations who had carried the same banners and sung the same songs. Public singing, voices raised in unison to a common cause, released powerful emotions. Even for those like the Protestant Liberals who trumpeted their commitment to freedom and independence, this commitment was most keenly felt when they joined with their fellow free and independent citizens singing together one of the rousing anthems of Protestant Britain.

The sectarian conflict of the war years and its immediate aftermath reinforced the already existing sectarian basis of the division between Liberals and Labor. The Labor Party emerged more Catholic, with Catholics more numerous and visible among its leadership; and the Liberals, now in the Nationalist Party, emerged identified with a militant Protestantism openly hostile to Catholicism, and more convinced than ever of the Catholic influence in Labor politics. The conflict over conscription and the meaning of loyalty had educated a whole new generation of voters in the dangers of

Popery and the virtues of Protestants on the one hand, or of the grievances of Catholics and the injustices of the Protestant ascendancy on the other. This renewed sectarianism provided Australian Liberals with a powerful base in commonsense and social experience for the next twenty years, as the political divisions were reinforced by increased social divisions between Protestants and Catholics. The Protestant churches and the Catholic parishes were the centres of social networks through which many Australians found their jobs, their marriage partners and their local tradesmen. As well, organisations like the Freemasons, which were becoming more important in the 1920s, provided Protestant men with a network of useful contacts to further their businesses and careers. Catholics formed parallel defensive organisations such as the Knights of the Southern Cross.[59] And the Irish origins of the great majority of Australia's Catholics made the mutual identification of Catholics and Protestants a relatively easy matter. A plan of operation for Protestant mobilisation in Victoria around 1920 includes the preparation of electoral rolls 'with all the RC names crossed out', so that Protestants in any electorate can be contacted 'at a minute's notice'.[60]

In the 1920s Protestant organisations reorganised to fight Catholic influence. The New South Wales Protestant Federation, established in 1921 with the support of most of the Protestant clergy, fought the 1922 state election campaign on the issue of Catholic control of the Labor government. An Orange Lodge advertisement in the mainstream press, headed 'Manifesto to Protestant Workmen. Rome's Campaign for Temporal Power', gave detailed analysis of Catholic power and influence in both the government and the Labor Party.[61] The Victorian Protestant Federation was established earlier than the New South Wales branch, in August 1918 with the financial backing of Deakin's son-in-law Herbert Brookes, and with Congregationalist minister the Reverend Walter Albiston as its General Secretary.[62] Brookes' shifting political interests and affiliations are instructive for understanding the relationship between Protestantism and the Liberal political imagination. Brookes entered the war a disappointed Deakinite Liberal and came out the other end a militant Protestant. He had closed *The Liberal* in 1914 shortly after war broke out and the Liberals had been decisively defeated by Labor. In 1916 he also closed down the People's Liberal Party, the organisation through which he and his wife Ivy had attempted to maintain a political presence for the Deakinite middle ground.[63]

The polarisations of the war destroyed in Brookes, as it did more generally in Liberal politics, the intellectual openness and commitment to the middle ground associated with Deakinite Liberalism. John Latham provides another example, with the fierce independence of his youth transformed into a stern, authoritarian conservatism.[64] The division of the political world inaugurated by Labor's convincing 1910 election victory became, under the pressure of war, a division between the loyal and the disloyal. Brookes was prominent in both conscription campaigns, serving on the executive of nearly every Melbourne-based major war organisation and helping to establish the Australian Protective League, which became the Australian Defensive League, to assist the Special Intelligence Unit in countering subversive and disloyal activities. After the defeat of the second referendum Brookes was swept up in the loyalist fury against Archbishop Mannix. Faced with what he saw as a militant Catholic Church in league with Labor, he decided to devote considerable of his intellectual energies, together with a good deal of money, to the cause of defending loyalism and Protestantism, which for him were one and the same thing. With Brookes' backing the Victorian Protestant Federation launched a weekly called *The Vigilant* in January 1920, which was relaunched in 1923 as the paper of the national body. At its peak, claims Brookes' nephew and biographer, Rohan Rivett, *The Vigilant*'s circulation was 12 000, with a good number of copies going into parsonages: 'It publicised to men who had an assured audience every Sunday, every action of Dr Mannix or his Church which, in the view of *The Vigilant*, could damage Australia or the British Empire'.[65] We don't know how much notice these clergymen took of *The Vigilant*, but Rivett points to the important ideological work the Protestant clergy did for the Liberals. They were its organic intellectuals, their weekly sermons in every suburb and country town throughout the land preaching the Liberal virtues of independence, self-discipline, duty, responsibility, loyalty and social harmony.

Sectional Grievances

The conflicts of World War I revealed to the Protestant Liberal political imagination another similarity between Catholics and the Labor Party. As well as shared disloyalty, both were prepared to put their selfish, sectional interests ahead of the interests of the nation as a whole, even in the midst of the gravest crisis the new nation had ever faced. Although accusations of selfishness were quickly subsumed into the larger and more emotive framework of shared disloyalty, they revealed an attitude to group-based identifications in Liberal political thinking that has lasted well beyond the decline of sectarianism and is still powerful in the contemporary Liberal Party's unease with multiculturalism and indigenous rights.

As already argued, the most persistent argument the Liberals put forward against the legitimacy of the Labor Party's claims to govern is that whereas the Liberals strive to represent and pursue the national interest, Labor represents only a sectional, class-based interest. In the war years, Labor seemed to behave true to form, with sections of the party pursing sectional demands despite the best efforts of Prime Minister Hughes to dedicate the Labor government to the overriding national aim of winning the war. Hughes abandoned a Labor commitment to hold a referendum on prices, and as prices continued to rise union members turned to industrial action. In 1916 it is calculated that 1.7 million days were lost to strikes in key industries,[66] stark evidence to Liberals of the selfishness of organised labour. Catholics too were similarly guilty of pursuing their own selfish sectional demands when they did not drop their agitation for the funding of church schools to pursue a united war effort. In the context of war, argues Patrick O'Farrell, the pursuit of claims which had long been seen as narrow and sectional became vastly more unpopular and offensive, evidence of such blind indifference to the unity of the nation that it could easily be seen as a form of disloyalty.[67]

The problem for Catholics, however, was that even when the country was not at war it was virtually impossible for them to organise politically as Catholics. The major grievance Catholics had as Catholics was the denial of state aid to their schools. This had begun prior to 1850 when the colonial states had funded both national and denominational schools. When in the 1860s and 1870s the state decided to fund only the national schools, the Catholic Bishops determined to keep their school system. They were able to do this by relying on religious orders for the teaching, and by increasing the pressure on Catholic parents to patronise the local Catholic schools. In this they were spectacularly successful; in 1950 75 per cent of Catholics attended Catholic schools.[68]

The separate school system entrenched sectarian differences in the institutional structure of Australian society and isolated Roman Catholics from the rest of the population. As well, the capacity of the Bishops to maintain the Catholic education system became for Protestants one more piece of evidence of the organisational power of the Catholic Church, and their success in recruiting children to their schools evidence of their power over their flock. The intensified sectarian identifications of the 1870s had seriously weakened the anti-sectarian, secular strand of liberal ideology in Australia. Protestants might use secular arguments about the separation of church and state, but their intent was sectarian rather than secular. The liberal secular commitment to a harmonious society and open public sphere became an argument to be used against Catholics who could be seen as putting the sectional interests of the part before the harmonious interests of the whole, and so threatening the achievement of that illusory harmony. Australian liberalism was seriously compromised by such arguments, and secular liberalism later took refuge in the Labor Party.[69]

Not, however, that Labor supported Catholic demands. Even within the Labor Party where politically active Catholics found a welcome, this was conditional, argues Patrick O'Farrell, on their not acting politically as Catholics: 'In so far as they were workers, Catholics would gain as other workers from Labor's efforts, but as Catholics they would gain nothing'.[70] Thus despite the consolidation of the association between Catholics and the ALP as the century progressed, the Labor Party made no efforts to redress Catholics' long-standing grievance over state aid to religious schools. It did, however, at least develop the manners to accommodate people of different religious beliefs inside the party. Liberals, with their belief in a common national interest, interpreted Catholic political demands as selfishly sectarian and un-Australian, and, as John Cramer found, were slow to develop good manners towards Catholics.

The ideal Liberal polity was based on independent, free-thinking citizens, who organised together on the basis of shared principles and commitments to the national interest. From this perspective there was no legitimate place for Roman Catholics as Catholics within the polity; any Catholic political activity was likely to be taken as evidence of the scheming ambitions of Rome, and any politically active Catholic was immediately suspect as a potential soldier of Rome. From this perspective, Catholicism was opposed to the Liberals' ideas of citizenship. The logic of this position is set out starkly in a 1925 editorial of *The Vigilant*: Roman Catholics are welcome in politics and in parliament, but only if they act as 'citizens and not as sectarians'. It is only 'when we see them sinking their citizenship in their sectarianism that we find it necessary to organise against them'. The editorial goes on: 'In this respect Roman Catholicism stands alone. Anglicans, Presbyterians, Methodists and other Protestants go into public life as citizens. They are to be found in all parties. They do not combine for sectional or sectarian purposes. But Romanists do.'[71] From this perspective, the social experiences and beliefs which shape the Protestant centre are invisible, while the secular liberal language of citizenship is deployed to render illegitimate the group-based claims and identity of Catholics.

Before World War II, Catholics were Australia's largest and most visible minority, the major social challenge, along with the class-based Labor

Party, to the Liberal's aspirations for a harmonious nation of free-thinking and independent citizens. Conveniently, the belief has been that these two challenges were really one and the same, that Catholics supported Labor because they were mostly working class anyway, and for those who were not their membership of a persecuted minority made them sympathetic to Labor's reforming, outsider status: Labor's concern with class grievance made it the natural home for other minority grievances. These are arguments from social structure. Whatever their merits, and to my mind they are less than has generally been granted, particularly the argument about the overrepresentation of Roman Catholics in the working class, they fail to take religion seriously as an agent in its own right, as a symbolic system which shapes the way people understand social and political reality. I have been arguing that the automatic suspicion of Catholicism carried by British Protestantism provides a more convincing explanation for Catholics' political preference for Labor than does the widely accepted class-based explanation. This is not about the reasons Catholics were attracted to Labor but the reasons they were not made welcome by the Liberals. For the most part, this is a story of sectarianism, but it is not just prejudice we are dealing with here. We are also dealing with fundamental historic differences between the Protestant and Catholic religious imagination, between the way the two faiths imagine the relationship between God, the individual and the world.

For Catholicism, with its roots in the premodern rural world, the individual relates to God as a member of a community, whereas for Protestantism the individual seeks and establishes his own relationship with God. For Catholicism the individual, however flawed, is embedded in social networks which already contain and reveal God, whereas for the Protestant imagination, the individual flounders in a Godless world until saved by his own acts of faith.[72] For Catholicism to leave the community, to be excommunicated, is to lose the connection with God, but the Protestant must always be prepared to defy the community to find God. These differences are embedded in the deep narrative structures of people's self-understandings, whether they are consciously religious or even regular church-goers, and they affect the way they understand the relationship between individuals and other non-religious groups and organisations. To see Protestantism and Catholicism as only about doctrine and institutional religion is to miss the pervasiveness of their cultural influence, particularly in the first half of the twentieth century when religion's social influence was much greater than today.

The underlying logic of Protestant liberalism with its emphasis on the virtues of free-thinking, independent men makes it difficult to recognise group-based identities as legitimate, as other than traps for the weak-minded and ignorant, or excuses for those who lack the strength of will and moral courage to take a stand. A political philosophy based on the fiction that society is a free association of individuals has no easy place for identity politics, for political demands which flow from social differences, which are always regarded as secondary, never primary, and whose assertion is thus taken as a threat to the logic which underpins the polity as a whole. Liberalism's individualism has thus led it both to a blindness to the social and historical conditions of its own formation, and to seeing all group-based political demands as potential threats to the achievement of a harmonious national interest. The fundamental position of individual choice and moral agency in the Protestant imagination makes it pre-sociological in a way the Catholic imagination is not, and helps to explain the difficulties later Liberals were to have with the demands of identity politics and of indigenous Australians. While, as has been argued, Labor had no more sympathy for Catholics' religious demands than did the Liberals, its acceptance of the class basis of identity created a potential for the possibility of the recognition of other social bases of identity – gender, race, ethnicity – when the time came. Nor did the Labor Party carry the same ambivalence about organisation, which for the Protestant imagination found its most extreme expression in the malignant image of an all-powerful Rome turning men into cogs. Labor's organisational demands and its language of loyalty and solidarity did not so readily offend Catholics as they did Protestants. Australian Liberals' anti-Catholic prejudice was bad manners, but behind the bad manners and giving them legitimacy were deep differences in the way individuals' relationships with others were understood.

4
Good Citizens and Public Order

Service

Australian Liberals saw themselves first and foremost as good citizens, and they firmly believed that it was on their virtues as citizens that the quality of the nation and, beyond that, the Empire was based. The previous chapter has argued that the Australian Liberal conception of citizenship, with its stress on independence of judgement, on loyalty, and on the subordination of self-interest to the national good, was based on Protestant conceptions of virtues in which Australia's Irish Catholics were regarded as deficient. Already suspect at the time of the formation of the party system and generally identifying with the only non-sectarian party on offer, Australian Catholics' alliance with the Labor Party was consolidated by the conflicts of World War I. While the polemical thrust of the previous chapter was to expose the patterns of sectarian thought and feeling Australian Liberalism brought to the formation of the Australian party system, it had another, more positive implication. Sectarianism in Australia before World War II was not mainly about fighting Catholic vices, but about affirming Protestant virtues. Most of the time, when anti-Catholic feeling was latent, Protestantism was still at work in the Liberal imagination, giving weight to Liberalism's promotion of the political, social and economic virtues of independent individualism and responsible citizenship against Labor's class-based understandings. Protestantism helped link Australian Liberals' political symbols with the deepest layers of people's experience of themselves in a way secular liberalism was hard pressed to do, and it strengthened the moral self-confidence that underpinned the Liberals' conviction that the Protestant middle class was the proper guardian of the nation and the source of its most responsible and valuable citizens.

Protestant Liberals' main opponent was not Roman Catholics and their church, but the Australian Labor Party and its political mobilisation of people's class-based identities as workers. The Liberals' conception of citizenship set it squarely against Labor's class-based mobilisation: 'the working man is not merely a working man, nor can all his interests be subsumed (classed) under the term Labour. The working man is and knows himself to be, the citizen of a great State'.[1] Liberals conceptualised people's political being first and foremost as citizens. This was a direct challenge to Labor's appeal to people's class consciousness and its understanding of relations between different social interests in terms of class conflict. Liberals set 'citizens', who entered the public world to promote the common good, against the 'workers', concerned only with the interests of a part. To act in politics other than as a citizen was illegitimate. Liberals were citizens and they thought everyone else should be too.

This meaning of citizenship is quite different from its contemporary use which refers almost exclusively to the individual's formal relationship to the state, and emphasises rights and entitlements conferred by the state rather than the duties and obligations of individuals to their political community. In the Liberal conception of citizenship, citizens and their rights exist before the state. The state is thus the creation of its citizens rather than citizenship being a status bestowed by the state. For example, Australian women argued for the vote not in order to become citizens but because they were already 'patriotic and law-abiding citizens' making a worthwhile contribution to the community.[2] In comparison with the limited, statist contemporary conception of citizenship, the Liberals' concept of the good citizen was as much moral as political. It provided at the level of the individual a corollary of the Liberal Party's claims to be non-sectional, and directly challenged Labor's advocacy of class-based politics as selfish. The good citizen was not just someone who fulfilled their political rights and obligations, the good citizen was also a good person and their fulfilment of their citizenship obligations was but an aspect of this goodness. Advising secondary school children on the obligations of citizenship, Deakin's first biographer, Walter Murdoch, stressed that good citizenship was not 'some special and peculiar kind of goodness … The virtues of the good citizen are just the plain, everyday virtues we learn in our own homes'. And the essence of this is 'the lesson of consideration for others'.[3] That is, it is the lesson of the proper relationship between one's own needs, desires and actions and those of the rest of the community. 'Be a good little citizen and give your sister a turn' a mother might say giving a lesson in sharing; 'Be a good little citizen and put away your toys', giving a lesson in responsibility.

Murdoch, a Scottish-born son of the manse, wrote voluminously for the quality newspapers throughout his long life and was widely read and admired. He said of himself that he had 'a commonplace sort of mind, a knack for putting into words what other commonplace people have thought but never said'. John La Nauze recommends him to future social historians as a window on to the thinking of his readers between the wars when his popularity was at its height.⁴ As Murdoch himself admitted, his essays were somewhat preachy, urging a little spiritual striving lest one settle down into an 'unadventurous, barnyard sort of life'.⁵ The popularity of Murdoch's secular sermons is evidence of the appetite for advice on moral self-improvement among his middle-class readers. His concept of citizenship was imbued with evangelical Christianity's commitment to the brotherhood of man, and its urgent sense of the world's wrongs. Good citizenship was something for which one strove. When in the 1920s the Young Women's Christian Association was looking for a name for a new organisation that would educate girls to become responsible and civic-minded young women, it chose the name 'Girl Citizens' because the word 'citizen' offered a challenge and a big vision. The chosen motto 'By love serve one another' linked this firmly to the obligations of service.⁶

The Liberal concept of citizenship spanned the distinction between the private and public spheres rather than referring solely to public virtues and so broke with earlier conceptions of citizenship based on the public masculine virtues of courage, honour and justice. This had its origins in the mid-nineteenth-century association of the middle class with domestic virtue and the propagation by evangelical religion of a middle-class morality as salient to the public as the private world.⁷ An important consequence of this was that citizenship was opened to women. As the doctrine of separate spheres developed during the nineteenth century, so too did arguments for the connection between civic virtue and domestic life. Women thus had a legitimate reason for excursions beyond the home to bring their special moral virtues to bear on the life of the nation and were urged to replace their merely domestic preoccupations with serious attention to the public world. 'How intimate is the connection which exists between the women of England and the moral character maintained by this country in the scale of nations', wrote one popular woman author in the 1840s.⁸ Women became, in Linda Colley's words, 'angels of the state', flocking to the various nineteenth-century moral campaigns from anti-slavery to temperance.⁹ Separate spheres, far from confining women to the home, gave those middle-class women who had the means a reason to leave it in order to advocate the relevance of their virtues and superior moral characters to the public sphere. This was far short of the equal citizenship for which later generations of feminists strove, but it underpinned the energy and conviction of most Australian women political activists until the very different postwar feminist campaigns for substantive equality and access to men's worlds.

Because women's chief qualifications for political participation were their virtuous characters and their sensitivity to moral issues, they became important bearers of the moral conception of citizenship. When Australian women gained formal political citizenship at Federation, they were far more likely to understand this in terms of service and obligation than rights and claims. Women political activists wrote and talked endlessly of women's new duties and responsibilities.[10] To women self-seeking was the greatest of all wrongs, and they were instinctively hostile to any political action which could be construed in terms of narrow self-interest. The West-Australian-based Women's Service Guild, one of the organisations set up in the wake of enfranchisement to promote women's political education, gave as one of its objects 'to seek public good and not personal advantage'.[11] Suffragist and life-long feminist activist, Rose Scott, regarded selfishness as the worst of moral and political failings; it was expressed in the vices of drink, gambling and immorality and in the aggression and self-interest of party government.[12] For women, goodness was equated with service and self-sacrifice, as in this wartime prayer of the Australasian League of Honour for Women and Girls: 'We shall turn to God with grateful hearts ... asking Him to forgive our thoughtless selfishness, and to make us strong to serve. We pray with a new zeal that the Empire may carry on this war without bitterness or self-seeking.'[13]

Marilyn Lake has argued that, because of women's deep uneasiness with the partisan and conflictual nature of party politics, the organisations they built to press the demands of Australia's newly enfranchised women citizens were determinedly non-party.[14] But the very language in which women couched their commitment to non-party, non-sectarian politics drew them into the Liberals' construction of the political world. The powerful Australian Women's National League (AWNL), the largest and most enduring Liberal organisation before the formation of the Liberal Party, was an avowedly party organisation, and it espoused much the same exalted view of women's potential political role as the non-party women's organisations. It too eschewed 'the strident voice of party politics'.[15] 'Its ends ... are neither personal nor sectional, but national ... For twenty-eight years it has been working steadily, continuously and without self-seeking.'[16] The party-oriented AWNL projected all the stridency, conflict and self-interest of politics on to the socialist Labor Party rather than on to men at large, giving their support to men of sound principle and broad national vision. If the middle class was the class defined by its possession of superior moral virtues, then women were the middle class par excellence, characteristically resolving the paradox of party discussed in the introduction in favour of the interests of the whole rather than the part.

The middle class's conception of citizenship was integrally connected with the concept of service. According to Murdoch, it is the 'eager and active spirit of service and sacrifice which makes the good citizen'.[17] What service primarily meant was putting the interests of the common good before those of the self, and the term had wide applications. One could give service to the school, the church, the cricket club, or any other organisation where one's voluntary individual effort made a contribution to a worthwhile collective endeavour. There were clubs specifically dedicated to service, such as Rotary with its watchword of 'service' and its commitment to seeking the best in people.[18] The administrative branch of government was called the 'public service'. Giving service was the way in which the efforts of individual units were integrated into larger collective efforts, it was not just people who gave service. The social or national role of institutions was also regularly described in these terms. The centenary history of the Launceston Bank for Savings is subtitled 'Established 1835, With an unbroken service of 100 years'.[19] Because such institutions were understood essentially in nation-building terms, laying solid foundations for future national prosperity, serving such institutions one also served the nation.

Duty, service and self-sacrifice were the themes of countless sermons, headmasters' addresses, speeches and obituaries throughout the first half of the twentieth century and well into the second half. For young people on the brink of their adult lives they were ideals to be striven for; when life was over they were achievements to be praised. The biography of Charles Hawker, the soldier politician who overcame crippling wartime injuries to serve his country as a member of parliament, records Canon Stephen telling the boys of Geelong Grammar that the school will be judged by 'the number of men who have sacrificed themselves and been of use to the world'.[20] The ultimate service a citizen could make was to sacrifice their life in war. Before World War I the Labor Party had supported compulsory military training for home defence as a necessary part of the obligations of citizens in a free state, but the bitter conflicts over conscription, its rejection in two referenda, and the split in the party weakened the link between citizenship and universally accepted obligations and considerably strengthened the Liberals' grip on the concept. Pro-conscriptionists used the term 'citizen' freely in their campaigns.

Service was also required of those who stayed behind, and women in particular threw themselves into voluntary work to support the war effort.[21] Knitting and sewing circles were formed, funds raised through button days, sales of work, and entertainments, support services organised for wounded soldiers, comforts collected and dispatched; amateur photographers were organised to take snapshots of relatives and friends for the men and nurses on active service. Women were at the forefront of this voluntary activity, participating as citizens giving voluntary service. The meeting at which the Lady Mayoress's Patriotic League was formed was described as 'a meeting of women citizens of Victoria' and patriotic citizens were invited to start local thrift branches.[22]

To the historian of the Australian home front, Ernest Scott,

> the amount of work done by women was a remarkable feature of the Great War, distinguishing it from every other war ... The recognition of the obligation of service by women in a great national emergency was something new. In a special sense it was an acceptance of the implications of citizenship.[23]

More recent Australian historians have misread the political meaning of women's wartime mobilisation around voluntary service. Distracted by the predominance of middle-class women in the various patriotic funds, Michael McKernan falls into the standard dismissive reduction of the meaning of middle-class political actions, concluding that their presence was the result of the time available to them, compared with more pressed working-class women, and the appeal of the social status of the activity.[24] Feminist historians have understood such work as extending and reinforcing women's traditional roles as mothers, wives and homemakers.[25] Focusing on what is absent in terms of later feminist agendas of the movement of women into paid work, they have missed the scale and energy of women's wartime mobilisation and its framing in terms of women's duties as active citizens. While some women sewed and knitted only for the male relatives or men they knew, most donated their services to the anonymous soldiers of the nation in the interests of the national war effort. The skills women practised may have been the same as those practised in the home, but they were being practised for national rather than domestic purposes and this was a crucial difference. The key message was not the one feminists have heard, reinforcement of the idea that women's place was in the home, but the one embedded in the liberal notion of citizenship as a category which spanned private and public: that domestic skills and virtues had a vital role to play in the survival and the future development of the nation, and that women as their chief practitioners were valuable citizens.

The war also provided ample opportunities for teaching children about citizenship. Frank Tate, the Director General of Education in Victoria, saw the war as giving teachers 'a capital opportunity to impress upon children their civic obligations, and to promote a zeal for social service'.[26] Scott reports in detail the range of ways Australian children gave service. Children in Victorian public elementary schools donated £410 000, and an enterprising pair of lads borrowed an acre of land from a farmer, fenced and ploughed it and raised a crop they sold for £12. Others raised eggs, sold rabbit skins, grew flowers, made sand bags, and fly nets for the soldiers' horses, did odd jobs and more. Scott's *Australia During the War* has a wonderful photo of the ninety or so children of the Warrnambool State School each nursing their gift of Christmas poultry for the sick and wounded soldiers in the Caulfield military hospital.²⁷

The country at war, all differences forgotten in the united service to a national cause, every citizen engaged in selfless service – this was the Australian Liberal's ideal polity in action, the fate of the nation depending on the moral quality of its members. It is this imagined link between the moral quality of the citizens and the strength of the nation that enabled the war to be seen by so many religious leaders as a moral test.²⁸ If the course of the war was to be determined by large, impersonal forces, such as the productive resources at the nation's disposal, or the structures of alliances between overseas powers, then the actions of individual citizens became largely irrelevant. Mannix's notorious description of the war as 'a dirty little trade war' offended so deeply not just because it cast doubt on the moral integrity of the British Empire and its allies, but because it threatened the relevance of the service of their citizens.

'Citizen' was the name under which unorganised people came together for political purposes. The various political organisations which sprang up during Australia's financial crisis of 1930–31 to support financial orthodoxy described themselves as leagues and associations of 'citizens'. Citizens' groups mobilised again during the campaign against Chifley's 1946 decision to nationalise the banks. The historian of this campaign, A. L. May, describes the process of mobilisation. Committees were formed from among the citizens attending a public protest meeting. These committees then proceeded to organise and address more meetings, prepare material for the local press and apply pressure to parliamentarians.²⁹ Protest groups still form along such lines and use similar tactics; for example the many resident action groups that have opposed both private and public developments in the cities, but they now rarely describe themselves as citizens.

For Liberals, citizenship was not primarily a status conferred by the state but a capacity of the individuals on which the polity depended. Its core meaning was the subordination of self-interest to the common good and this was manifest in people's dealing with each other as well in their relationship with the state. 'An Australian citizen? What should one look for as the characteristics?' asks Rohan Rivett introducing his biography of Herbert Brookes, which was titled *Australian Citizen*. And he answers:

> Probably ever since the days of the Greek city state the best citizen has needed a quality apart. He has needed to subordinate personal interest – putting the community interest before self – not simply in war-time or in moments of mass emotion, but throughout the ordinary practices of everyday.³⁰

Citizenship was something which Liberals both aspired to and already embodied, and which was enacted not just in their narrowly political actions like voting, but in their active involvement in the affairs of the community. Being generally law-abiding, Walter Murdoch made clear, was not enough; good citizenship was an active not a passive state.[31] Contemporary concepts of citizenship see it primarily in terms of individuals' rights, entitlements and obligations vis-à-vis the state, whereas, as should by now be clear, an understanding of citizenship that centred on the proper relationship of individual members of society with each other was widespread in Australia before World War II. This broader concept of citizenship was expressed through people's participation in the voluntary associations of civil society which provided practical training in the techniques of self-management on which good citizenship depended.

Meetings

> Mother would return home from an afternoon meeting, and, not even stopping to take off her hat, would get the tea, make a couple of sponge cakes, sandwiches or biscuits, eat and rush off again to an evening meeting ... She ate most evening meals with her hat on.[32]

Voluntary associations in the form we know them today emerged in the eighteenth century, as aristocratic control of public life waned and society became more complex. Independent of both the family and the state, they enabled people to come together for a wide range of purposes.[33] Their formation intensified in the first half of the nineteenth century and Australia's nineteenth-century colonists were well familiar with them. Building communities in the new land, they had even more need for them here than at home. With no traditional ruling classes to rely on, if anything were to happen they had to make it happen themselves. Like the settlers in the United States, they were building a new society and Alex de Toqueville had observed on his visit to America in the 1830s the range and effectiveness of American associational life.[34] In new areas of settlement, both rural and urban, public resources were limited and the provision of many essential services, such as hospitals or fire brigades, depended on voluntary effort, or on convincing the government of the local area's urgent need. By the end of the nineteenth century the typical Australian country town and suburb had a plethora of community organisations: sporting clubs (such as cricket, football, horseracing, tennis and lawn bowls), musical societies, literary and debating clubs, mechanics institutes and subscriber libraries, agricultural societies to organise the annual show, and so on. As well, there were the churches, which supported their own range of organisations, and the women's auxiliary fund-raising organisations attached to institutions such as schools, hospitals, fire brigades and children's homes. There were also associations with an economic purpose, trade unions, chambers of commerce, farmers' groups. A survey during the early 1940s of 180 Victorian country towns ranging in size from 250 to 10 000 found well over 3000 social organisations and 1700 sporting organisations, as well as boards, councils and trusts and the more formal organisations of political and economic life.[35]

De Toqueville famously argued of the United States in the 1830s that the American people's enthusiasm for voluntary associations was the basis for their successful democratic life, that 'In democratic countries knowledge of how to combine is the mother of all other forms of knowledge'. There has recently been renewed interest in the links between the quality of democratic public life and citizens' engagement (or not) with community organisational life. The focus of this work has been on the way participation in voluntary organisations builds what has become known as 'social capital', networks of reciprocity and reservoirs of social trust which enhance communities' abilities to solve their problems, and on the likely consequences of the recent dramatic decline in such participation. But participation in such organisations also taught more direct political lessons in citizenship. It taught people how to run a good meeting, and in so doing it taught them about the links between personal character and public order, between the ethics of self-control and the effective pursuit of collective outcomes, between the principles needed to run a good meeting and those necessary for a good society.

There were thousands of Australians who knew how to run a good meeting, thousands who were competent minute secretaries, thousands who could keep accounts books and prepare annual financial reports, and tens of thousands who were well-versed in the manners and procedures of meeting participation. Particular skills and knowledge were needed to participate effectively in organisations, whether they be the tennis club or the local Chamber of Commerce, and these were as much moral as political. Australian Liberals' concept of citizenship as the subordination of self-interest to the collective good was central to the organisational practices of voluntary associations and their many meetings. Citizenship's core virtue was thus as likely to be learned in the avowedly non-political organisations of church, school or sporting club as in the electoral leagues or political parties.

Meeting procedures developed as part of the broad historical process of the pacification of politics in which rule-governed talk was substituted for force and violence as a way of settling disputes within increasingly large territorial units. Their history includes the increasing need for orderly and coordinated decision-making procedures among the European ruling elites of church, town and state, the Reformation and the Protestant Meeting Order which spread meeting discipline among the lower classes, and the emergence of national parliaments as deliberative bodies in which conflict is settled by talk rather than force, a process sometimes referred to as 'parliamentarisation'.[36] By the twentieth century the meeting based on simplified parliamentary procedure was the major vehicle for cooperative social endeavour throughout the western world. To participate successfully in society one thus needed a rudimentary knowledge of its rules and procedures. Meeting manuals began appearing in large numbers during the nineteenth century to instruct people in the manners and procedures of meeting participation. These manuals served a similar function to etiquette manuals, instructing the lower classes in forms of behaviour already developed among the elites, and they are a valuable source for understanding the values and self-understandings associated with this new form of behaviour. As they make clear, to participate in a meeting, and above all to chair it, required social, political and moral knowledge carrying attitudes to aggression and self-control, the balancing of self-interest and community interest, and to public order. These amplified and gave form to the middle class's understanding of itself as the bearer of political virtue, able and obliged to give 'leadership'. There was a match between the good meeting and Liberals' view of the good polity, such that meeting participation was a practical training ground in the Liberals' central value of the subordination of sectional self-interest to the general good.

Before the 1970s when women turned their attention to representation in the parliament, the meetings of civil society were the main sites of their political participation. Few women were in the various organisations of the economy such as trade unions, chambers of commerce and business associations. Women at home, however, could exercise their political rights as citizens by joining political organisations and attending their meetings, and the political ethic embodied in their procedures resonated with the morality of consideration for others which was central to ideals of women's domestic role. Such participation reinforced women's commitment to constitutionalism and proper procedure as the prime means for resolving conflicts in society. This is not surprising; after all it was the replacement of conflicts of physical force with conflicts of words which produced a sufficiently pacified public space to enable women's participation in politics.

The early manuals focused as much on meeting manners as on procedural issues such as the order of motions. One should not arrive late or depart early, fall asleep, fight, shout or swear, but should rather endeavour at all times to listen attentively to the views of others and to maintain a calm and dispassionate demeanour when stating one's own.[37] Meetings were about rational talk, and to participate in them successfully one had to learn to talk and listen in appropriately reciprocal ways: to take one's turn, to control one's outbursts of scorn or temper, to subordinate one's own interests and views to those of others, or at least to appear to do so. As innumerable meeting manuals told their readers, 'Common sense and common courtesy are the foundations of good meeting procedure'.[38]

As meeting manners became more widely known attention shifted from instructing the membership to advising the chairman, the person ultimately responsible for the effective and orderly conduct of the meeting. Again, as the advice made clear, knowing how to run a good meeting is knowing far more than knowing formal procedural rules; it is knowing how to balance competing interests and views; how to achieve an effective outcome; how to handle a potentially disruptive outburst of anger, or even violence; how, that is, to maintain public order, prevent it from descending into chaos and still get things done. Meeting manuals thus mix exposition of various procedural rules with advice to the chair on such matters as how to control aggressive impulses, hostile feelings, passions and passing impulses in oneself as well as in the meeting under one's charge. *Robert's Rules of Order*, the standard United States manual, concluded its list of 'Parliamentary Don'ts for the Presiding Officer' with 'Don't lose your calmness, objectivity and impartiality'.[39] A displayed capacity to govern oneself provided one's authority to govern others.

A person's ability to provide political leadership was thus a manifestation of their general moral capacities. An obituary to Mrs Crocker, founding member and president for four years of the AWNL, slides easily between her capacities in office and her general character: 'The outstanding qualities of Mrs Crocker were, to my mind, her wonderful sense of justice, firmness and wisdom. To my knowledge she never gave a ruling without considering the question from all points, and also consulting those with whom she was associated.'[40] When the chairman of the inaugural meeting of the Middle Class Party claimed that the middle class supplied probably 80 per cent of the organising and executive ability of the community he was clearly exaggerating.[41] There is plenty of evidence of organisational ability in the labour movement and in working-class communities. He was, however, expressing a widely held middle-class conviction not only that it was their obligation to lead, but also that because of their superior moral qualities, in particular their self-discipline and self-control, they had a near monopoly on the qualities necessary to lead. As well, of course, the middle class were far more likely to have the skills and confidence necessary for successful public presentation.

Complementing the personal morality of the meeting was a historical narrative which linked the meaning of the meeting to the evolution of the British parliament. Most meeting manuals include brief histories of meeting procedures, and although the development of meetings was a European-wide accompaniment to industrialisation and modern state formation, English manuals generally present it as an exclusively British development, beginning with the Anglo Saxon moots, through the emergence of parliament and the gradual transfer of legislative and executive power from the monarch to the parliament.[42] Thus 'Parliamentary procedure represents the distilled common sense of centuries'[43] and so can carry the full weight of British pride in their constitutional system of parliamentary government, and its evolutionary development.

> On the basis of common sense and fair play the British Parliament slowly, through the centuries, evolved a system of rules and conventions upon which are based the procedure and usages of all free parliaments.[44]
>
> The word 'Parliament' ... embodies the spirit that has characterised the British people at home and abroad, through the generations.[45]

To participate in a meeting was thus not only to enact the obligations of citizenship and manifest one's virtuous character; it was also to participate in the wisdom of the British race and its civilising mission, as one followed in local meetings procedures developed in the mother of all parliaments at Westminster. The smallest and the greatest meetings of the land were thus linked by their shared deliberative procedures. *Robert's Rules of Order* has a frontispiece with the three simple words: 'CHURCH – CLUB – GOVERNMENT'. His *Rules of Order* are sufficient for each, a shared woof and weft which weaves society into a single cloth.

Meeting procedures embedded in the day-to-day life of the community knowledge of and commitment to parliamentary proceedings. Australian Liberals' commitment to parliament and to parliamentary procedure as the way of settling political conflicts was thus not a weak or abstract commitment to a distant institution. It was a commitment enacted in every meeting they convened or attended, and it informed their hostility to any political action which made unlawful use of force or physical violence. This hostility was, I am arguing, not primarily a hostility fuelled by fear and self-interest; there was, after all, very little likelihood that a violent picket line would really threaten middle class property holders. Rather it was hostility based on the confidently held conviction that this was not the way civilised people went about settling their differences. In this conviction there is a clear line of implication running from the government of the self through to the government of the community and the nation. Only if individuals learn to put the interests of others before the interests of themselves will it be possible to govern in the interests of all. This lesson may have begun in the home and the school, but it was given its most convincing political form in the countless meetings attended by Australians from all walks of life as they built and maintained their social worlds. Participation in the many meetings of civil society gave form and substance to Australian Liberals' understanding of citizenship and demonstrated to the middle class its possession of both the political skills and the qualities of character which legitimised its self-understanding as 'the backbone of the nation'. The links between voluntary associations and democracy are thus not simply to be found in the beneficial social effects of participation in meetings – the establishment of networks of reciprocity and the building of social trust, for example. Rather they are in the very form of the meeting itself in which people learn to discipline their emotions, self-interest and passing impulses within an externally-imposed system of constraint and so learn the lessons necessary for successful living in an increasingly interdependent society. For Liberals these were the lessons of good citizenship.

Order and Anarchy

The 1920s and 1930s were the heyday of Liberal citizenship. The ALP came out of World War I with its claims to legitimacy badly shaken. Apart from the brief and disastrous Scullin Labor government (1929–31), Liberals formed the national governments, first as the Nationalist Party and after 1931 as the United Australia Party, as well as the governments of most states. The overt sectarian conflicts of the last years of the war lapsed back into entrenched patterns of social separation, and industrial conflict became the key issue of public order, with a new and much more threatening face lurking behind the Labor Party's commitment to the parliamentary road to socialism. The principles of order and service on which Liberal citizens ideally based the government of their selves, their homes and their communities needed defence in the public realm if civilised life as they knew it was to survive.

In 1892 the rural politician and future Victorian premier J. B. Patterson had summed up the political scene thus: 'there might be many sections and groups of parties, but in his opinion the central consideration after all was that there were two distinct parties in this community. One must be regarded as the party of order ... the other ... the party of anarchy'.[46] To describe the Labor Party as 'the party of anarchy' was to dismiss outright its claims to political legitimacy: a party of anarchy could never take on the law and order maintaining responsibilities of government. From Federation to World War I such representations of Labor's political role had had slight purchase. Labor's electoral successes had moved it quickly from the political margins into the heart of the parliamentary contest. It had cooperated with the governing party, had won two general elections in its own right, and the country had not descended into anarchy. The fact that Australians were prepared to elect a Labor government at the outbreak of the war is evidence of just how firmly Labor had established its legitimacy as an alternative party of government. The main attacks on it had been in class terms, attacks on its policies as favouring one section of society above another, and on its representatives for having insufficient education and experience to provide good government. George Reid had attacked the Labor Party as socialist in 1906 and anti-labor interests had rallied under the banner of anti-socialism, but most voters had shared Deakin's lack of response to the 'bogey-breeding epitaph' of socialism, preferring to judge the Labor Party in terms of its practical policies and the quality of its government. But the war and the Bolshevik Revolution in Russia changed all that.

The industrial conflict of the war years and the two conscription referenda had given Labor's early association with disorder new lease of life, and so heightened the Nationalists' identification with order. Opening the New South Wales Nationalist Party headquarters, in 1921 Joseph Cook said: 'This solid old building, standing like a Rock of Ages, is a fitting symbol of the solid, sane and square principles Nationalism stands for'.[47] Throughout the 1920s the Nationalists were the party of authority, and respectability. The 1920s are the decade which best fits Eggleston's description of the Liberals as the residual party in Australian politics, the party based on the desire to 'maintain the pattern of Australian life' against what were seen as the extremist demands of the parties of 'vested interests'.[48] The Nationalists were the party of cautious commonsense, defined less by what it was for than what it was against. The reforming optimism of the period before the war was gone, and with it much of the basis for Labor's electoral support. As the Nationalists' 1922 campaign slogan put it: 'For Safety First Vote Nationalist'.[49]

Nationalists conceded Labor's prewar popularity and idealism, but, they argued, the prewar party was not the same party as had emerged from the war. Then its leaders had ideals: 'They were earnest and sincere men ... [their] mistakes due more to their intellectual limitations than to innate wickedness of heart'. But now the party was 'a degenerate dogfight' and 'its policy was one of unconstructive negatives'.[50] A pamphlet endorsing Captain S. M. Bruce for the 1919 federal election explains the difference: the prewar Labor Party 'stood for great principles, which, however one may have disagreed with some of their views were sane, and were designed to advance the position of the workers of this country by Constitutional means'. By contrast, the party in 1919 was composed of two sections, 'one of extremists, who are controlled by no sense of responsibility, and care nothing for the welfare of the country. The other ... those who still follow Labor because they have been born and bred to believe in the principles of the old Labor Party and who have not recognised the terrible changes that have come over the situation'.[51] The strategy was to identify the contemporary Labor Party with the extremists and so discredit the legitimacy of Labor's claims to government.

In the years immediately after the war the Nationalists continued to attack Labor for its opposition to conscription in the two referenda and its association with the disloyal Irish Sinn Feinians. At the 1919 election the Nationalists pursued the claim on which their formation was based: that they represented the burying of partisan and sectional differences in loyalty to the nation as a whole. Billy Hughes concluded his policy speech by invoking the 'Spirit of Australia': 'I appeal to all of you who love your country to forget your ancient party differences and stand side by side in this crisis – to be guided by the spirit of Australian nationalism which animated our soldiers'.[52] In contrast with the Nationalists' all-out effort to win the war, Labor's commitment had been less than wholehearted. Why else would it have opposed conscription? The Nationalist Speakers Handbook supplied quotations from Labor Party and unionist spokesmen to illustrate Labor's dubious loyalty. For example, Senator Stewart had expressed the hope that at the end of the war all Crowned Heads 'including our own' would be dethroned; and Mr Brookefield, a New South Wales Labor MP, was quoted as saying 'The red flag is the only flag I'll ever spill my blood for. As for this British Flag they talk about – the Union Jack – I'll never spill a drop of blood for it.'[53] Attacks on Labor's loyalty re-ran the divisions of the second conscription campaigns, and the presence of the returned service men together with the grieving of the bereaved ensured it retained its emotional power.

As the 1920s progressed, accusations of disloyalty against Labor based on the wartime conflicts waned and attacks on Labor's legitimacy increasingly focused on its Bolshevist sympathies and associations. The boundaries between loyal and disloyal Australians created by the sectarian conflicts of the war and early 1920s were overlaid with another way of distinguishing between loyalty and disloyalty – apparent sympathy for Bolshevism. And in the overlay, features of the Roman Catholic Church as the centre of a nefarious worldwide conspiracy to undermine democracies and exert world domination slid easily over on to the Communist Party. Eventually Moscow came to replace Rome as the ultimate signifier of disloyalty, though in the meantime Liberals were alert to connections. An article in *Fighting Line* (the publication of the New South Wales branch of the Nationalist Party) on the history of the Red Flag reminds readers that although nowadays red is an emblem of revolution, it was originally the recognised colour of the Catholic Church militant and still figures prominently in papal and cardinal vestments.[54] Anti-communism, however, was much more congenial to Nationalist propagandists than sectarianism. Where sectarianism risked disqualifying a significant proportion of the Australian population from full social membership, anti-communism well-suited the logic of scapegoating, in which a small, alien group can be seen as responsible for all the ills of the loyal national mainstream and targeted for expulsion and destruction, or simply for marginalisation.

Australians knew little about Russia. When the Tsarist regime fell it was at first welcomed cautiously as a step for the backward Russian people towards liberty and self government, as well as a more determined war effort. But when the first revolution was succeeded by the second, and the Bolshevik government sued for peace on the eve of the second conscription referendum, Bolshevism became synonymous with extremism and lawlessness.[55] Most Australians knew even less about the ideas of Marx and Lenin than they did about Russia, and saw Bolshevism in terms of anarchism, the abandonment of all self-restraint, and the overthrowing of the conventions of respectable, orderly society. George Reid's 'will-o'-the-wisp' of socialism had taken form in Russia, and its horrors went far beyond the dangers of a little too much planning and government control.

The 1919 election was the first at which these dangers were widely presented to the Australian people. The 1919 Nationalist Speakers' Handbook, after discussing the way the Nationalist government had helped, among others, the sugar, butter and rabbit-skin industries, turned its attention to 'Bolshevism and Official Labour', claiming that 'Official Labour has adopted Bolshevism in all its horrors'. The first of these is that Bolshevism does not merely stand for majority rule, but for the 'Nationalisation of women'. There followed claims about the abolition of marriage and of unmarried 18-year-old girls being required to register at the 'Bureau of Free Love of the Commissariat of Surveillance'. The source given for these claims is 'The Anarchist Soviet, City of Saratov'.[56] Liberal women's organisations picked up these claims and circulated them in their publications, ensuring that they reached the ears of women already anxious about the effect of the war on the sexual morality of men. *The Woman's Voice*, the publication of the Women's Reform League, for example, repeated the story about the fate of 18-year-old Russian girls, and *The Fighting Line* featured the claims prominently on its women's page.⁵⁷

The Bolshevik Revolution gave anti-socialist rhetoric a living example of the loss of life, liberty, property and social order under a communist government. Bolshevism became an image of extremist lawlessness to strike fear into the hearts of law-abiding Australians, and in 1920, when the Australian Communist Party was established, 'Communist' joined 'Bolshevik' in the Liberals' lexicon of threat. Party propaganda remained preoccupied with the iniquities of Bolshevism and communism throughout the 1920s and 1930s, and with establishing the connection between communism and the ALP.⁵⁸ In a 1922 cartoon in the *Australian National Review*, captioned 'His Master's Voice' after the famous trademark for HMV recordings, the dog of the Federal Labor Party has its ear to the gramophone's trumpet to receive instructions from Moscow: 'The Federal Labor Party's platform includes the Soviet doctrines of socialisation of industries, Councils of Action, etc. The close connection between the Red International at Moscow and the Australian communists who dominate the ALP is obvious.'⁵⁹ 'Under which flag?' asks a 1928 election leaflet showing the Union Jack crossed with the Red Flag. Another claims that 'The objectives of Communism and the ALP are identical'.⁶⁰

This was not, however, simply scare tactics. The Labor Party itself gave plausibility to the association when it adopted the socialist objective at its 1921 Federal Conference. The Bolshevik Revolution had given new confidence to radicals throughout the world. An All-Australian Trade Union Conference recommended to the 1921 Federal Conference that the party's objective be simplified to 'The socialisation of industry, production, distribution and exchange'. The objective was carried, against strong arguments from pragmatists who realised what an electoral liability it would be. At the very end of the conference 'The Blackburn Declaration' was adopted, which considerably modified the objective and committed the party to industrial and parliamentary action in clear rejection of the unlawful, violent means used by revolutionaries.⁶¹ But it was foolish to think that opponents who were happy to confuse Russian Bolsheviks with Irish nationalists would read the fine print of Labor's platform, or take care to distinguish between the parliamentary and revolutionary roads to socialism. Labor had handed its opponents a powerful weapon by giving plausibility to their association of Labor with Communist threats to property and so made it harder for Labor to get a hearing from the middle class. Until the 1970s when the debacle of the Vietnam War forced Australians into a more realistic assessment of the nature of Asian communism, associating the Labor Party with Communism could be relied on to scare Liberal stragglers back across the line.

Order/disorder, loyalty/disloyalty, Australian/unAustralian: these simple pairs of opposites presented the difference between the Nationalists and the Labor Party in terms of a stark, black-and-white choice in which the Nationalists found it hard to concede the ALP any legitimate basis for its political existence. This reiterated their faith in the possibility of one party able to represent a unified national interest. Under the pressures of war many on the Liberal side gave up even the pretence of believing in the necessity of opposition for the Westminster system. Herbert Brookes in his 1918 presidential address to the Associated Chambers of Manufactures urged the assembled gathering to replace their commitment to Profit (a sectional demand) with a commitment to Service: 'We shall then have ONE GREAT NATIONAL PARTY OF AUSTRALIA, and we shall know how to deal out their desserts to the disloyalist and sectarian traitor and Bolshevik in our midst'.[62] Brookes here takes little care to distinguish among the different bases of disagreement with the Nationalists, or different classes of enemies. Such conflations were common: for example, on the issue of Britain's relations with Ireland, loyalists regularly conflated Catholicism, Irish nationality, constitutional Irish nationalism, support for the Sinn Fein and armed insurrection, legal criticism of Empire policy and actual treason.[63] Enemies were always assumed to be acting in consort: Bolshevism 'was made in Germany',[64] and the Russian Soviet was behind the Irish Red Republican Army.[65]

Rejection of the legitimacy of opposition in the name of commitment to a unified national interest was an important strand in non-labour politics in the 1920s and 1930s. While the Nationalist Party itself soon settled back into the rhythms of parliamentary democracy, some non-labour supporters continued to reject the inevitable conflicts and compromises of democratic, party-based politics and to hanker after non-party solutions, either government by a national non-party government, or, more extremely, some form of 'strong' non-parliamentary government such as Mussolini was providing in Italy. Such ideas circulated among the right-wing militia groups in which ex-soldiers sought a national cause to defend as simple and clear-cut as the one for which they had so recently fought. They achieved wider popularity in the crisis of the depression.[66]

In the aftermath of the war, Australians pulled the boundaries tight around themselves and the lines of division opened up by the war hardened. There were good social and psychological reasons for this. The war had been far more traumatic than could have been imagined when the first recruits flocked to the bugle call of Empire in August 1914. Of the approximately 417 000 men who had enlisted, 60 000 were dead and 160 000 wounded.[67] Family and friends built memorials in towns and suburbs all over Australia, as they grieved for the loss of so many young lives. Staying loyal to the values these young men had died for helped make sense of their deaths, as did the transformation of the digger into a national hero and the landing at Gallipoli into the Anzac legend. As well, society had to reintegrate the surviving soldiers who were rejoining a world innocently remote from the horrors of Gallipoli and the Western Front and where the unity of purpose to which they had marched away had been lost in the conflict over conscription. Returned soldiers were ready recruits for loyalist demonstrations which rallied to the defence of God, King and Country against perceived threats from the left.[68]

But yearn as people might to return to the certainties of prewar life, the years immediately after the war were chaotic. There were the sectarian rallies and demonstrations already discussed. In 1919 there were street riots in both Brisbane and Melbourne, and violent industrial clashes throughout the country. The year 1919 was a highpoint for industrial action as the pent up demand released by the end of the war fuelled inflation which in turn fuelled wage demands: 6.3 million strike days were lost to production, more than in any other year till the 1970s. In Fremantle, striking waterside workers clashed with police in a pitch battle in which one man was killed. And on top of all this, an epidemic of Spanish influenza killed 12 000 people.[69] In such circumstances, it was not hard to make the world look a frightening place to small property holders, and to women who felt physically intimidated by the threat of violence and lawlessness on the streets. The election year of 1919 was the most chaotic of the postwar years, and the Labor Party was easily defeated.

For Australia emerging from the chaos and grief of the years immediately after the war, Britain and her Empire provided a reassuring foundation on which to rebuild order and prosperity, and a solid platform from which to participate in the affairs of the world at large. With Labor fatally associated with disloyalty, the custody of Australia's imperial relationship seemed safest in Nationalist hands, as Billy Hughes told electors in 1922: 'The National Party stands for the maintenance of Empire; that is the rock on which its house is built, the cross to which it clings'.[70]

The confident Australian nationalism of the 1880s and its flirtation with independent republicanism had well and truly disappeared by the turn of the century. The depression of the 1890s destroyed the illusion of Australia's capacity to deliver boundless prosperity and revealed it as a small trading economy hostage to larger economic forces. Its export income was derived overwhelmingly from primary commodities and when world prices for these fell Australians suffered. As well, it was an importer of capital and so depended on retaining the confidence of foreign investors who were mostly British. The lesson drawn from Australia's vulnerable position in the world economy was that membership of a strong Empire was in Australia's best economic interests. It was also in her best strategic interests as the islands to Australia's north attracted the interests of Britain's rival European powers, France and Germany, and as Japan's power grew.

At Federation few Australians doubted the wisdom of Australia's remaining in the British Empire, and this conviction only increased in the period up to and during World War I. At its end, the Empire still seemed Australia's best security. Billy Hughes, who had deserted Labor because of his imperial convictions, was not however the one to oversee this. No one doubted his loyalist credentials, but many doubted his capacity to preside over a stable and orderly government. His role in the two conscription referenda had left him associated with rancour and division, and he carried none of the gravitas or level-headed commonsense associated with the best British practices of good government. As well, the alliance on which the Nationalist Party was based was inherently unstable, formed in the heat of passionate wartime loyalties but bound to falter when peace brought cooler economic issues back into the centre of government concerns. The Nationalists' business supporters felt the government needed men of sound business and financial experience, and this conviction was given added force by the appearance of a new player in federal party politics, the Country Party.

Farmers' organisations had been active in state and federal politics since before World War I but it was only with the introduction of preferential voting for the 1919 federal election that a federal organisation was established. Preferential voting enabled rival non-labour candidates to trade preferences and so avoid splitting the non-labour vote. Eleven representatives were elected from variously named farmers parties in 1919, and fourteen in 1922, which left the now-named Country Party holding the balance of power and able to demand terms for joining a coalition. Its most dramatic demand was for a new leader. Country Party leader, Earle Page, was not prepared to be a member of any government led by Billy Hughes. After futile attempts to stave off the inevitable, a humiliated Hughes eventually resigned and the Country Party formed a coalition government with the Nationalists under the leadership of Stanley Melbourne Bruce.

From that point on the Country Party was a permanent presence in Federal Parliament, sharing power for forty-three of the next sixty-three years. In terms of the Liberals' claims to national government, the formation of the Country Party required some adjustments. Liberals now had to both differentiate themselves from the new party, and explain why, whatever its faults, it was still more deserving of support than Labor. The first task was relatively easy. Like the Labor Party before it, the Country Party was formed to advance sectional demands; and like Labor it advocated government-based solutions to various of its constituency's problems. Small farmers had long felt neglected by both the city-based parties of big business, finance and the urban middle class, and by the Labor Party which had little to offer the small rural property holder except the threat of arbitration fixing farm wages. Small farmers wanted reductions of government spending and taxation, the freeing up of trade in primary produce (in particular the abolition of price fixing which delivered cheaper food to city consumers), the abolition of tariffs on items used in primary production, and the establishment of cooperative marketing boards. Eggleston compared the Country Party 'as the machinery of a vested interest' with Labor, and the Country Party's support for government assistance for primary production led to frequent complaints about 'Country Party Socialism'.[71]

Such criticisms did not, for the most part, prevent the Liberals from entering into coalition governments with the Country Party at both state and federal levels. Small farmers were implacably opposed to socialism and to the union movement, and as small property owners and small businesses they were responsive to stories about the importance of independent, self-reliant, productive activity. The County Party developed a specialist inflection to this story. Don Aitkin has called this 'countrymindedness', a set of views about the moral and social virtues of country life and the crucial importance of rural production to Australia's economic wellbeing.[72] This gave Country Party supporters the basis for their conviction that in pursuing their economic demands they were also pursuing values and principles of importance to the nation as a whole: the nation rode on their backs, and so had to take care of its backbone. From the point of view of the Liberals, cooperative arrangements with the Country Party boosted their claims to be a non-sectional party capable of harmonising competing demands and hence the only legitimate representative of a unified national interest.

Prime Minister Bruce

The man who replaced Hughes as the Nationalist leader and as Prime Minister was everything the irascible, unkempt little Hughes was not; tall, grave, immaculately dressed and impeccably polite. He spoke in measured, ponderous prose and could be relied on to 'do the right thing' according to the conservative social and political conventions of the day.[73] The *Australian Manufacturer* summed him up thus: 'Bruce is a capable but not a particularly brilliant man. He does not say new things, nor does he say the old ones in a new way. He is in fact a very average person, and that is the secret of his success.'[74]

Born in Australia but educated in Britain, Stanley Melbourne Bruce was an Australian–Briton able to pass as well as any Australian ever could as a member of the British governing classes. Bruce's father, John Munro Bruce, was one of the poor immigrants who made a fortune during the golden age of Australia's economic growth after the goldrushes, and by the time Bruce was born in 1883 the family owned a large and successful importing and warehousing business. Bruce left Australia at nineteen to go to Cambridge, where he studied law and gained a blue for rowing. He served with the British army during the war and was wounded at Gallipoli, and again in France. In 1917 he was repatriated and awarded the Military Cross. He returned to the family business and while visiting Melbourne was recruited by the Nationalists for a by-election in the seat of Flinders. The National Union (which provided the party's financial backing) in particular felt the government needed men of sound business and financial experience to counter the Hughes' government's propensity to extravagance and support for government enterprise. And to add to Bruce's credentials, he was a wounded officer. Bruce won the seat and held it at the 1919 election, and in 1921 was offered the position of Treasurer by Hughes who was coming under increasing pressure from business demands to reduce government expenditure.[75]

Bruce's easy movement between Australia and England was reassuring to those who wanted to believe in the continuities of the two societies. Bruce was a 'gentleman', from the tips of his patent leather shoes to his measured speech and impeccable manners. To Australians unfamiliar with the cruelties of the English class system he could easily represent all that was best about the British. Selecting Bruce as leader of the Nationalist Party, Australian Liberals were attempting to stabilise their political identity around enduring values. Deakin's tolerant, open-minded liberalism had not survived the polarisations of the war, and the Nationalists became a conservative party, its identity based squarely on the defence and perpetuation of the status quo: White Australia, the British Empire, constitutionalism, sound finance and a continuing commitment to Australian nation-building. Bruce's personal attributes fitted him well to be the leader of such a party: business experience, first-hand familiarity with Britain, and honourable war service.

The 1920s is the period for which my decision to use 'Liberal' as a continuous name for the political tradition which this book is about is most problematic, in which the word 'conservative' comes more naturally to the pen.

Describing Australia's major non-labour party as 'conservative' draws much of its plausibility from aligning Australia's party system with Britain's, seeing the opposition between Labor and non-labour in Australia in terms of the opposition between the British Labour and Conservative Parties. Such a reading, however, only becomes possible in the 1920s when Labour emerges as the fulcrum of British politics. Before 1920 the major cleavage in British politics was between the Liberals and the Conservatives, and the British Labour Party, which began to make an electoral impact in 1906, operated essentially as an appendage of the Liberals. After the war the Labour Party adopted a specifically socialist constitution, broke its pact with the Liberals and struck out on its own. It won 22 per cent of the vote in 1918 and by 1922 had increased its share sufficiently to become the official Opposition. British politics thus reformed around the two poles of Labour and anti-Labour as Australian politics had done over a decade earlier, with many Liberals joining the Conservatives as the most effective vehicle for countering Labour.[76] Although the Liberal Party continued to exist, it was now a third party and Australian Liberals identified themselves with the Conservatives. Both shared the major political responsibility for combating the dangers of socialism and organised labour in their respective countries.

As well, to tackle Labour more effectively the British Conservative Party was transforming itself from the old Tory Party of the aristocracy and landed gentry into a broadly based Conservative Party of consensual popular nationalism. Such a party was a much more congenial point of identification for practical colonial Liberals, as was the party's new leader. The emergence of Labour as Britain's official Opposition required a Prime Minister in the House of Commons. Stanley Baldwin, who became the leader of the Conservatives and British Prime Minister after the 1922 election, was a commoner and a provincial industrialist, who prided himself on being a practical man of business and sound commonsense. Bruce, himself a practical man of business, was easily able to recognise Baldwin's virtues,[77] as was Menzies a decade later who constructed him as the authentic voice of the plain English man's instinctive decency.[78] Baldwin pitched the party's appeal to the cautious, middle-class property owners of the suburbs, the men on £500 per year who responded to Labour in terms of deeply held stereotypes of a militant and greedy working class.[79] Class relations in Britain had a visceral quality lacking in Australia's more open social structure, but nevertheless the parallels were sufficient for both

Australian Labor and Liberal politicians to look to the homeland for guidance. During the 1920s both the British Conservative Party and the Australian Nationalists promised to put 'Safety First', and presented themselves as the only party able to represent their respective national interest. In 1931 after the Liberals had re-formed again as the United Australia Party, their new leader and another ex-Labor man, Joe Lyons, chose 'Tune in with Britain' as a campaign slogan. Australian Liberals were no longer leading the way in developing strategies to combat the Labor challenge. With the re-formation of British politics in the early 1920s, they became followers of 'Britain's Grand Example'.[80]

When Bruce first stood for parliament he said he stood not as a politician but as 'a plain business man and as a plain soldier'.[81] In the face of the manifest conflicts and divisions within Australian society, Bruce believed in the unified national interest he had served as a soldier. For him the resolution of the paradox of party was easy and he simply collapsed the party into the nation. He was thus committed to keeping the Nationalist Party inclusive and resisted moves from people like John Latham to revive the Liberal identity of the government and drive out the Labor element. He insisted, for example, on the inclusion in his government of ex-Labor minister George Pearce.

Bruce defined the unified national interest in the overwhelmingly materialist terms to which his business background disposed him. He believed that increased wealth, prosperity and happiness depended on increased production and that the nation could only be made more productive through the application of good, sound business principles. Who, after all, could argue with the goal of development? He increased incentives to producers, whom he regarded as the real engines of economic growth, established various marketing schemes, and attempted to improve the efficiency of the national economy. In the early 1920s there was much talk among men of affairs of the need for 'clean' government, a modernist image of a streamlined, efficient government, shorn of the irrationalities of special pleading, political deals, and inefficient traditional practices.[82] In a statement which was to be echoed many times in the 1980s, Bruce insisted: 'We were guided not by ideological motives, but by strict business principles'; and he supported the selling of government-owned enterprises with the claim that it was not the function of the government to compete in the open market but to govern. For Bruce 'strict business principles' did not bear class or partisan values, but were simple and transparent agents of a practical and impersonal rationality which could be directed towards the common good of national development.[83]

The Bruce–Page government picked up the prewar agenda of nation building, but without the same optimism and consensus with which

Australians had embarked on the new century, and with perhaps an even greater dependence on Britain. Men, Money and Markets was the theme: to expand the population through migration, to attract capital investment, and to expand the markets for Australian exports. All this was to take place within a secure and strong imperial framework in which Australia was a proud white, British dominion, 'an outpost of Empire [in which] our chief task is to keep alive the traditions of our race'.[84] This strategy, however, was only partially successful. The assisted migration schemes were costly, as were the associated schemes to settle the 'empty' land with the expanded population, and governments borrowed to sustain them. Nor did Britain see the role of trade in the maintenance of imperial family ties in quite the same way as Australia; after all, the British government's first obligation was to British consumers not high-waged Australian producers, and imperial preferences were not expanded as Bruce had hoped. As well, Australian governments borrowed heavily during the 1920s to provide the expanding urban population with the infrastructure of modern life. About 70 per cent of capital inflow during the period was borrowing by governments. When added to the still unpaid loans used to finance World War I, this debt greatly expanded governments' international interest commitments.[85]

Signs of trouble with Bruce's vision of Australian prosperity were apparent by 1925 as the economy began to stall. Australia headed into the second half of the 1920s with rising levels of foreign debt and stagnating export income from primary industries hobbled with high costs by protection. By 1926 the accumulated foreign debt had risen from £419 million to £562 million, and the annual interest bill from £7 million to £26 million. It was not a happy situation, and London financiers were starting to ask 'Is Australian finance sound?'[86] Bruce was convinced that high wages were a major cause of Australia's economic difficulties, and that it was agitators in the union movement who stood in the way of the industrial relations reform necessary to enable the downward adjustment of the cost of labour. As the decade progressed he became increasingly focused on industrial relations and on the influence of 'alien' agitators. With Attorney-General John Latham he made various legislative attempts to control what he saw as unlawful industrial action. Although these were largely unsuccessful in stopping industrial action, they created a climate of conflict and distrust around the government which ensured it a place as a ruling-class government in the demonology of Labor history.

Bruce saw strikes as caused by a few militant union leaders intent on spreading revolutionary, Bolshevik or communist ideas and causing the ultimate overthrow of the capitalist system, rather than as directed to the limited industrial ends of the improvement of wages and working conditions. He assumed they had little rank and file support and that if the leaders could be removed then the strife would disappear. He made reform of industrial relations the central issue of his first election campaign in 1925. Consistent with the Nationalists' projection of itself as the party of safety and stability, Bruce framed his approach to industrial relations within the Nationalists' general commitment to constitutionalism and the rule of law, in opposition to the unlawful use of strikes to achieve political ends. The echoes of the British conservatives' appeal to 'the constitutional classes' are everywhere apparent.

> We feel that when the supremacy of Parliament is challenged, our constitutional and democratic institutions are subverted and law and order threatened, we should at once appeal to the people and place the issue clearly before them.
>
> The laws of this country have been defied, and constitutional authority challenged. An attempt has been made to subvert Democracy to domination by a few extremists. At the period of our greatest prosperity and most glowing opportunity, there are wreckers who would plunge us into the chaos and misery of class war.[87]

The 1925 election was the first of Australia's full 'red scare' federal election campaigns. Centre stage was the spectre of 'the communist and extremist' who sees in the great institutions of the trade union movement 'a ready instrument by which to effect his illegitimate purposes. He has bored into and white-anted many of them and is today endeavouring to use them not for the advancement of the worker but for his own nefarious purposes'.[88] As when Bolsheviks made their first appearance at the end of the war, communists were presented as unmotivated agents of pure hate and destruction, outside of any identity-giving social institutions: 'they recognised no distinction of nation, race or colour'; they were 'fanatics who want to bring the upheaval they cause in Russia to the rest of the world … Whenever there is strife – national or industrial – you will find the paid agents of Bolshevism – the harbingers of hate, the disseminators of poison'. Even inside the British Empire troubles in India or Egypt were to be directly traced to their activities; 'they have a malign hatred for the British Empire because it stands as a sure and stable rock in a world faced with chaos'.[89]

In contrast to the heated language Bruce used to describe the dangers of Bolshevism, he presented the Australian voters with a view of themselves as simple folk needing guidance and reassurance:

> Amidst all this turmoil, the ordinary citizen, whose life is far removed from political controversy, finds himself utterly confused and knows not where to

turn for guidance ... And when I speak of the ordinary citizen I speak of those who constitute the overwhelming majority of our people ... It is to these men and women of moderate and sane views that I would address myself tonight.[90]

Sanity, Safety, Stability – these were the Nationalists' key symbols for the moderate, sensible, middle way which would reconcile competing interests in the national interest and resolve political conflicts within the orderly processes of parliamentary democracy. Such appeals were particularly resonant for women. Industrial conflict could wreak havoc with women's household duties, but deeper than this inconvenience was its threat of male violence. Industrial labour spoke the language of militant masculinity; strikes and pickets were its weapons and violent demonstrations made the streets unsafe. As I argued earlier, women's support for law and order and constitutional means of settling conflicts may well be the result of fear, but it is rational fear, based on the knowledge that only if public space is pacified and orderly will women be heard.

For all Bruce's connection with reassuring British values and constitutional traditions, however, there were dangerous gaps between his experience and that of the ordinary Australian men and women to whom he spoke. A 1927 report of a function to welcome him and his wife back after one of their trips abroad shows his constituents working hard to fit the Bruces' wealth and peripatetic existence to their own more humble life-experience:

> Although in the past five months the Prime Minister has been present at many wonderful functions ... and has been entertained with a display of grandeur and circumstance befitting the representative of a great nation ... no event ... could compare in its deep heart [sic] appeal with the simple and informal conversazione at the Dandenong Drill Hall ... It was a home coming in the true sense of the word. There was that comfortable atmosphere of a heart to heart talk between the members of a family or clan, an atmosphere in which all present felt perfectly at ease ... After the Goodnights ... Mr and Mrs Bruce drove away amid cheers for home sweet home, where they had not slept since September.[91]

But their sixteen-room Spanish-style mansion with baronial hall, recently built at a cost of £20 000, was a far cry from the homes of the solid citizens and farmers of Dandenong and Western Port.[92] Bruce was more at home with the political traditions of a wealthy patrician class than with the temper of popular democracies where political leaders are required not just to deliver good government but to represent their supporters' experience.

His major leisure activities were golf, horse-riding and motoring, hardly sports of the people, and his social life centred on the leather armchairs and well-furnished tables of the Melbourne Club. There were very few Australians who could see themselves writ large in the aloof, wealthy man in spats and plus-fours leaning nonchalantly against the door of the latest model motor car, and as the 1920s headed into the depression this was an increasing liability.

The 1928 election re-ran the red scare campaign, but not quite so floridly as in 1925, nor quite so successfully, and the government's majority was reduced. It appealed again to Australians to vote for 'sane and safe Government, combined with sound progressive policies', and it again blamed the lack of progress on continuing industrial trouble.[93] But by 1928 it was becoming clear that more than industrial trouble was blocking Australia's road to prosperity. Unemployment was 11 per cent, and the 1927–28 budget had a deficit of nearly £5.5 million.[94] Bruce had no new ideas as to how to tackle the downturn. He hoped it would be temporary, but when it failed to pass, he became increasingly bewildered and frustrated. A team of economic experts invited from Britain attacked Australia's high tariffs, the expensive rural settlement schemes, the practices of loan financing, the arbitration system and the bounties to encourage production. These were the core policies on which Bruce had built his vision of an expanding national productivity. And if the national cake was not going to expand but to contract, then difficult political decisions would have to be made about the distribution of pain. When the government dropped prosecution proceedings against a wealthy coal mine owner, John Brown, for an illegal lock-out, the contrast with its pursuit of unions for breaches of the industrial relations law was glaring and confirmed the government's class bias in the eyes of many of its working-class opponents.

Out of panic about the deteriorating economic situation and frustration at the continuing inability of the government to prevent industrial action, Bruce introduced legislation to hand most industrial relations powers back to the states. Nothing had been mentioned of these plans during the election and in fact Bruce had earlier sought increased Commonwealth powers over industrial relations. The legislation was defeated when Billy Hughes finally took his revenge on Bruce and led an assorted group of opponents across the floor to vote with Labor. Bruce called another election, less than twelve months since the last, in which he campaigned almost exclusively on the necessity of restoring power over industrial relations to the states.[95] Bruce may have believed that this was the magic solution to the country's mounting economic woes, but no one else did, and he was humiliatingly defeated, losing not only the government but his own seat of Flinders in a landslide victory for Labor.[96] The reserved and fiercely independent John Latham replaced him as Nationalist leader and Labor leader Jim Scullin replaced him as Prime Minister.

Stanley Melbourne Bruce was an unimaginative man, with few points of easy identification with ordinary Australians nor he with them. When first elected his embodiment of Britishness was reassuring to many Australians who saw him as a representative of solid British values and British imperial power on which to build both Australia's prosperity and its security. And the sense of service to a unified national interest which he took from his wartime experience held out the promise of a national harmony of interests to combat the divisiveness of class politics. If people did their duty and worked hard, not asking for too much and obeying the law, prosperity and public order would prevail. But as the depression loomed with its sharpened class conflicts and its threat of economic chaos, Bruce's lack of understanding of ordinary people was an increasing handicap. He had little grasp of the experiences which animated trade union politics and reached too readily for the language of scapegoating when confronting industrial militancy. Nor was he able to see his own class interests as part of the broad national picture. This is not unusual among the wealthy, but it is a great liability for the leader of a political party which claims to represent the interests of the nation as a whole, particularly once the going gets tough. Not only was Bruce widely seen as too close to the interests of the employers in his handling of industrial relations conflict, but his wealth and limited social experience rendered him unable to identify with the economic insecurities of thousands of Australians and they with him. As the depression developed, this would have been a major liability. As it was, it was Labor that led Australians into the full brunt of the depression and a major political crisis in which not only their livelihoods but their reputations in the eyes of the British were threatened, which was the only part of the world most of them cared about.

5
Honest Finance

War Bonds

A 1922 Nationalist election pamphlet titled 'The Savings Snatcher' depicts a cigar-smoking Communist boss snatching a mother's bank passbook with one hand and a man's war-bond certificate with the other. Reacting to a threat by Labor leader Matt Charlton to reduce interest on war loans proportionate to any fall in the cost of living, the caption reads: 'The same argument applies to savings bank interest. Hundreds of thousands of earners of small incomes have money in both war loans and savings banks. They can protect their savings only by voting National and "Safety First".'[1] When they promised to put Safety First, the Nationalists were not just promising safe streets and industrial order; they were also promising safety for the nation's finances. The class-based model of the Australian party system has given pride of place to economic self-interest as the basis of party identity and electoral support. Here surely is its proof. People with property voted Liberal, Nationalist, UAP and Liberal again because these parties promised to protect their homes, businesses and savings from the greedy, extravagant or incompetent hands of Labor governments. If, in the final analysis, politics is based on hip-pocket nerves, then this shows Australian Liberals' claims to moral virtue for what they are – excuses by mean-spirited, anxious people to hang on to their money.

There is of course something in this, for financial self-interest is a powerful motive; but it is not by any means the whole story. Money has never been simply about material things. It has always been experienced within complex moral and social frameworks which imbue its presence or absence, its superfluity or its dearth, the various ways it has been acquired and its competing uses, with a wealth of meanings. To understand the role that money and property have played in Australian Liberals' electoral support we have to go beyond crude materialism to probe the moral meanings money and its handling carried for the people of small means who were the Liberals' electoral backbone. The safety of the nation's savings was a constant theme in Nationalist party propaganda throughout the 1920s and the chapter begins with an analysis of the moral and political meanings of saving. In the early 1930s issues of savings and financial management moved from a minor theme to the centre of a national crisis over honest finance and the repudiation of debts. The people who mobilised behind Honest Joe Lyons' stand against debt repudiation and the mildly inflationary policies of Labor Treasurer Ted Theodore were not acting in any simple way out of self-interest. They were rallying to save the nation's honour. What were the historic processes which had brought them to this point of identification with the nation's financial predicament? How had they come to imagine themselves as part of a national economy as well as a nation? Why were they so quickly and confidently able to link the conviction of their own financial virtue to the nation's? The answer to these questions begins with the campaigns to raise money to fight the war. Both the housewife and the war-bond holder were bearers of virtue not just of threatened apron or hip pockets. As savers both clearly practised the virtue of thrift, and to this the war-bond holder added the virtue of patriotism. The pamphlet is eloquent on the virtues of those who invested in war bonds: 'these people lent what they had, and schemed and pledged their properties and incomes to get more, because it was for the soldiers at the war'.

At the outset of the war, Prime Minister Andrew Fisher had promised that Australia would fight 'to the last man and the last shilling'. Not only physical sacrifice would be called for but also financial, yet in 1914 when Fisher made this confident pronouncement Australia's capacity for financial sacrifice was largely unknown. Australian governments had well-worn paths to the London money markets to raise money for their ubiquitous development projects, but no government had previously attempted to raise a loan through a public campaign. Once the British government made clear that Australia would be expected to finance its own war effort, raising money from Australian domestic sources became the only available option. And, as with recruitment, Australians rallied: 'the war galvanised into activity the vast latent resources and financial potentialities of the Australian people' comments the Loan Organiser, Captain Dash.²

The Commonwealth floated seven war loans between July 1915 and August 1918, and three peace loans after the war ended, raising £250 172 440 of the £376 993 052 the war cost the Commonwealth government between 1914 and 1919. The loans were mostly fixed interest at 4.5 per cent per annum and exempt from state and Commonwealth taxes. The first loan in 1915 was raised easily with comparatively little organisation and publicity, but as loan followed loan, greater efforts were needed to mobilise the nation's savings. The first tactic was to make it easier for people of small means to buy bonds by introducing instalments; this led to a fourfold increase in the number of subscribers for the second loan. War Savings Certificates were also introduced so that small wage earners could participate. The second tactic was to increase the publicity and organisation of the loans.

Campaigns to mobilise the nation's savings required strenuous efforts by the public authorities in many ways parallel to the recruitment campaigns, with public launches, speeches, posters, banners, and gimmicks to attract public interest, such as giant barometers in each capital city to measure the progress, and a large model tank lumbering through the streets. Although all the loans were in fact oversubscribed, the numbers subscribing fell away by the fourth and fifth loan, spurring a massive escalation of effort for the sixth and seventh. The Commonwealth Bank, which had the responsibility of floating and managing the loans, appealed to professional and commercial organisations like the Commercial Travellers' Association for help. Captain Dash said of the campaign to raise the Sixth War Loan that 'It is doubtful if any public campaign was ever more spontaneously helped by every section of the community than the Sixth War Loan campaign ... The scenes of enthusiasm ... in every part of Australia will not readily be forgotten ... hardly a public meeting of any kind was held but some speaker was ready to make an appeal for the Cause.'[3]

For the Seventh War Loan in September 1918 spontaneous patriotic activity was largely replaced by a comprehensive national organisation of locality-based committees, coordinated in each state by a Central War Loans Committee which allocated quotas to the various shires. Competitions harnessed local loyalties to the national effort. In case exhortation to patriotic duty was insufficient, there were plans to compel every person to subscribe a sum based on their income tax, and it was likely that the terms would not be as favourable as for those 'who have voluntarily put their money at their country's service'.[4] In the event, the loan was oversubscribed, with an estimated one application for every four Australian households, and the plan to conscript the nation's savings was dropped.

Duty, sacrifice and service were the major themes in the advertising for war bonds. Huge banners with the simple words 'Save and Serve – Buy War Bonds' were strung across the fronts of prominent buildings such as Melbourne's State Treasury building at the top of Spring Street[5] or the Commonwealth Bank in St Martin's Place. In some advertisements saving money in order to buy bonds was presented in terms of one's moral duty to support the soldiers at the front: 'Each individual Australian must save and pay, work and lend to his last penny before he can truthfully say: "In this at least I have done my share".'[6] Spending freely put one in the same category as the despised shirkers, exposed to shame and the censure even of one's children. A variation of the famous recruiting poster 'What did you do in the war, Daddy?' has a curly-haired little girl clutching a war bond certificate saying 'My Daddy bought me a War Loan Bond. Did Yours?'[7]

The equivalence was not just one of different forms of sacrifice, of every one doing what they can; in some of the advertising the equivalence was deeper, as if one's money was a surrogate for one's self fighting on frontline. 'Money is a good soldier – Invest in the war loan' was stamped on government envelopes and letters;[8] 'If you can't fight your money can. A Bond may save a life.'[9] In one poster a fountain pen lies like a rifle across an open cheque book, its cap off ready for action; the caption reads 'Your Weapons Against Germany. Strike Here?'[10] The symbolic equivalence of a person's money with the deepest layers of their identity had been established by the Protestant ethic's ambivalent relationship with money, whereby the worldly pleasures it could buy were forsworn, yet its accumulation was external evidence of one's inner spiritual state. Here, in the call to sacrifice one's savings, that virtue was made manifest; only those whose self's energies had been accumulating in their bank balances were now in a position to put that self at the service of the nation.

Many of the investments in war bonds were made by businesses and firms or by individuals with potential investment capital. The first couple of loans were filled easily by tapping funds already available for investment. But as the net widened to include the small wage and salary earners, the pool available to invest had to be increased by the active encouragement of domestic saving. 'There is no one in Queensland who earns money who cannot afford at least one Bond, and thus become a shareholder of Empire. By this form of investment you combine THRIFT and PATRIOTISM.'[11] The exercise of thrift thus became not just a morally desirable attribute of individuals but a national duty, confirming for Australian Liberals another strand in the reciprocal relationship between the virtue of the individual and the strength of the state: 'As thrift builds on the best in individual character, so must it also build up the best in the national character. National thrift depends upon individual thrift.'[12]

Much of the exhortation to thrift was directed to women, who were advised on the choice and care of clothes, economical, nutritious cooking and ways of economising on household expenses.[13] Such advice had always been available, but the practice of thrift was no longer simply a means to the establishment of personal independence or the maintenance of the family's material well-being, though these were still worthy secondary goals. Its major purpose was to contribute to the nation: 'If you can add to your individual wealth, you add to the Nation's, and if having added to your wealth you lend some of it to the Nation, you help Australia'.[14] The

National Council of Women, the Australasian League of Honour for Women and Girls, the YWCA and the women's branches of the various non-labour parties all launched 'Thrift Weeks' to raise money for war bonds and the various patriotic comfort funds.[15] Through the campaigns for thrift the eyes of the state reached deep into the nations' households, and in particular into the shopping baskets, kitchens and wardrobes of the women who ran them: whether one sought out the bargains, saved the matches, turned a collar, or re-used the cooking fat became potentially political acts.

Women of small means had been used to such practices to make ends meet, so it was simply a matter of reframing them as patriotic activities. For women who were comfortable and accustomed to some level of discretionary income, they were novel and required more elaborate justification. An address delivered to the Victoria League in Adelaide explains the shifts in moral thinking about the economic relationships involved in the politicisation of the nation's savings. The speaker posed the question: 'How can I curtail my spending without injuring somebody else, who will generally be poorer than myself? If I reduce my staff of servants, what will the dismissed housemaid do? If we eat less meat, what will the butcher say?' The answer: 'The point missed by the argument is that, in the national economy, the saving of individuals does not mean less spending, but different spending, spending on different objects'. There follows a detailed explanation of how shifting the labour of the housemaid from the home to the munitions factory and using the money saved on her wage to buy war bonds involves not a 'diminution of work but a transfer'. Not spending stimulated the transfer of labour to the public services and by investing in the war loan one helped the state to pay for this transferred labour.[16]

Liberals had long possessed a model of the harmonious interdependence of the productive economy, labour and capital working hand in hand, people in different jobs each contributing their skills and talents and fulfilling their allotted tasks, the wheels of industry turning and the whole business of production humming along; but imagining the national economy in terms of flows of money required more abstract reasoning. The lesson of the housemaid-turned-munitions worker was that to understand one's economic responsibilities one had to move beyond the relations of economic interdependence embedded in the household and its immediate community to the interdependence of the national economy mediated by the state. In imagining oneself as a member of a nation one also had to imagine oneself as a member of a national money economy.

Historians seem to have largely overlooked Australians' patriotic mobilisations around money during World War I. Although Scott gives them their due, later general histories of the war barely mention them.[17] But they have important general implications for understanding later historical developments. They prefigure both in their arguments, and in their form of organisations, the mobilisations around money in the early 1930s. Having been drawn into an involvement with the nation's finances by the war loan campaigns, people retained a psychological investment in the handling of the nation's financial affairs. The war loan campaigns forged links between the private morality of the way people handled their own money and the financial standing of the nation, creating the pathways along which the moral panic of the early 1930s flowed to link codes of personal honour to the honour of the nation. They also created groups of people skilled in the organisation of public campaigns around money, from the officers of the banks, to the people who ran the war loans committees established in every municipality by the seventh war loan. Through them the nation's savings were politicised in ways which lasted at least until the campaigns against bank nationalisation in the late 1940s, and the moral discourse around money took on much more overtly political meanings.

Thrift campaigns continued into the interwar years, though not with the same political urgency. The focus shifted from the national back to the household economy, as organisations like the Housewives' Co-operative Associations sought ways to help women stretch their housekeeping budgets.[18] The State Savings Bank of New South Wales established a Thrift Department, with a Thrift Service Director, Jean Mitchell, who promoted various ideas from the United States savings banks. Where organisations like the Housewives Associations encouraged the economical practising of the domestic arts – the more one made at home the less one needed to purchase – Jean Mitchell's attention was on the way the housewife handled her money. 'Women are the nation's purchasers ... and it is essential to the prosperity of the nation, that this purchasing power be wisely used'.[19] Women were encouraged to keep strict account of their household income and expenditure, and to prepare budgets to guide future spending: 'The value of the personal budget is to make clear to the individual his own ideals and objectives, to adjust proportionately his needs to his income. The very process of budgeting ... is in itself an aid to economy and indirectly tends to develop a sense of proportion in spending, which ... develops stability and good citizenship'.[20]

The budget was yet another tool for the inculcation and display of virtue, and budgeting was added to the repertoire of training in citizenship. Banking facilities had been provided in schools since before the war. These had the dual goal of encouraging saving and teaching banking procedures. Through such means the commonsense link was established in people's minds between the managing of the household and the national economies. As the *Australian National Review* said when reporting on the State Savings Bank's Thrift Department: 'private economy is as important as national economy. Indeed, wide private thriftlessness almost connotes government extravagance.'[21] From this perspective the nation's savings could be constructed as a measure of national virtue: 'the tidy little provision against a rainy day' in the State Savings Bank or the Commonwealth Bank was evidence 'that there is a considerable proportion of the public content to shun the allurement of the ponies and the two up school'.[22] In 1934 Alex Cook, the General Manager of the State Savings Bank of Victoria, described it as a 'monument of thrift and self-denial'.[23]

With less urgency and ease than in the wartime savings campaigns, it was however still possible for these banks of personal virtue to be firmly tied to national purpose. Savings bank deposits were invested in government loans and these funds were used for nation-building purposes, to finance the development of rural and urban infrastructure.[24] Savings bank deposits were also used to pay for the building of domestic dwellings and shops through special purpose loans on lower interest rates. The aim was to provide low cost loans for people with an income of £400 or less (at 1920 value), and Australian cities' nineteenth-century centres are surrounded by the suburban developments of the 1920s and 1930s in which people of modest means paid off their Californian bungalows. The result of the capacity to save for a deposit and service the loan, the houses too became symbols of the interdependence of personal and national virtue, at the same time manifestations of their owners' inner strength and a contribution to the nation's housing stock.

Of course, such personal virtues were easier to practise in some social and economic locations than others. The key divider was not so much the actual level of disposable income, as its reliability. Clerks might begin their working life on incomes no higher than skilled workers, but the comparative permanence of white collar employment and the prospect of regular advancement meant they could contract debt and so acquire property. The prudent handling of money both required and inculcated the respectable virtues of thrift and self-restraint, but crucial for its practice was a reliable income which made the careful handling of money over the long term a rational response. Where income was irregular, unreliable and insufficient, quite different practices seemed rational. The manual classes also had to plan and save but their time horizons were of necessity shorter: the weekly wage not the annual salary. And they had to put money aside against periods of ill health and unemployment. In a study of the saving and spending patterns of the British working class Paul Johnson has argued that middle-class commentators on the needs of the working class to develop better financial habits had little appreciation of the precariousness of their weekly incomes; that insecurity of income prevented the adoption of long-term saving plans across a lifetime characteristic of the middle classes.[25] Australia's prewar house ownership patterns bear out his argument. The expansion of home finance in the 1920s was of little use to low income earners, although the skilled working class and tradesmen fared better in Australia. The deposits required were substantial by today's standards, at least 25 per cent of the home's value, and the interest rates were between 6 and 7 per cent. In 1929 a fully employed male factory worker earned an average of £200 per year when even the cheapest land and house package cost about £600.[26]

For white collar employment one needed both education and a good character. The latter requirement disguised for the middle class the structural basis of its economic good fortune. One achieved the positions which gave one the regular income with which to practise the virtues of regular saving and prudent money management because one already had the steady, disciplined and self-denying character which would make good use of the opportunities to save and accumulate. From this perspective it was easy to read the straitened economic circumstances of those without regular work as the result of their unsteady characters. This was not just the familiar workings of the Protestant work ethic, it was also, as Stefan Collini has argued, an expression of deeply held beliefs about the role of habit in the formation of the settled dispositions of the person, and in their capacity to restrain impulse. Character was formed over the long haul, from an accumulation of tiny acts of strength or weakness of will: 'Every smallest stroke of virtue or of vice leaves its never-so-little scar,' wrote William James, a sentiment echoed in the stringent moral puritanism of the Australian Catholic Church. Character could be trained and strengthened like a muscle, or grow flabby from want of use. Attention was thus shifted away from a person's present circumstances and capacities, both to imagined past actions which had left them well or ill-prepared to face life's challenges, and to a future where they would reap the costs of their present indulgence through their weakened characters.[27]

For both the moral middle class and for the bankers and financiers the rallying cry of the depression was 'Sound Finance'. Ross McKibbin has argued for Britain of the same period that the bankers, financiers and Treasury officials made economic and financial policy on the basis of underlying assumptions which differed very little from those of 'the plain man in Tunbridge Wells': 'The political economy of the Blacketts, Normans, Hopkinses, Niemeyers or Fishers was inspired by a series of precepts (not living beyond your means, paying your way, safety first) ... which ... as rules for life meant more to the middle than to the working classes'.[28]

The plain men and women of Australia's moral middle class – of Hawthorn, Ashfield, North Adelaide and Claremont – were not quite the same as the plain folks of Tunbridge Wells, and there were proportionately more of them. In Britain by 1931 manual classes made up slightly more than three quarters of the working population; in Australia it was about half.²⁹ Class relations in Australia lacked the hard edges which separated the middle and working classes in Britain; the lower middle class blurred into the skilled working class and crossing the boundaries did not carry the same fears of loss of caste. McKibbin puts the weight of his argument on the middle classes' hostility to the working class, arguing that the middle classes shared a largely negative ideological social unity held together more by a shared negative conception of the working class than by positive shared beliefs and practices.³⁰ In Australia, it was the Labor Party and the unions which bore the brunt of middle class hostility, particularly once Jack Lang hit his straps as a promoter of debt repudiation, and the invitation was always open for respectable workers and their wives to identify with middle class values. For Australians, the commonsense precepts of sound finance were not simply about the projection of certain vices on to the working classes; they were also about the affirmation of middle class virtues in which the way one handled one's money was as much a moral as a financial matter and had been given national political meanings in the mobilisation of national savings in World War I.

Bonds of Honour

In November and December 1930 Australia's savers were again called on to contribute to an urgent national cause: to save the nation's honour in the face of threatened repudiation of a loan. A government loan fell due on 15 December and the Labor Caucus had voted at a meeting in early November to postpone its repayment. Joseph Lyons, acting as temporary Treasurer, defied the Caucus. As far as Lyons was concerned, postponing the repayment of the loan amounted to repudiation, the dishonouring of a government's contractual obligation by forcing the bond holders to retain their bonds. In response to the vote, he sprang to his feet shouting 'I will not do it! You have done this thing but I will not be a party to it'.³¹ Scullin was in London at the Imperial Conference and Treasurer Ted Theodore was temporarily out of Cabinet awaiting the investigation of accusations of fraud in relation to the sale of the Mungana mine. Lyons cabled Scullin, and with his support proceeded to defy the Caucus resolution by launching a public loan to raise £28 000 000 to cover the debt. Australia's honour was at stake, her national reputation, and the confidence of the British investors on which Australia's ability to weather the depression depended.

Lyons had entered federal politics in 1929 after twenty years in the Tasmanian parliament, including serving as Treasurer, Leader of the

Opposition, and from 1923 to 1928 as Premier, during which time he had restored Tasmania's finances using the principles of sound finance. He had pruned government expenses, reduced loan expenditure, raised new taxes, and presented honest and transparent state accounts.[32] And, he had succeeded. Sound and honest finance had worked in Tasmania, and he was convinced that adherence to its principles was the only path to an honourable national financial recovery. As well, as shown by his defiance of Caucus, he held the interests of the nation higher than those of the party. When later censured by the Tasmanian State Labor Conference for his failure of 'discipline', he said: 'Outstanding among the things for which I was condemned was the statement I made recently that I would put the interests of Australia before my Party … I am out for Australia and the interests of its people.'[33] Although Lyons' stance was against the Labor Party, it struck a wider chord. As the depression deepened disillusion with parties and politicians of all persuasions was increasing.

C. J. Dennis, the creator of Ginger Mick, published a poem in the Melbourne *Herald*, 'Under which Flag?'. This was a common question on Nationalist Party pamphlets in the 1920s, strung above the crossed Union Jack and the Red Flag.[34] Dennis' question was more allegorical: was Australia to meet its troubles beneath the flag of honour or the flag of shame?

> 'Haul down the country's flag!' they said,
> 'Haul down our flag, and, in its stead,
> Break this, the banner of our shame,
> That to the world Australia's name
>   Be e'er disgraced.
>
> …
>
> 'What tho' this starry flag has flown
> Proud o'er this land we call our own;
> Flown o'er grim fields where men have bled,
> The winding sheet of glorious dead?
>   Now let it drag
> Thro' mire because we fear the cost,
> Because we count the battle lost—
>
> …
>
> And when the people, put to test,
> Win freedom, surely they shall wrest
> This staff from out these weakling hands
> And show the world Australia stands
>   On Honour's side.[35]

The verse is lame, with none of Ginger Mick's irreverent wit, but its sentiments were widely shared. Surely the fighting spirit and valour displayed on the battlefields of World War I had not deserted the country. Surely Australians were not prepared to dissipate their newly won reputation as a nation through financial recklessness.

The Scullin government had been elected in October 1929, just as Wall Street began to slide. It inherited a weak economy, with increasing unemployment, an accumulated deficit of £6.5 million,[36] and a time bomb in the fixed interest overseas government loans. Of particular concern were the short-term loans which had accumulated rapidly throughout 1929 as longer term loans became harder to raise. By 1930 the debt had grown to £23.1 million with little prospect of conversion to a long-term basis. The Wall Street crash had triggered a collapse in world prices of the commodities on which Australia's export income relied, wool and wheat, thus making the servicing of the debt all but impossible. As a proportion of government debt fell due every few months, the Federal government was continually engaged in negotiations for renewals of loans with financial institutions both here and in London.[37] This provided regular opportunities for orthodox bankers to exert pressure on government policy, in particular to stress the need for the reduction of government expenditure in order to balance the budget. Chief among these was Sir Robert Gibson, the Chairman of the Board of the Commonwealth Bank, who repeatedly reminded the government of the dangers of straying from the principles of 'sound finance'. The central principle of 'sound finance' was that credit could not be created, but had to be backed by solid assets. Saving must always equal investment, and if the money was not saved, then it was not available to spend. Any artificial expansion of credit would inevitably lead to inflation, and inflation could quickly develop into hyperinflation and risk the integrity of the entire financial system. Meanwhile, as the depression worsened domestic political pressure mounted for some relief for the unemployed and the most distressed farmers.

In early 1930 the Commonwealth asked the British government for temporary deferment of a payment of interest due on the war debt, a debt which, as Labor radicals pointed out, had been incurred by Australia helping to defend Britain. The British government referred the proposal to the Bank of England which in turn wanted to know more about Australia's financial position. In particular it wanted to know how the Australian government proposed to resolve its financial difficulties. In the end the Bank of England sent out one of its own to see for themselves. Sir Otto Niemeyer arrived in July 1930 on a visit of inspection, and after a month's fact-finding met with the Premiers to instruct them on the nature of Australia's economic and financial problems and the means necessary to repair them.

The message was simple: Australia had been living beyond its means. Out of this meeting came the Melbourne Agreement in which the representatives of the state and Federal governments agreed to reduce government expenditure, balance their budgets, desist from overseas loans until the short-term external debt was completely dealt with, and only raise internal loans for income-producing schemes. Any further raising of loans to service the already existing loans was ruled out. Just how they were to manage to balance their budgets, however, was left unclear. Boris Schedvin suggests that, even as they signed, the assembled premiers knew that the terms of the agreement were politically impossible for them to meet. Uppermost in their minds however was the need to impress this representative of the Bank of England and the London money markets with their financial good intentions.[38]

The Melbourne Agreement was closely followed in October by the New South Wales state election in which Labor, led by Jack Lang, vehemently attacked the capitulation of Labor governments to the demands of foreign bond-holders. Lang campaigned against the Melbourne Agreement, with Niemeyer as his special target, the personification of British capital lording it over honest Australians, unconcerned whether they lived or died so long as the banks and bond-holders got their pound of flesh. Niemeyer was Jewish and there was more than a tinge of anti-semitism mixed in with Lang's defiant Australian nationalism.[39] A populist demagogue, Lang simplified the complexities of Australia's financial and economic difficulties, offering tough talk and the promise of decisive action against visible enemies whose defeat would bring salvation. He won the election, greatly increasing the confidence of Federal Labor members unhappy with the government's capitulation to Niemeyer and the banks in the Melbourne Agreement. Scullin's inexperienced Labor government was caught between the pressing political demands for relief from the social misery being caused by the depression and the demands of the bankers for substantial reductions in government spending as the price for an extension of credit. The ensuing political crisis split the Labor government. By the end of 1930 three positions were apparent inside the Federal Labor Party: to maintain deficit expenditure through an extension of credit from the Commonwealth Bank in order to provide some relief to the unemployed and the most distressed farmers; to default on external interest payments in order to spend more on unemployment relief; and to reduce expenditure in order to balance budgets as was being demanded by the banks.[40] Lyons held the last of these.

When Lyons defied the Caucus repudiators and launched the conversion loan appeal only one month before it fell due, he was defying the odds. Secretary to the Treasury, J. T. Heathershaw, cautioned that conversion loans were normally issued three months prior to maturity, and that there had never been a successful issue of this magnitude in a period of less than two months. Given the general lack of confidence among investors, he gave the loan scant chance of success.[41] Compounding the problem, as a consequence of the government's commitment to 'equality of sacrifice', it was to be issued at rates less than the current market yields. Yet the alternative seemed worse. If the campaign were to fail and some form of postponement of repayment become necessary, Australia would seem set on the path of repudiation and inflation which spelled both moral and financial ruin. Those who believed in sound methods of finance were on trial and must make the loan succeed.[42]

Announcing the loan to parliament, Lyons claimed that 'Not even in the war time were the financial problems of Australia more formidable than they are today'. Leader of the Opposition John Latham offered the full support of the Opposition: 'It will be a test of the confidence of Australians in their own country ... to make this loan a success [is] a patriotic duty'.[43] Those who held bonds were exhorted to renew them, thus proving 'that the patriotism of war time was absolutely genuine'.[44] The campaign drew on the tactics developed during the war loan campaigns: public meetings and rallies, extensive advertising in the press, on the radio and at the new cinemas, and various schemes to assist people of small means to do their patriotic duty. The Commonwealth made arrangements for its officers to subscribe to the loan with deductions from their salaries of ten equal parts deducted over ten pay days.[45] Banks and large business houses made similar arrangements for their employees, in some cases contributing a portion of the purchase price, and banks made liberal advances to those wishing to subscribe.[46] Lyons was helped considerably in the campaign by the group of Melbourne men who were to orchestrate his emergence as leader of a reformed non-labour party only a few months later. These included Staniforth Ricketson of the stockbroking company J. B. Were who urged Were's clients to subscribe, and Robert Menzies, then in Victorian politics, who organised the Young Nationalists to speak at rallies and meetings.[47]

The text of an advertisement which appeared in major papers over Lyons' signature combined appeal to a sense of national moral obligation with appeal to sound financial practice, but as the final slogan made clear, it was the appeal to national obligation which was the stronger.

> AS A MATTER OF HONOUR –
> Australia must raise £28 000 000 by 15th December. This
> amount is an obligation that must be met and met punctually
> in order that our credit abroad and our own
> self-respect may be maintained.

AS a MATTER of SANE, SOUND, BUSINESS
Australians should provide this amount.
The loan offers gilt-edged security and a
good rate of interest ...

BUY A BOND OF HONOUR[48]

As with the war loans campaigns, the campaign provided the occasion for community and institutional cooperative action. Newspapers reported contributions from firms, municipalities and organisations, as well as from wealthy individuals: 150 staff at the department store Buckley & Nunn contributed a total of £4 000;[49] the Limbless Soldiers Association subscribed £2800 from funds raised in an appeal in 1928 and since held in trust; the scholars at Richmond Technical School 'spontaneously agreed' to forgo the annual prize distribution and speech night festivities to buy two £10 bonds.[50] The culmination of the campaign was 'All for Australia Day' on the closing day of the loan, Friday 12 December. The ear-marking of a special day was another of the techniques borrowed from the war loan campaigns. Accompanied by rallies and promotional gimmicks, these created a sense of festive collective action in the face of a common threat. Many businesses agreed to donate their day's takings and Lyons urged people to do their Christmas shopping on that day to ensure the takings were good. The Air Force put on a spectacular display of brilliantly illuminated planes silhouetted against the night sky.[51]

In Lyons' final appeal to the people the comparison was again with the war:

> Never since the dark days of the war had Australia been faced with such a critical position, never has there been more urgent need for spontaneous outburst of patriotism ... Let the world know that the heart of Australia is sound, that her fighting people possess the same fighting spirit in peace as they showed in war, and that they will not repudiate their obligations.[52]

Speaking to a monster lunchtime rally at the Melbourne Town Hall, Lyons told an audience, whose memories of wartime patriotic endeavour in a shared imperial cause had been kindled by the organ playing 'Australia Will be There', that 'A sacred duty devolved upon us' to redeem the debt. 'We had to uphold the name of this great country of ours. Unless we allowed confidence in ourselves we could not expect people on the other side of the world to have confidence in us.'[53]

Against all the odds the loan conversion campaign was oversubscribed by nearly £2 million, a remarkable result, due as much to the many small subscriptions of £100 or less as to the large institutions.[54] The number of subscribers was nearly 100 000, and although the strongest support was in Victoria (roughly 44 000 contributors to New South Wales' 18 000) there were subscribers from all parts of the Commonwealth, which Lyons interpreted as 'a bulwark of security against wild cat schemes'.[55] As *The Woman* pointed out, the result was an expression of patriotism rather than financial calculation as current Commonwealth securities were selling on the open market at prices which gave the buyer a substantially higher interest.[56] Boris Schedvin argues that in comparison with the war loan campaigns the achievement was far greater. In war, appeals to patriotism were comparatively simple. As well, in contrast to wartime economic conditions when profitability was good and consumption restrained, in 1930 profits were virtually non-existent and many people's wages had been reduced to levels scarcely sufficient for their living expenses, 'Only savings remained', writes Schedvin and that these were used so lavishly is evidence of the psychological impact the depression had already made.[57] It is also evidence of the extent of the psychological, emotional and moral identification many Australians had made between national and personal financial honour.

One Small Honest Man

Joe Lyons' success in mobilising the nation's savings in defence of the nation's honour was the precursor to his role in the much larger citizen mobilisation which gained momentum in the summer and autumn of 1931. He had become a national hero, and by mid-April the *Adelaide Advertiser* could write of 'the rousing of the nation by one small honest man'.[58] An awkward piece of verse from the Hobart *Mercury* compares Lyons with the wise man of the New Testament parable who built his house upon the rock.

> The Ultra-Reds may mock,
>   When the storms financial beat
> 'Tis good to have a rock
>   Beneath one's trembling feet.
> Be theirs the house upon the sand,
>   But you and I, old friend, will stand
> And face whatever gale may blow
>   With Joe.[59]

After Scullin's return from England in January, his government quickly unravelled. Although Scullin had supported Lyons in the loan conversion, his immediate reinstatement of Theodore as Treasurer was not a vote of confidence in Lyons who promptly resigned from Cabinet. Lyons recoiled from Theodore's inflationary policies and regarded his membership of Cabinet while his name was under a cloud as a breach of standards of public administration.[60] Abandoning Scullin to the left were followers of New South Wales Premier Jack Lang, whose various proposals breached every accepted tenet of sound and honest finance: suspension of overseas interest payments, reduction of interest on domestic public loans, and abandonment of the gold standard. Supporters of Lang sat in the parliament as the Lang Labor Party. They supported the government until November 1931 when they voted with the Opposition and precipitated an election. Lyons sat on the backbench until 13 March when he and four other Labor members voted with the Opposition on a no-confidence motion.[61]

Lyons' speech in support of this no confidence motion was effectively his speech of resignation from the Labor Party. He knew that expulsion would quickly follow this breach of party discipline. In one of the best speeches of his life, Lyons spoke of the 'deep pain and sharp mental suffering' of breaking with 'the associations of a life time'. Yesterday he had 'completed twenty-two years of service for the workers of Australia'. As the speech continued, its focus shifted from 'the workers of Australia' to 'the men and women of Wilmot' (his electorate), and with it Lyons' sense of accountability. As Frank Brennan pointed out: 'The honourable gentleman appears to have overlooked the fundamental fact that has always been recognised by the Labour party ... that loyalty to the party postulates sacrifice in regard to detail and subordination of self to the considered views of the party as a whole'.[62] Lyons' resignation from Labor made him the Australian Liberals' ideal representative, appealing to his conscience in defiance of the dictates of his party, putting the representative processes of parliament and the good of the nation above the claims of the party, acting from a sense of service and duty, rather than ambition and self-interest. Lyons was flooded with letters and telegrams from grateful citizens. For example, W. G. Ashford of the Congregational Church, Summer Hill: 'On behalf of the thousands of inarticulate people who are poor but honest, I venture to say Well done! and Thank you!' Another wrote: 'As a nobody citizen in this Commonwealth I feel that my small acknowledgment of the task to which you have set your hand is an act of duty ... we are watching and appreciating your endeavour to do the right thing in the best interests of every citizen'.[63]

Lyons' resignation from the Labor government made him a hero with the increasing numbers of Australians who believed that the existing parties and their incumbent politicians were completely inadequate for the crisis facing the nation, and that new forms of action and organisation were called for. Non-labour supporters could be expected to see the federal Labor government as wanting, but they also turned on the Nationalists, and to a lesser extent on the Country Party. Between December 1928 and December 1933 incumbent state governments, whatever their colour, fell before the electorates' anger at their inability to protect incomes and living standards, and new political organisations proliferated.[64] Non-party political organisations are a permanent presence on the Liberal side of politics in Australia, where the paradox of the party's partisan claim to represent the unity of the whole is more keenly felt than on the Labor side, and where activists are always keen to assert their independence in the name of 'non-political' values such as patriotism or the Constitution or a vaguely defined unified national interest. Peter Loveday has described this tradition as 'Anti-political political thought'.[65] Its adherents grew during the summer of 1930–31 in a spontaneous ground swell of citizens' movements: the All for Australia League in Victoria and New South Wales, and the Citizens' League of South Australia, a secessionist movement in Western Australia, and new state movements in the Riverina and northern New South Wales.

The Adelaide Citizens' League, which Lyons later saw as the origins of the citizen movement, was formed in October 1930 when more than thirty members of the Constitutional Club met to discuss 'the criminal procrastination of the Federal Government'.[66] Constitutional Clubs had been formed in the mid-1920s during the Bruce government's campaign for industrial law and order. They presented themselves as non-partisan, concerned to promote the cause of constitutional government, to inculcate members with the spirit of patriotism, and to provide them with opportunities to learn about and discuss political issues.[67] They were appropriate convenors for meetings of citizens concerned to express their dismay about the state of the nation and to discuss what should be done. The Adelaide League was hugely and quickly successful, claiming a membership of over 20 000 by mid-1931. Strong on protest and indignation, it was weak on policy, but its rapid growth in membership showed the numbers of people who felt they should be doing something to help solve the national crisis. As its leading spokesman, World War I officer Captain E. D. A. Bagot, described it at its inaugural meeting, it was not a political party and had no desire to become one, but was rather 'a conscience, a sentiment, a force, the force of public opinion, public sentiment, public conscience, which awakened at last by the crisis that confronts us, attempts to make itself both heard and felt'.[68]

Citizens' Leagues formed in Melbourne and Sydney in mid-February, following Lyons' resignation. The pattern followed was similar to that in South Australia: a small meeting of prominent citizens formed a committee to organise protest meetings and recruit a mass membership. In Melbourne the initial organisation was done by members of the Citizens' Committee, which had been instrumental in the success of the loan conversion campaign and was closely linked with the Victorian Branch of the National Party.⁶⁹ In Sydney the initial organisers were businessmen members of the Sydney Rotary Club. In both cases the growth of membership was spectacular. By the end of March the membership of the Melbourne League was 24 000 and 120 branches had been formed. At the end of May at the time of the League's first convention, the Victorian All For Australia League had 80 000 members and 320 branches.⁷⁰ The Sydney League which had the added impetus of hostility to the Lang Plan reported a membership of 130 000 by the end of June.⁷¹

The urban citizens' movements were concerned with the state of the nation and adopted the name 'All for Australia'. The New South Wales new state movements and the West Australia secessionists showed the fault lines in the federal compact. Demands for new states in the New England, Riverina and Monaro regions had been an important theme in New South Wales politics during the 1920s. In 1925 a Royal Commission had rejected the proposal and the movement had languished, but the decline in rural incomes combined with Lang's increasingly radical proposals renewed calls for the country regions to cut free from Sydney.⁷² In February 1931, 200 delegates attended a conference in Armidale where, invoking precedents from the United States, a committee was established to draw up the boundaries of the new state and start framing a constitution.⁷³ In Wagga, a good-looking and energetic young timber merchant, Charles Hardy, addressed monster meetings on the banks of the Murrumbidgee which voted enthusiastically for 'the right of the Riverina to determine its own affairs and control its own destiny, if necessary by secession'.⁷⁴ Intertwined with the secessionist movements were longstanding rural grievances about tariffs, taxation and high government expenditure. These movements combined, in the words of their historian Ulrich Ellis, 'a fierce crusading zeal and confusion concerning practical objectives'. Hardy, for example, was a political amateur. Although he achieved instant national notoriety as 'a man of force and courage', he lacked the two basic essentials for politics, 'enduring patience and a clear sense of objective … and at all stages in his spectacular career he was subject to unstable and often unsuitable influences'.⁷⁵ Ellis' description could apply equally well to Pauline Hanson, another political amateur who for a time also aroused the potent combination of rural and regional grievance but was equally unable to turn it to lasting political effect.

Western Australia had been the most reluctant member of the Federation. As the depression deepened and commodity prices fell, popular support for secession grew there too. Particularly galling to the primary producing West Australians was the tariff which they saw as discriminating in favour of the more industrialised eastern states, but secessionists also feared that the Commonwealth Labor government was weakening imperial ties. 'The Dominion League of Western Australia' was established in May 1930 and became a major focus for non-labour political discontent for the next three years, arguing that 'Freedom will best be served when none are for the Party and all are for the State'. It promised to support any parliamentary candidate, Labor or Nationalist, who would pledge himself to the cause of secession.[76] A referendum in 1933 was decisively won by the secessionists, but the British Parliament refused to receive the handwritten petition some 8 metres in length, arguing that the bonds of the Federation could only be dissolved with the consent of both parties to the compact.[77]

Nationalists watched these citizen mobilisations with alarm. They welcomed the increased pressure on the government, but realised that they were fast losing the initiative to Lyons in leading the opposition. In February a public meeting sponsored by the Citizens' League of South Australia passed a resolution calling on Lyons to form a government with the support of the Federal Opposition.[78] After his resignation from Labor in March, such calls reached a crescendo. In April he and his wife Enid embarked on a national tour, beginning with a triumphal visit to Adelaide. The train arrived to a packed, cheering platform. From the steps of the train Lyons made an impromptu speech, quoting the Protestant martyrs Latimer and Ridley: 'We shall strike a match tonight which will blaze throughout Australia'.[79] The enthusiasm and support Lyons generated wherever he went was remarkable. On the return trip to Melbourne he gave impromptu addresses to people gathered at railway stations and sidings, and there were more huge meetings in Ballarat, Melbourne and Sydney. After his visit to Adelaide a tacit understanding developed that Lyons was now the leader of the All for Australia Movement, which encompassed the All for Australia League of New South Wales and Victoria and the Citizens' League of South Australia.[80] He was now de-facto leader of the Opposition and the pressure was on the Nationalists to make it legal.

Events were moving quickly for Lyons. Since his resignation he had been in discussion with the informal group of Melbourne men who had helped him with the conversion loan. Calling themselves 'The Group', they sounded him out about becoming leader of a reformed opposition. The two separate streams of events, the one taking place in the full glare of public meetings and mass rallies, the other in the discreet privacy of the clubs and dining rooms of the Nationalist powerbrokers, converged in mid-April. John Latham succumbed to pressure to resign as the leader of the Nationalist Party and Lyons took his place as leader of the Opposition, shortly re-formed as the United Australia Party. When the Scullin government was finally brought down in November by Lang Labor and an election called,

Lyons led the new party to a resounding victory.⁸¹ I will discuss the organisational transition from Nationalists to United Australia Party in the last section of this chapter. For now I want to look more closely at the reasons for Lyons' tremendous popularity in this period of national crisis.

A great deal is known about the working-class politics of the period, but the various citizens' movements have on the whole been overshadowed by the drama of their radical paramilitary extremes: Eric Campbell's New Guard and the White Army ready to take up arms to fight the communists and unemployed.⁸² What was the perspective of the people of small means who rallied to Joe Lyons and the cause of honest finance, to what Henry Gullett described as 'his homeliness and his spontaneous practical patriotism'?⁸³ Their views and actions cannot simply be understood negatively, as reactions of fearful self-interest and confusion, though these were certainly involved; they also drew on convictions of their moral worth based on experience and on deeply held self-understandings. Lyons became their public representative, their man in parliament, facing the nation's problems as they faced their own. Here is how his effect on a public meeting was described by the *Adelaide Advertiser*:

> The meeting was an amazing demonstration of the feeling of confidence Mr Lyons inspired in people that he is the leader Australia is seeking. The picture thousands carried away from the meeting was of a solid, clear minded man of the people whose simple conception of right and wrong had been bred in the normal atmosphere of family life, whose measure of life was the welfare of a gallant wife and a household of happy children … Here was someone who thought and felt as they did, who had a home like them to lose or save, talking to them in a conversational way.⁸⁴

Pastoralist South Australian MP Charles Hawker proffered a very similar description in a private letter:

> Lyons … has the really conservative habit of mind which twenty five years of democratic training has quite failed to alter … He approaches everything from a man in the street position which in no way cancels the conservatism, although it gives it a popular basis … This man is a conservative of the men with small savings and a home of their own. It is in his bones.⁸⁵

'Small', 'little' and 'honest' are the adjectives most frequently associated with Lyons, and the diminutives refer not to his height but to his financial means and social position. They were the Australian equivalents of the 'petit' in petit bourgeoisie, and resonated with the common description of the time of tradesmen and shopkeepers as 'the little man'. Barry Humphries sardonically reports his puzzlement that although the local grocer, chemist and butcher all seemed to be of normal height, his mother always referred to them in the diminutive.[86] The term was a description of their financial weight, the size of their stake in the country, the amount of influence they could expect to exert. These were not the big men from the top end of town but the little men from provincial towns and modest suburbs, who owned a house, a family farm, a shop, or a small business, and a life insurance policy. They were used to handling money, albeit in small amounts, and regularity and habit had contributed more to their financial standing than vision, entrepreneurial risk-taking or luck. They knew what it meant to balance the books, were familiar with terms like credit and bond, had mortgages and bank accounts, and so had the experience to make confident judgements on the way the nation handled its finances. The conclusions they drew were that the nation should handle its finances as they handled their own.

As Lyons told the parliament, his was not the expert opinion but that of the ordinary honest man who dealt with problems on the basis of the commonsense solutions that had worked in the past: 'There is no escaping [the] fact. We have to go back to honest, straightforward methods ... I have spoken, not as a financial genius; not as one who has any visionary schemes ... visionary schemes will avail us nothing. We must do what the ordinary citizen would do in similar circumstances.'[87] And this meant reducing expenditure. The war had familiarised people with the idea of national savings by encouraging them to relate the impact of their patterns of saving and spending to the nation's financial resources. The depression introduced them to the idea of the national income. Australian economists saw the core of the crisis as the loss of national income and how this loss was to be spread among the various producer groups. They were remarkably successful in transmitting this idea to the public. Copland reports an incident from early 1931 of a conversation between an economist and a railway clerk who approached him on a platform: was his salary part of the national income? After five minutes or so of discussion the clerk went away accepting some loss of income as inevitable and fair in the circumstances.[88] Just as a household dealt with hard times by reducing its expenditure, so too should the nation. The thrifty habits which in wartime contributed to the nation's savings would now help it deal with its reduced income. As Lyons' wife Enid told many public meetings, women had a special role to play:

> when a family's income dropped the housewife cut her costs in keeping with the loss. Shin of beef and Irish stew replaced the steaks and sirloin roasts until better times returned ...

> Who is the greatest financier in Australia? Mr Scullin? no. Mr Theodore? I doubt it. Mr Lyons? Certainly not! I know him! ... The little mother of a family making one shilling do the work of two![89]

It was not just that the 'little' mother, the wife presumably of the little man, was a good budgeter, she was also a specialist in the foresight and restraining moral qualities the nation needed:

> When the baby cries father will give it anything in the world to stop it. Mother won't. She thinks of the tummy-ache that will come later. It is the inherent commonsense and restraint of our women that will help us through the national crisis as it does the domestic.[90]

Growing understanding of the interdependence of the national economy was accompanied by the widespread belief that the pain necessary to restore its health must be shared. 'Equality of sacrifice' was crucial if the government were to gain acceptance for tough economic measures. The Premiers Plan which was adopted in May set out the plans for reducing government expenditure in order to reduce the deficit. The state and Federal governments agreed to reduce their adjustable expenditure (which included wages, salaries and pensions), to some increase in taxes, and to reduce interest rates on internal loans.[91] For Labor the inclusion of the last point was vital. Only if the bond-holders also contributed did the plan have any chance of popular acceptance; but it was also the most controversial. The Group was not pleased, and Ricketson and Menzies led the Melbourne business community in attacking 'the repudiation of contracts'. This was not Menzies' finest hour. He told a Pleasant Sunday Afternoon gathering at Melbourne's Wesley Church that 'If Australia were to surmount her troubles only by the abandonment of traditional British standards of honesty, justice, fair play and honest endeavour, it would be better for Australia that every citizen within her boundaries would die of starvation during the next six months'.[92] Lyons, however, who was responsible for leading the response of the parliamentary opposition, supported the government and steered the necessary legislation through the Federal parliament, including the Senate. He was his own man, committed to finding points of consensus from which Australians could work together rather than aggravating conflict. For the remainder of 1931 Lyons was civil and cooperative towards his former colleagues. He eschewed anti-Labor and anti-socialist slogans, emphasising instead the positive principles for which the new party stood in order to attract Labor voters opposed to unorthodox financial and economic policies.

The Menace of Inflation

The financial crisis of the early 1930s raised the question of how one dealt with adversity. Lyons' answer was clear: one remained true to oneself. In his resignation speech, for example, Lyons reminded the parliament of his loyalty to Scullin. He had 'held the fort' while Scullin was away, had 'stayed at his position … trusting always that when he came back he would be what he was when he went away'. But when he returned Scullin was changed, he was listening to Theodore and entertaining ideas of the inflationary expansion of credit and Lyons could no longer give him his confidence. Consistency is what Lyons had looked in vain for in Scullin, and consistency is what he now offered himself: 'I realise that I have been out of step with a number of members of the party for some considerable time. I have kept travelling along the road upon which I started, and I intend to keep to that road, whatever the consequences may be.'[93] What Lyons was enacting in his resignation speech was how one deals with life's adversities: one faces them fairly and squarely and does what one thinks is right. What is true for the individual life is also true for the nation and he offered himself as the rock on which the nation could rely.

And it is true for the financial system. The issues of financial morality in the 1930s had deep psychological roots in the belief that the stability of the nation's financial system was ultimately grounded in stability of character. Just as a man's word was his bond, so was a nation's. To go back on one's words, to breach a contract, was to damage one's reputation for reliability and consistency. The face-to-face world from which banking began was still present, at least metaphorically, in these understandings of the trust implicit in financial transactions. The integrity of the financial system relied in the last analysis not on any regulatory framework but on the moral character and integrity of those who borrowed and lent. This implied a certain fixity of personal character within a stable moral order, that the persons with whom one entered into a contract would stay the same in their relevant moral qualities for the duration of the contract, that the people to whom one entrusted one's money to hold for perhaps half a lifetime would not change in their essential character and betray one's trust. Hence the symbolism of solidity evoked by all things to do with banking, the imposing brick and stone buildings in the main streets of every suburb and town.

Repudiation was the first threat to sound finance to mobilise this complex amalgam of commonsense financial and and moral beliefs. The second was the radical proposal for ameliorating the depression through a mild expansion of credit. In early 1931 Theodore was proposing to take Australia off the gold standard and print a special note issue of £18 million,

£12 million to finance public works and £6 million for the wheat-growers. From the hindsight of experience with Keynesian economics, Theodore's proposals were moderate and creative moves to use an expansionary monetary policy to stimulate the economy; for many at the time, however, they were dangerous and illusory solutions, and in this too Lyons was representative. He told a meeting at the Sydney Town Hall:

> Under the cloak of high sounding jargon about monetary policy and credit control this plan seeks to impose upon the people the doctrine, that a Government which has refused seriously to cut its own expenditure in the face of colossal deficits, has the right to demand that the people's savings shall be handed over.[94]

Credit expansion was simply the government taking the easy way out. If banking and credit policy were to become subject to political control, politicians' self-interested propensity to buy favour would be a constant danger, a genie which if let out of the bottle threatened to unravel the moral fabric of society.

In early March 1931 Archibald Grenfell Price, Master of the Anglican University College, St Marks in Adelaide, published a pamphlet on 'The menace of inflation' which warned of a menace 'more dangerous and subtle than frank and dishonest repudiation'. Repudiation will cause crisis and dishonour, and people will eventually realise they must economise and pay their interest; 'Inflation, however, will involve a slow strangulation, a long-drawn-out descent into an almost inescapable mire'.[95] The hyperinflation of Germany and Austria after the war was a recent, shocking example of the potential depths to which a country might sink once a government started to tamper with the currency. As with the earlier anti-Bolshevik propaganda, women were reminded of their particular vulnerability to the breakdown of social order: in Germany as inflation soared, 'Husbands saw their wives and daughters driven wholesale on the streets; an entire group of relatives would depend on one woman's shame'. Even without reaching these depths of moral disgrace, inflation threatened to unsettle the economic moral order of savers and spenders by enhancing 'the survival of the unfit': 'Governments impoverish those who work and save to provide for the future and reduce them to the level of the loafer, the wasters, and those who make no effort to avoid falling upon the charity of the nation in their old age'. By reducing the value of their capital, 'Inflation ruined the sane, the thrifty, and the hardworking classes. The reckless and the lazy survived.'[96] Former Prime Minister Bruce, just returned from a trip abroad, even claimed that the effects would be worse in Australia than they had been in

Europe, because here wealth was more evenly spread. He said we had 'great savings banks, enormous life insurance companies and hundreds of thousands of people buying their own homes ... Do not let us listen to the cry "Print more notes" ... If once inflation comes all this will vanish; all that these people have struggled for will disappear.'[97]

The arguments mustered against inflationary policies show the moral weight savings carried in the early 1930s. It was not just that the erosion of one's current savings put one in a difficult financial situation, although this was undoubtedly the case. It was that the difficult financial situation of the savers was given more moral weight than that of the unemployed or those forced to take a cut in salary. The superior claims of capital were most easily defended when they could be turned into the claims of the small bond-holders and savers whose capital accumulation could be clearly linked to their own efforts. Attacking proposals to tax income derived from property, Senator George Pearce described the effect of 'this crushing taxation' not on the income of the capitalist, the wealthy man, but on the 'deserving section of the community who, through long years, have been saving so that they would not have to ask for an old age pension in their declining years'.[98] To such deserving savers, their capital was not just evidence of their character but its embodiment, its slow accumulation the result of a myriad of small calculations and daily self-sacrifices, each bank deposit and life insurance payment a pleasure forgone or temptation avoided. For inflation to undermine the value of such sacrifices was not simply to make one's present and future life insecure, it was to render much of the effort of one's past life meaningless. Earned money existed in the present, in relation to current potential spending and pleasures; saved money was from the past, the storehouse of the energies and pleasures of youth, and an affirmation and display of one's past virtues. In contrast with Marx's labour theory of value which regarded capital as the accumulation of human labour which had not received its full value, the moral middle class carried what might be described as a savings theory of value, in which the renunciation of consumption added value to the work which went into the earning of the money. This gave saved money its moral edge over earned money and made the steady savers the 'deserving section' of the community.

Savings were points of fixity for people, anchoring their present situation to their past efforts, linking their current good character to the steady habits of a lifetime, and providing the stable and secure foundations of their world. This was the psychological bond between the small savers and the bankers' and financiers' central principles of 'sound finance' – that credit could not be created, but had to be backed by solid assets, that saving must always equal investment, and that if the money was not saved, then it was not available to lend or to spend.⁹⁹ In his speech of resignation from the ALP Lyons voiced the commonsense view of any proposals to expand credit:

> I am sorry that the Government has lost the confidence of the people of this country and therefore has to fall back on the tricks of the conjurer ... The rehabilitation of industry can be effected only with real money. I say that real money is that which comes from the accumulated savings of the people, and that is dependent upon confidence and credit.¹⁰⁰

Any expansion of credit not backed by equally expanded savings was depicted as an illusory solution: inflation was the 'Menace of False Finance' and 'Labor's Promises mean False Finance and Faked Money'.¹⁰¹ The conjurer was a common representation of Labor's economic policies in political pamphlets: circus-master Theodore presented a bloated illusionist 'Professor inflationski' who would 'reduce your savings to nil and make it appear that they have been increased by millions'; 'Balloon Man' Scullin held aloft a bunch of balloons with words like 'dreams', 'promise', 'talk' and boast' on them: ''ere you are, sir, all filled with gas!'¹⁰² Inflation was delusion at best, deception at worst. One cartoon had milkman Theodore responding to a woman's demand that she have her usual quantity of milk despite insufficient supply by topping up his bucket from a tank marked Inflation: 'Well, thank Gawd, if we can't give her milk we can give her water and CHARGE her for milk'.¹⁰³

The contrast between reality and illusion, 'real' and false money, runs right through the public campaign against the 'artificial' expansion of credit. The fiduciary notes themselves became images of trickery and dishonesty and political leaflets and dodgers were produced in the form of bank notes, particularly in the 1932 New South Wales campaign against Lang. A 'Starvation Debenture' to the value of 'One Lang' promised to pay £121 million ('which he has not got');¹⁰⁴ 'Lang's Note' payable on demand, had a face value of nothing.¹⁰⁵ Another from the federal campaign had one side labelled 'Fiduciary Inflation Note', with snarling cameos of Theodore and Scullin, their eyes averted. It was overstamped with rising values like the worthless German bank notes and the bold final warning 'DANGER'. On the other side the reassuring, smiling face of Joe Lyons looked directly at the viewer from under the slogan, 'Hands off the Note Issue'.¹⁰⁶ In these dodgers, there is an exchange of qualities between men and money: fiduciary notes take on the cunning smiles of artifice, pretending to be what they are not, while good people acquire the reliable qualities of solid gold. Both the financial and the moral world depended on the belief in unchanging values, and the threat to the value of one flowed into a threat to the other. Thus Theodore's mildly inflationary proposals could invoke moral outrage and resistance disproportionate to any likely financial consequences.

The gradual acceptance of Keynesianism which decoupled the logic of the household economy from that of the nation's also began to decouple the stability of the personality from the stability of the financial system. Looking back on her life with Joe in the 1930s from the perspective of the 1960s Enid Lyons comments wryly on the change:

> Neither Joe nor the thousands who heard him speak were conscious that within a few years a new theory of public finance would be universally accepted; that by 1960 the whole world would be fiduciary, from the Smiths on the basic wage with their fiduciary TV set and washing machine to the young man with his fiduciary sports car; from the girl with her fiduciary record-player to the man who would never own his own car although he would drive one registered in his name to the day he died of fiduciary heart disease. None of these things could they foresee; that night they cheered for honesty, for honest men and honest government. They cheered for the better times they longed for and for which they were prepared to pay. They would take the hard way out of the depression but the honest one.[107]

The United Australia Party

Latham's resignation from the Nationalist leadership in favour of Lyons was only the first step in the formation of the United Australia Party. Between April and June 'Unity' conferences were held among representatives of the various non-labour organisations to discuss forms of cooperation.[108] The Nationalists needed to tread carefully. The party's credibility had been badly damaged by the debacle of the 1929 election, particularly among 'the middle vote' and 'decent wage earners'.[109] The leadership of the citizens' movements was politically inexperienced and suspicious of anything that looked like a return to party politics. Relations between the Nationalists and the All For Australia League were good in Victoria, but much cooler in New South Wales, the home of Archdale Parkhill's efficient political machine, particularly after Parkhill's description of the UAP as 'a party of spare parts' was published in the *Daily Telegraph*.[110] The Country Party led by Earle Page resisted all invitations to cooperate, as it was to do a decade or so later when the Liberal Party was being formed.

At the parliamentary level, the UAP was a simple realignment in which the Nationalist MPs were joined by Lyons and five other ex-Labor men. The coalition of the Nationalists with the citizens' movements offered the opportunity to build an effective new extra-parliamentary organisation which combined the movements' activism and passion with the Nationalists' organisational skills. This did not happen. Although Lyons was the accepted leader of the All for Australia Leagues, he had no organisational base. In fact by becoming leader of the Opposition he defused the sense of crisis which had brought the Leagues into being and their strength quickly waned. The promise of a mass base for the new party failed to eventuate. When the dust settled the organisational core of the new party was that of the old, though weaker and more fragmented than it had been under Bruce. It was more than ever dependent on the personal qualities and energies of its leader and on the unaccountable executives of the finance committees – the National Union in Victoria and the Consultative Council in New South Wales. These were small, secretive committees of influential men who raised donations from business to support the party and to ensure that the men who entered parliament were generally understanding of the businessman's perspective.[111] The Victorian body was the more powerful and the more overt in its exercise of influence. It had participated in the courting of Lyons and he consulted with them regularly.[112]

Far more than was the case with Labor, in the UAP as in the Nationalist Party before it, the state branches were the party, assisted by leagues and committees that had varying constitutional relations with the party proper. The organisation was messy and fragmented. It had moved well beyond the circles of family and friends which provided the core of Deakin's organisation, but it still relied heavily for its coherence on personal networks. There was no federal administrative structure to support the federal parliamentary party (the National Union refused to pay for one), and the party lacked a federal platform. Lyons ran the federal election campaigns from his private office, in consultation with the state branches.[113] Lyons' biographer, Philip Hart, has argued that Lyons himself was the main link between the federal parliamentary party, the National Union and the Consultative Council, and the state organisations, and so was the most important single element in the party's federal structure. It was his genial personality, his commitment to consultation and consensus and his skills as a mediator that held the federal party together. And it was his personal popularity that won the federal elections in 1934 and 1937.[114] By this last the political energies of the party's birth had well and truly faded. The ALP was overcoming the divisions of the depression and the government was drifting with little clear sense of policy objectives, and with its financial backers more obvious than ever. Lyons' reassuring, moderate leadership, however, continued to win people's trust. But on Good Friday 1939 Lyons died of a heart attack and the federal party lost not only its popular leader but the mainstay of its organisational coherence.

Robert Menzies, who had been deputy leader, was elected by the parliamentary party as the new leader, but for the man destined to become Australian Liberals' most important Prime Minister his support was less than overwhelming. He was clearly the most able of the federal parliamentarians, but he was arrogant and many doubted his capacities to win elections. Some thought his undisguised ambition had contributed to the strains which had caused Lyons' death. Country Party leader Earle Page attacked him for his lack of a war record and made clear he would not serve under him. The National Union tried to persuade Bruce to return but he would only come back as leader of a non-party government. The New South Wales branch backed Billy Hughes and Menzies defeated him by only four votes.[115]

Without Lyons the federal UAP began to disintegrate. Within five months of his death war was declared and Menzies had no time to worry about party organisation. From Australia's perspective the war began as a re-run of World War I: Australian soldiers were sent to support the Empire on distant battlefields in Europe and the Middle East, and civilian life went on more or less as normal. In August 1940 three of the government's senior ministers were killed in a domestic air crash. A general election in 1940 returned a hung parliament with the UAP–Country Party coalition government depending on the votes of two independents. Menzies' clear preference was for some form of national or coalition government, but Labor's leader John Curtin continued the traditional Labor rejection of alliances. Party differences were not to be suspended for the duration of the war. Despite his precarious hold on national political power, in early 1941 Menzies went on a four month overseas trip. His main purpose was to represent Australia's interests at the centre of empire, and in particular to press the cause for a continuing British naval presence in the Pacific. Australians were increasingly apprehensive about a war with Japan as it moved from China into Indo-China. The trip further weakened his domestic political support and he returned to a disunited and bickering government. The contrast with Churchill's wartime national government was striking. 'It is a diabolical thing', he said, 'that anybody should have to come back and play politics … at a time like this'.[116] Within a few months he had resigned as party leader and as Prime Minister. He was replaced as Prime Minister by Deputy Prime Minister and Country Party leader,

Arthur Fadden, and as UAP leader by the aged Billy Hughes. Fadden's government lasted two months till it was defeated on the floor of the house by the two independents and John Curtin was invited to form the government. The responsibility for Australia's war effort went to Labor. The Curtin and Chifley governments became high points in Labor's twentieth-century history and evidence for the comforting belief that in times of crisis the Australian people turned to Labor.

Sidelined, the Australian Liberals spent the war on yet another party reformation as Labor steadfastly refused to form a national government. The UAP had been formed to deliver national leadership to Lyons in a national emergency and the state organisations had accommodated themselves to its existence with varying degrees of enthusiasm and effectiveness. Most still used other names, calling themselves the UAP only for federal purposes. The loss of government precipitated a new round of splits and realignments; for example the New South Wales party split three ways, two parts of which then formed an alliance; in Queensland much of the Liberal vote was captured by a new party, the Queensland People's Party.[117] The 1943 election was contested by six separate non-labour groups, including the Country Party. Their combined vote was 33 per cent, with the UAP contributing just over half with 16 per cent of the vote.[118] This was a disaster. Unless something were done a successful and united Labor Party would quickly surpass the Liberals as Australia's preferred party of government. The first move was to replace Billy Hughes as leader with Menzies, which was done when the parliamentary party met. The second was to build a new party.

6

From Menzies' Forgotten People to the Whitlam Generation

Robert Menzies and the Formation of the Liberal Party

In 1944, Menzies and other leading Liberal politicians moved to reform the fragmented non-labour political organisations into a new national party. As Menzies told the first of the conferences on party re-organisation:

> The picture ... is one of many thousands of people all desperately anxious to travel in the same political direction but divided into various sects and bodies with no Federal structure, with no central executive, with no co-ordinated means of publicity or propaganda, and, above all, with no clearly accepted doctrine or faith to serve as a banner under which all may fight.[1]

By comparison with the Liberals, the ALP was born national, with its origins in the national organisation of the new unionism and the radical nationalism of the 1890s. The Liberals' organisational roots were deep in colonial political experiences and their state organisations with their supporting leagues and committees still acted on assumptions of state sovereignty which made the national polity a secondary consideration. World War II, however, changed all that. Alan Davies has argued that one of the key moments in Australian political history is when the national polity displaced the states as the focus of political attention and energy.[2] The psychological impact of the national emergency and the national war effort is part of the story, but of more lasting importance are the national institutions of governance which resulted from the war, and in particular the strengthening of the national economy. In 1942 Labor took over the states' income taxing powers for the duration of the war and unified the rates across the nation. This arrangement outlasted the war and made the national government the major focus for debates about the role and rates of taxation. It also gave the national government a powerful tool for the exercise of the new Keynesian macro-economic management. The political centre of gravity was shifting to the national polity. This required that as well as building a national organisation to more effectively compete with Labor for national government, Liberal ideology had to be reworked to accommodate the greater expectations of the role of government which were taking shape during the war.

Two conferences were held in October and December 1944, to which were invited representatives of all the major non-labour political organisations, including the Country Party. The Country Party declined the invitation and continued to maintain its independent identity. The others resolved to dissolve their identities into a new organisation, the Liberal Party of Australia. The agreement of one of these, the Australian Women's National League, was particularly welcome. It was perhaps the strongest of the organisations represented at these conferences, and certainly the oldest, having been formed in 1904. It had a large membership (averaging 30 000 during the 1930s), a separate branch structure and financial resources, and its members did a good deal of the Liberals' electoral leg-work. It had been courted before but had always held that it could best serve women's interests within the broader Liberal cause by maintaining a separate organisational identity. But now under the leadership of its President Elizabeth Couchman, it realised 'the urgent postwar need for unity of Liberals to combat socialism' and dissolved its identity and its assets into the new party.[3] War, and the impending threat that a socialist Labor government would oversee the peace, focused the delegates' minds on their common cause. As Menzies said in his address to the first conference at Albury, a new party was needed to 'give impetus to ... a great movement of Liberal deliverance in Australia'.[4] It also needed to build a mass base, with a branch structure to provide it with an independent financial base. The UAP had been damaged by suspicions of the influence of its financial sponsors, in particular the National Union.

From these conferences emerged the decision to form a new party, the Liberal Party of Australia, with Robert Menzies as its leader. During 1945 branches were formed and a federal organisational structure established, with the party officially launched in August 1945.[5] The new party contested the 1946 election, but the result was disappointing. Labor won a second term of government for the first time ever, and an unassailable majority in both houses. Between 1946 and the next election in 1949, however, the new party's fortunes looked up. People's individualism was reasserting itself after the collective efforts of the war. As well, the onset of the Cold War, and the transformation of the Soviet Union from wartime ally to enemy of the free world, marked the return of communism as a salient domestic political issue. In 1947 Chifley pressed ahead with his ill-judged and fateful plan to nationalise the banks. Here was a plan for socialism in action, showing Labor's true ambitions to maintain and extend wartime controls into peacetime. Here was a cause which dramatised Australian Liberals' differences from Labor and gave them a chance to regain the high moral ground lost in the last years of the UAP. Here was an issue which linked the ALP with the threat of international communism. As the Cold War intensified the new Liberal Party's opposition to socialism was given powerful impetus.

Labor's Bank Nationalisation Bill mobilised many of the same groups and sentiments aroused by the financial crisis of 1930–31, and the banks' capacities for political organisation were again swung into action with a coordinated campaign against political control of banking. Bank clerks fearful for their jobs were energetic foot soldiers against the threat of socialism and many were given leave to work full-time against the Bill. The campaign quickly widened from the issue of banking to the broader issue of socialism and the role of government in postwar Australia. The trading banks embarked on a well-organised campaign to ensure the defeat of the Chifley government at the next election, hitching their cause to threats to 'The Australian Way'.[6] 'The Australian Women's Movement Against Socialisation' was formed under the energetic leadership of Millicent Preston Stanley Vaughan to rally women to the defence of freedom.[7] The mobilisation around bank nationalisation gave plausibility to the new party's presentation of itself as a new political movement rather than the old party with a face lift. By the end of its life the UAP had been seen as too close to its business and financial backers, so clear evidence of support from ordinary people was crucial. The new party's first success was the voters' rejection in 1948 of a referendum on prices and rent control.

Menzies later described this period as 'the Great Australian Liberal Revival'[8] and others talked of the 'Liberal Movement', presenting the new party as the expression of a broad social movement in the way Labor had been at its beginning, able to tap similar sources of political energy and idealism. By the 1949 election campaign such claims were looking increasingly plausible as political energy gathered behind the new party. Led by the bank clerks, 'the white collar men' were fighting, as a small army of clerks and salesmen were dragged from their 9 to 5 routine into electioneering.[9] Over 1300 new branches had been formed, and there were more than 150 000 members.[10] Alexandra Hasluck describes the spirit which animated these new members, young men and women 'impelled by a sense of longing to do their best for Australia … We all knew we were a body concerned with the good of Australia. Ours was the patriotism of Peace, after the War'.[11]

For the 1949 election the Liberal Party sought younger candidates with a strong commitment to public service, preferably shown by their war record, though not exclusively. Paul Hasluck describes being tapped on the shoulder to stand as a Liberal candidate for Curtin. Expressing reservations about his capacities to be an unquestioning supporter of the Liberal Party, he was assured that Liberalism did not require bondage and he was not expected to subscribe to everything Bob Menzies said.[11] In 1910 Liberals had despaired that youth and idealism were flooding to Labor; in 1949 the situation seemed reversed. The government benches, according to Alexandra Hasluck, were

> full of ... splendid young men returned from the Services, decorated for bravery in battle, many with university degrees, or with expertise in some form of public life or other ... The atmosphere was charged with vitality. By contrast most of the Labor Party looked old and tired after the war years, and they could boast few young members with a university education.[12]

The Liberals had thirty-nine new members with an average age of 43 and twelve under 40.[13] There weren't many Catholics, though. Although the Liberal Party had made a conscious pitch for the Catholic vote by stressing its opposition to atheistic Communism, John Cramer was the only Catholic elected. Protestant anti-Catholicism was still strong in the party, particularly among the members who controlled pre-selection.[14]

The 1949 election restored Australia's Liberals as the dominant party of government. This dominance was not, however, consolidated till the 1954 election. John Murphy has argued persuasively that the 1950s of popular memory, of easy affluence and domestic peace, did not really begin until after the middle of the decade when fears of economic instability were eased and Cold War tensions had moderated.[15] But even as the good times flowed and the Labor Party split in 1954–55, the Liberals continued to worry that their electoral support was weak. Despite the split and the erratic behaviour of its leader Dr Evatt, Labor held a solid core of loyal support, winning nearly 5 per cent more of the primary vote at the 1955 election than the Liberals. Liberals viewed this with a mixture of dismay and admiration. Labor's voters stuck with their party when times were tough, whereas the Liberals always feared that their own vote was as much a vote against Labor as the result of deeply held conviction; that the Australian people only turned to them when Labor was unelectable. Could the Liberals ever overcome their negative description as anti-labour?

Would they ever be seen as the party of initiative, the national party based on a permanent liberal tradition?[16] This fear was as old as Labor's dramatic rise to electoral power in 1910 and successive election victories failed to quiet it among Liberal organisers.

The Liberal Party did have Menzies, however. After the initial doubts about his lack of popular appeal faded, his hold on the leadership was assured. Winning seven federal elections in a row, he seemed to dominate the nation as he came to dominate the party, and many of our historical understandings of his period of government are filtered through interpretations which centre on the representativeness of his values and beliefs. Since my book *Robert Menzies' Forgotten People* was published in 1992, it has become common to refer to the busy, family-centred homemakers of the 1950s and 1960s as 'the Forgotten People', to see Menzies' radio broadcast made in early 1942 just after the fall of Singapore as a remarkably prescient foreshadowing of the Australia that was to come, particularly his claim in the most frequently quoted section of the speech 'that the real life of the nation ... is to be found in the homes of people who are nameless and unadvertised, and who, whatever their religious conviction or dogma, see in their children their greatest contribution to the immortality of their race'. But to read the speech only in terms of what was to come is to miss the continuities of experience and aspiration which it expressed. Menzies' elaboration of the home's manifold virtues looked back to the suburban expansion of the 1920s and 1930s, and beyond that to the colonial liberalism of his Wimmera childhood and the family-based life of his Ballarat-born parents, as much as it looked forward to the modern homes of the 1950s.

Homes for Everyone

Australia's postwar history has been so successfully periodised by journalism and popular history – particularly the decades of the 1950s and 1960s – that it can be hard to see more enduring patterns. When we take a longer time span, however, the decades do not look so self-contained, particularly if our interest is in political culture, the slowly shifting relationship between dominant political ideas and people's lived, day-to-day experience. The 1950s may have a distinctively modern and streamlined look, but many people were still living in houses with 1920s, 1930s and 1940s interiors and facilities. And the young couples forming their households and families in the new suburbs were fulfilling aspirations which had deep roots in Australia's experience: first of the land-hungry goldrush immigrants, and then of the suburban nation which developed in the long boom from 1860 to 1890, in which the working man's longing for a plot of land and a cow was transformed into the aspiration for a home of one's own and a garden. And it was a remarkable feature of Australia that this aspiration could be more readily fulfilled here than anywhere else in the world at the time.

For the most part, this aspiration was fulfilled in the suburbs of Australia's capital cites. In comparison with crowded and expensive inner-city property, the suburbs offered affordable homes of one's own in healthy, peaceful, semi-rural surrounds. Decency, good order, health and domestic privacy were at the heart of the suburban ideal. By the late nineteenth century the combination of high wages and cheap, easily serviced land had made suburban home ownership more affordable in Australia than in Britain or most parts of the United States.[17] By Old World standards, property ownership was diffuse. Graeme Davison estimates that in the early 1880s, 45.5 per cent of Melbourne households were owner-occupiers, which was exceedingly high by contemporary world standards.[18] With a different history and a geography less hospitable to easy development Sydney's rate was lower, at 30 per cent. The rate for Australia as a whole in the second half of the nineteenth century is estimated as between 30 and 40 per cent, and observers were struck by the number of working men among the home owners.[19]

The suburban ideology which developed in the land boom of the 1880s stressed the advantages of the settled life to woo restless immigrants from their wandering life, and the suburban way of life became a permanent rival to the nomadic romance of the bushworkers for the allegiance of ordinary Australians.[20] In terms of national mythology, the suburbs lost to the rural-based mythology of the Australian legend, but in terms of the voting feet of the population they won a clear victory, as the overwhelming majority of Australians settled on the coastal fringe, with almost 40 per cent living in the six capital cities by 1900. A writer for the 1888 *Building Societies Gazette* was clear as to the political advantages of home ownership: 'To have a home which he himself reared or purchased – a home which he has improved or beautified – a home indeed which, with honest pride or natural love, he calls his own, will make any man a better citizen'.[21]

Property qualifications for voting had long linked the obligations of political citizenship to property ownership, and although the Australian colonies all had manhood suffrage for lower house elections by the end of the nineteenth century, property qualifications remained for participation in upper house and for municipal elections. But the property qualifications inherited from an England in which democratic rights were wrenched from the landed gentry and aristocracy took on very different meanings in a settler society. In the new land of opportunity it was far more plausible than in the Old World of hereditary wealth and social position to present property ownership as an indication of achievement and hence of the desirable citizenly qualities of independence, hard work and resourcefulness. As well, property ownership became a sign of property owners' commitment to the future of the colony, their building of 'a stake in the country'.

The left have often interpreted the phrase 'a stake in the country' to mean that property ownership was a conservative tool to make one supportive of the status quo. But in a settler society like Australia that needed people to settle – to commit their futures to the future of the colony and not to come, make a pile and go home again – the phrase had an additional layer of meaning. To build a house, a stake in the country, showed one intended to stay, and as the writer for the *Building Societies Gazette* makes clear, it mattered little whether one built it oneself or paid someone else to do it. Again the more democratic meanings of colonial home ownership are clear. The home owner may or may not depend on the labour of others, and the suburban owner builders and handymen were linked by their independent practicality to the rawhide and stringybark resourcefulness of the men on the land.

The depression of the 1890s ended Australia's first long boom, 'the glad confident morning' in which boundless resources seemed to offer boundless opportunities to new immigrants, and to promise a society free from the miseries and fixed class divisions of the Old World. As the depression struck, people's futures closed in and class divisions hardened.[22] The failed great strikes of the 1890s and the formation of labour parties challenged colonial liberalism's optimistic, nation-building individualism with the politics of class, and Australian Liberals had to make the unwilling accommodations with which this book began. Australian Liberals' ambiguous thinking about class is clearly evident in Menzies' 1942 speech. He uses the word only reluctantly – 'if we are to speak of classes' – and evokes the optimism of Australia's nineteenth-century settlers with his claim that 'In a country like Australia the class war must always be a false war'. But then he proceeds to define the middle class in terms of the clear and easily recognisable social indicators of middle-class life (home ownership, higher secondary and university education, opposition to organised labour) that marked the boundaries between the middle and working classes in the first half of the twentieth century. Menzies was born in 1894 and grew up into the class-divided Australia that resulted from the depression of the 1890s. He was a young adult during the industrial conflicts of the 1920s and saw the working class suffering in the depression. As a successful member of the professional middle class, Menzies wielded middle-class imagery in the context of the class-based social experience of the 1920s and 1930s. But this is imagery which, in its appeal to values rather than to overt economic interests, is able to appeal to people across social locations. When the good times came again in the 1950s Menzies' arguments and images were lifted somewhat clear of the class meanings carried in the 1920s, 1930s and 1940s, to regain the more general relevance Liberals had always claimed for them. As Australia again began to experience a long economic boom, aspirations for home ownership, on hold since 1890, were able to be satisfied and the rhetoric of Australian Liberals was given new, more general relevance.

The rise in home ownership after the war was dramatic, the result both of pent-up demand and, after the Liberals' 1949 election win, of government policies which favoured private ownership over public provision.[23] In 1947 the Australian rate of home ownership was 52.6 per cent of households, but with fewer new households buying it was set to decline as the buyers of the 1920s died. Within a decade the trend had been reversed. By 1954 the homeownership rate had leapt to 63 per cent and by 1961 it was 69.9 per cent with the greatest change occurring in urban areas.[24] In Melbourne the rate of home ownership by 1961 was 82.3 per cent,[25] with even higher concentrations in the newer suburbs, such as working-class Clayton where, in 1968, 94 per cent of houses were owner-occupied.[26] Most of these new owners were also new households. After the war the marriage rate soared, and those coming of age in the 1950s became Australia's most married generation.[27]

Interpretation of the political meaning of the postwar housing boom and of the 1950s more generally has been coloured by the preference of some left commentators for publicly provided housing and their identification of citizenship with state entitlements.[28] But it is wrong to see the 1950s' focus on home building as a retreat from citizenship, to see domesticity and the private as in opposition to citizenship and the public. Rather it was a reassertion of the link between home ownership, character, citizenship and nation which had long been self-evident to Australian Liberals. As argued in chapter 4, Liberals' notions of citizenship had always bridged the public and the private in their assertion of the relevance of domestic virtues to the public sphere, and in their construction of the home as a key site in the formation of the strength of character on which good citizenship depended. To build a home was to build a stake in the nation, a secure place to raise future citizens who would have the independent mindedness and strength of character on which the future of the nation depended. Liberals had always dreamed that such secure bases would be available to everyone.

The public, nation-building meanings of home ownership are clear from the energetic suburban community-building that accompanied it. The new homes built in the 1950s and 1960s were in new suburbs created from the orchards and market gardens that surrounded the capital cities. Unsewered and with few made roads, the infrastructure may have been adequate for small semi-rural communities but was woefully insufficient for the rapidly increasing population. Voluntary effort was needed to make good the deficiencies. Churches, halls and sports clubs were built or facilities expanded, and money was raised to support the local schools. People even banded together to improve roads and drains rather than wait for action by overstretched councils. In Blackburn, the Malcolm Street Citizens Group was formed, with a weekly levy and regular working bees to improve the road surface, build nature strips and install culverts.[29] John Murphy describes women in Oakleigh, 'sick and tired of walking through the slush and mud to do their shopping', picking up the shovels and wheelbarrows themselves.[30]

While the scale of the activity was unprecedented, and the locations were new, the models were not. Una Taylor who moved with her husband Keith into Nunawading in the late 1940s said 'we were sort of like pioneers'.[31] Both had grown up in country Victoria and the patterns of community participation and sociability they and thousands of young couples like them recreated in the new suburbs were the familiar ones of community building in a new land. The land had been more or less cleared, but there was still plenty of improving work to do. They were linked to the pioneers too by the hardships and privations many experienced in the early years. The acute housing shortage in the decade immediately following the war was compounded by a shortage of materials. Many people, including many of the new immigrants, simply took matters into their own hands, living in garages or makeshift dwellings as they built their house in their spare time with whatever materials they could find. About a quarter of the 700 000 new houses built in the decade after the war were built by owner-builders, who bridged the gap between their dream and their finances with their own labour and privation.[32]

Graeme and Barbara Davison have argued that Australia's postwar owner-builders and suburban community-builders can be seen as a last fitful expression of Australia's pioneer legend, the celebration of the courage, enterprise, hard work and perseverance of the first settlers.[33] Postwar home ownership was more broadly based than the interwar housing expansion. In the 1920s and 1930s, the capacity to buy a home was the result of one's credit worthiness which in turn depended on regular employment and on the strength of character to save. Homes were symbols of respectability and steady character. The dominant historical interpretation of the expansion of postwar housing has been that middle-class cultural forms were generalised to the working class who were the subjects of a generally conservative process of embourgeoisment.[34] In this argument, the 1950s are primarily seen in contrast to the obviously class-based social experience of the 1920s and 1930s. But if we take a longer perspective, the homes built on weekends by strong and resourceful young couples can be seen to reach back over the cautious conservatism of the 1920s and 1930s to the energies and opportunities of the pioneering nineteenth century and to the resourceful practical masculinity of the Australian legend. And as Robin Boyd's well-known description of suburbia as the Australian ugliness testifies, the old middle class did not experience the postwar housing boom as a welcome swelling of their own ranks so much as a general lowering of taste. Instead of seeing the postwar housing boom as the embourgeoisment of the working classes, it is more accurate to see it as the democratisation of home ownership in which the aspirations of ordinary Australians are at last realised.

Crown and Race

Robert Menzies is a transitional figure in Australian political culture, a hinge in the middle of the century between its Edwardian beginnings and constrained interwar years and its expansive postwar modernity, as the 1950s are a transitional decade, a point of separation between an old and a new Australia.[35] Menzies bore the values and experiences of the Australian moral middle class with assurance and aplomb: their self-confident belief in their own virtue; their faith in their independence of judgement; their sense of civic service and obligation; their distrust of credit and easy affluence; their solid, well-formed personalities; their commitment to the habits, work and institutions of a lifetime. But during his long time in office, the seventeen years from the 1949 election to his retirement in 1966, Australian society changed and the people growing up under his governments were very different from their grandparents born at the turn of the century, and different in significant ways from their parents born between the wars.

In the 1960s Donald Horne captured Menzies' unrepresentativeness of the Australia he governed:

> It was a feature of Menzies' long rule that little of what he did seems to matter much ... The positive characteristics of his Age – the spread of affluence, the considerable relaxation in social styles, the increase in national self-assurance, the continued migration programme, the beginning of an interest in Asia

and the growing tolerance of Asians resident in Australia, the demands of technology, the increasing power of overseas investment in Australia – were not of the kind of thing that Menzies has 'stood for' and some of them are the opposite of what he had hoped when he came to power.[36]

Much the same complaint might be made about any political leader in power for so long until such an advanced age – Menzies was 72 when he finally retired. What is of interest is the particulars of the lag between Menzies' representativeness and Australians' changing values and social experiences.

Some aspects of this lag are familiar. Menzies was born in 1894 when Queen Victoria was on the throne, in what he later described as 'the outer Empire', and grew up during the resurgence of British imperial fervour before World War I. Britain was the centre of his world, the source of the power, the wealth and the people that had established white society in Australia and of the institutions, values, and ideas on which it had been built. High political office in Australia gave him the chance to visit and then become familiar with a place long revered in imagination, and his long Australian Prime Ministership made him a familiar figure in Britain, a representative of the old white dominions who reminded the British of the days when the sun shone on their Empire. Although Menzies was an active advocate of the new British Commonwealth, it was to the Empire and its monarch that he had given his heart. When in 1954 the young Queen Elizabeth and her husband Prince Philip visited Australia, the first reigning monarch ever to do so, he led millions of Australians in a rapturous welcome. By the early 1960s, however, the crowds were thinning and they continued to diminish until, by the end of the century, only a few elderly women, mostly British migrants, turned out to greet royal visitors. By the time Australia voted on the referendum to become a republic in 1999, monarchists centred their arguments on the constitutional role of the Crown and said almost nothing about loyalty to the monarch or the royal family.

Also familiar is the lag in attitudes to race which Menzies represented. Menzies carried into postwar Australia the attitudes to race of the turn of the century which underpinned Australia's racially restrictive immigration policy and its exclusion of Aboriginal people from the nation. These attitudes are more complex than is often recognised, and included deeply held beliefs about the impossibility of civilised racial co-existence, as well as beliefs about white racial superiority. Nations were understood as based in racial homogeneity, and any loosening of racial restrictions was seen as inviting inevitable civic and political discord. Menzies and his government continued the postwar immigration program begun by the Labor government to build Australia's population, which included large numbers of non-English-speaking Europeans alongside the familiar British and Irish immigrants. The hope was that these people would assimilate to Australian ways, and for the most part they did, although Australia had to give up its self-description as a British nation and become instead a multicultural one.

The disintegration of the unifying symbolic structures of Crown and race are familiar stories. By the 1980s they had left the Liberals high and dry, struggling to find a language of social cohesion to bind the millions of individuals who inhabited Australia. This was before John Howard and his successful revitalisation of the Liberal Party which will be discussed in the final chapter of this book. These familiar stories however do not get us very far in understanding the larger historical forces of which they are a manifestation. They are essentially moral tales, generally of enlightenment and progress, told by those who approve the direction of change or were its agents, and occasionally by those who disapprove. But the lag Menzies represented was a lag of far more than attitudes to Crown and race. It was a lag in ways of experiencing the self which disguised the impact of postwar change on the constitutive experiences of Australia's moral middle class and its political expression in Liberal ideas and values.

When in 1954 the Liberal Party put forward as a central tenet of its philosophy that 'We believe in the Individual. We stand positively for the free man, his initiative, individuality, and acceptance of responsibility', it put it forward as a statement of self-evident and unchanging values. The individual was the same in 1910 as in 1954 as in the foreseeable future. This individual was held securely in place in a society of individuals by shared, overarching symbolic structures, by the mutual obligations of active citizenship, and by substantive racial and cultural similarities anchored in a shared history. As a result, the many free-thinking individuals who made up the nation could be expected to come to roughly similar independent judgements on many important questions, and were easily recognisable to each other. But the meaning of the term 'individual' was different in important ways by the end of the century from its midpoint after the war. The visible overarching symbolic structures of the British Crown and shared British race patriotism had largely gone, but so had much else that bound mid-century Australians to each other and to their government. Beneath the familiar stories of the melting of the British Crown's symbolic glue, and the way Australians learned to live with cultural difference, are larger stories about changes in the way people experienced the balance between their individual and collective identities, and changes in the ideas and experience of government. From Deakin to Menzies, both the moral middle class and Australian Liberals were based in Protestantism, Liberal ideas of citizenship and the conservative habits of sound finance. Postwar changes transformed the experiential foundation of Australia's moral middle class, and fragmented it in ways the Liberal Party is still trying to comprehend.

The Decline of Protestantism

In chapter 3 I argued that the Australian Liberals' political imagination was essentially Protestant; that the individual in which they believed was the Protestant individual of free judgement who would never willingly subordinate this freedom to the dictates of a party organisation. And I argued that this foundational belief in freedom of judgement carried an inevitable anti-Catholicism which pushed Australian Catholics towards the Labor Party. The Australian party system at mid-century still had a clear religious dimension, revealed both in the first postwar voting studies, and in the religious affiliations of parliamentarians. Two developments began to erode this. The first was the Split in the Labor Party over communism; the second the sudden collapse of habits of religious observance in the 1960s and with this the decline in the moral and social centrality of the Protestant churches.[37]

The complex and dramatic story of the Labor Party's Split over communism has been told many times. Catholic trade unionists, alarmed at the growing power of the communists in the union movement during the war, began to organise into Industrial Groups ('Groupers'). The Catholic Social Studies Movement, later known simply as the 'Movement', was also formed. Using the parishes as an organisational base, the Movement was an informal lay organisation to organise Catholics within the trade unions. It operated with the blessing of Archbishop Mannix and was led by the law graduate son of an Italian greengrocer, B. A. Santamaria. By the end of the war well-organised factions were struggling for control of the union movement, and much of this spilled into the Labor Party itself as the Groupers opposed candidates for pre-selection or party office seen as too close to the communists.

In 1950 the Menzies' government passed a Bill to outlaw the Communist Party. The ALP was divided over how to respond. On the one hand it did not want to appear soft on communism and many of its Catholic members were vehemently opposed to communism's godless atheism; on the other, there was a fear that the attack on communism would broaden into a general attack on the left and on the Labor Party's support for the parliamentary road to socialism – which simply meant a little more state enterprise. The Communist Party and several unions challenged the Bill's constitutionality. Bert Evatt, the Deputy Leader of the party and an experienced barrister, accepted a private brief to appear on behalf of the communist-led Waterside Workers' Federation. After the High Court rejected the Bill the electorate was asked to vote on a referendum to give the government the power to ban the Communist Party. Ben Chifley died shortly before the referendum and Evatt became leader. Evatt threw himself into the 'No' case with a passion. It was his finest hour as he argued the cause of civil liberties, and in a month turned a 73 per cent majority for the banning into a narrow defeat for Menzies.[38] The cause was won, but the cost to the Labor Party was immense in bitterness, suspicion and recrimination.

Menzies abandoned the attempt to ban the party, but communism continued as a visible issue, flaring to prominence again in the lead up to the 1954 election when a minor Soviet diplomat, Vladimir Petrov, defected with allegations of a spy ring in Canberra. The economy was still unsettled, and Evatt had expected to win the 1954 election. When Labor lost, Evatt became convinced that he had been robbed of victory by a conspiracy masterminded by Menzies. In the subsequent Royal Commission into Petrov's allegations, a member of Evatt's personal staff was implicated and Evatt became increasingly paranoid and erratic. His paranoia was directed at Menzies, and at Catholic anti-communists in the labour movement. In a fateful press release in October 1954 he lashed out at 'a small group of members' who had adopted methods which 'strikingly resemble both Communist and Fascist infiltration of large groups'. They subverted Labor policy and Labor leadership 'with the inevitable and intended result of assisting the Menzies government'; and the bombshell – 'It appears certain that the activities of this small group are largely directed from outside the Labor Movement. The Melbourne *News Weekly* appears to act as their organ'.[39] *News Weekly* was the paper of the Movement and B. A. Santamaria. Here was the familiar structure of sectarian anti-Catholicism – secret Catholic conspiracies, small groups subject to the control of priests and bishops – but this time within the Labor Party itself. Evatt's outburst was greeted with dismay, and the party's division along complex fault lines of religious and party loyalty deepened, with tensions particularly severe in Victoria. With bitter accusations and recriminations the party split soon after. The Anti-Communist Labor Party was formed and subsequently became the Democratic Labor Party (DLP).

Communism was an issue of high salience to Catholics. Not only was it a godless doctrine, but Communist governments banned religious observance and persecuted Christians for their faith. Catholic voters began to swing away from the ALP at the 1949 election, although with significant state variations. In 1955 after the Split, the ALP lost a large proportion of its Catholic support, particularly in Victoria. One influential interpretation argues that the formation of the DLP was a convenient stepping stone for upwardly mobile Catholics to move away from their traditional Labor support on the way to becoming Liberal.[40] This argument reduces the passionate anti-communism of the men who split from Labor to an expression of status aspiration. It refuses to take religious belief seriously as an agent in its own right, and provides a dismissive explanation of the Groupers' motives to warm the hearts of old Labor. And, as I argued in chapter 3, it depends on an argument about the working-class character of Catholic support for Labor for which there is, at best, only fragmentary evidence. John Warhurst has argued, far more convincingly, that anti-communism itself was the decisive factor in the decline in Catholic support for the ALP. That the decline was greater among middle-class than working-class Catholics was because active, church-going Catholics were more middle-class than Catholics in general.[41]

The formation of the DLP changed the religious dynamics of the party conflict. Catholics were no longer seen as inevitably aligned with Labor, and Labor was no longer seen as free from sectarian suspicions. The Liberals came to rely on DLP preferences which effectively kept the ALP from power. In 1963 Menzies announced that all secondary schools, government and private, would receive federal funding for science blocks. This was the beginning of state aid for church schools, the first breach in the wall that had kept the government and church school sectors divided since the mid-nineteenth century, and the first move in the redress of Catholics' longest-standing political grievance. And although there was no immediate influx of Catholics into the Liberal parliamentary party, the social and religious barriers dividing Catholics and Protestants were softening. Revolutionary moves towards ecumenicalism within the Catholic Church removed the prohibition on Catholics participating in other forms of worship, and the reforms of Vatican Two, which brought Catholics' liturgical practices closer to those of the Protestant churches, allayed Protestants' suspicions of the mumbo-jumbo of Popery.[42] The mass was no longer said in Latin, the priest faced the people, and nuns gradually abandoned their medieval-style dress. At the same time the social reach of the Protestant churches was shrinking. Religious historian, Ian Breward, claims that liberal Protestantism collapsed in the 1960s.[43] The collapse was sudden, and it came after a decade of unprecedented expansion.

The resurgence of Liberal ideas of citizenship after the war was accompanied by a resurgence in the Protestant churches. From the mid-1950s, after a long lull, the active membership of the Protestant churches increased. Funds were raised to provide churches and Sunday School halls in the new suburbs. Sunday School enrolments reached their numerical peak in the early 1960s, indicative of the social reach of the churches beyond the core of active parishioners into the families who, attending only rarely themselves, saw Sunday School as a useful supplement to their children's moral education. The view of the churches' role was conventional, little different from its prewar understanding: religion provided a divine legitimation of conventional morality, a firm basis for self-discipline, character building and concern for others. What was new was the zeal. Churches embarked on missions, campaigns and crusades to attract converts, increase commitment and raise funds.[44] In the new suburbs the churches became busy social hubs for young families and their active community building.[45] In the 1950s the Protestant churches continued to support central Liberal values, underpinning the moral middle class's political convictions with religious belief.

Some time in the mid-1960s this phase of expansion suddenly ended and Protestant congregations began to decline from about 30 per cent reported weekly attendance in the early 1960s, to 20–25 per cent a decade later, to the current level of about 13 per cent.[46] David Hilliard dates the turning point at 1963–64 with the emergence of radical theology and a wave of doubts about the relevance of religious institutions to modern life. The biggest change was among the young. Sunday School enrolments fell sharply, and church-based youth groups began to collapse for want of new members. In the early 1960s organisations like the Presbyterian Fellowship of Australia, the Young Anglican Fellowship, and the university-based Student Christian Movement were vigorous and exciting; by the end of the decade they had been swept away by the youth movements which grew from the opposition to the Vietnam War. According to David Hilliard:

> Almost an entire generation of teenagers and young adults seems to have dropped out of the Protestant churches, as the churches came to be seen as one of the conservative institutions propping up an oppressive social order. The socialisation process by which religious affiliation was transmitted from parents to the next generation broke down.[47]

The causes of so dramatic a generational break in habits of religious observance are complex and still only imperfectly understood by historians, but the church has been pushed from the centre of moral discourse to become one source of moral guidance among many others. Secular sources of moral value, such as a rather generalised humanism, have become more significant, and have interacted with sociological understandings of identity to challenge the language of duty and responsibility at the heart of conventional religious moral discourse. The churches too have changed in response to this, and since the 1960s there has been a perceptible shift in their attitude to social questions. Century-long preoccupations with gambling, alcohol and the preservation of Sundays from commercial activity have given way to concern with social justice issues such as poverty, racial discrimination and capital punishment.[48] One political impact of the general decline in religious belief has been to make the difference between the religiously observant of all denominations and the secular majority of greater political significance than denominational and sectarian differences among the religious. Regular church-attenders, whatever their denomination, are more likely to support the Liberals. Catholics are still more likely than non-Catholics to support Labor, but if they are regular church-attenders they are more likely than non-attending Catholics to support the Liberals.[49]

Despite the religious changes of the 1960s, the Liberal Party's sectarian suspicions of Catholics lingered into the 1970s. Philip Lynch, a junior minister in the coalition governments of the late 1960s and early 1970s and Treasurer in the first Fraser government, believed that because he was a Catholic he could never get the top job.[50] By the end of the century, however, John Howard's Liberal government contained a number of Catholic Cabinet ministers, most prominently Richard Alston and Tony Abbott. Recent work by Marion Maddox on federal parliamentarians' religious beliefs suggests that religion is more significant among current parliamentarians than one would expect in an as avowedly secular society as Australia. Parliamentarians' religiosity seemed, however, to be more a matter of personal faith than visible social identity, operating in complex personal and idiosyncratic ways quite different from the well-organised socio-religious blocks of the first half of the twentieth century and at a greater distance from the cultural mainstream.[51]

From Duties to Rights

Australian Liberals' conceptions of citizenship were centred on the obligation to cooperate and to subordinate self-interest to the common good, whether this be in the family, the community or the nation. This sensitivity to one's communal obligations, this readiness to serve, flowed from the moral qualities of the citizens. It was on these, ultimately, that the strength and prosperity of the nation depended. World War II strengthened Australian Liberals' ideas of citizenship. It reminded people of their common fate, and called on their obligations to the nation. When peace came, Australia's nation-building agenda was picked up again, just as it had been after World War I, although people were anxious that larger historical forces might again intervene to stall the project, that peace and prosperity might be short-lived. Robert Putnam, writing of a similar surge in identification with traditional ideas of citizenship in the United States, has called this 'the civic-minded World War II generation'.[52] For members of this generation, as for their parents and grandparents, citizenship was still about obligations and duties rather than rights and entitlements, and the relationship of good citizenship to good character and the strength of the nation was still self-evident. They brought their children up with ideas of service and obligation similar to those of their own youth.

The charge to the new members of the Nunawading Branch of the YWCA Girl Citizens in 1962 expressed sentiments which would have been easily recognisable forty years earlier when the organisation was formed, but forty years later seem to come from another world. 'Girl Citizens everywhere are bound together in one common purpose, the tasks of building up a girlhood in our country which holds the highest ideals of citizenship and gives itself in service'.[53] Brownies and Cubs, Guides and Scouts, pledged to honour and obey, to do their best, and to serve other people at all times. The mottoes and uniforms of the new high schools built in the 1950s and 1960s reproduced the sense of order, common endeavour and moral purpose of the prewar secondary schools, both public and private. Headmasters and visiting dignitaries addressed the students on the importance of the habits of youth for the development of character and backed up their exhortations with stories of bravery in war. But just as the generation coming of age in the 1960s deserted the Protestant churches, so the way an older generation understood their social and political obligations rapidly lost its hold over their children.

Nowhere was this clearer than in the generational revolt against conscription to the Vietnam War in which sons of the men and women who had fought World War II refused to serve their nation. They appealed to conscience, and pitted their independent-minded evaluation of the threat to the nation against the government. And in the countercultural and social movements which followed, they championed the authenticity of individual experience. The slogan of the sexual and women's liberation movements, 'the personal is political', captures the new relationship between private experience and the public domain in which the barriers that had separated and protected sexuality and family life from various forms of public intrusion were dismantled, and women renegotiated their social roles in order to take greater control of their lives. Many conventional notions of duty and obligation were swept away by arguments for the rights of particular groups of individuals (women, homosexuals, Aborigines) to greater personal autonomy and opportunity of experience.

The social movements of the late 1960s and early 1970s also spread more sociological understandings of the person. Ideal Liberal citizens were active. They had views, made decisions, exercised reason or perhaps prejudice, and took responsibility for their beliefs and actions. Members of social movements were active too, but they were motivated by their opposition to society's power in shaping and limiting people's capacities for thought and action. They were expanding the already existing concern of working-class politics with the way economic inequality limited and deformed people's lives to encompass other dimensions of inequality, in particular gender, race and ethnicity. Hence the women's movement argued that individual women's problems had social rather than individual origins and so required political solutions. In the Australian context this led activists down the path Labor had previously followed – to seek state-based solutions to the inequalities and constraints the various movements identified. Like Labor, they came to the state as claimants and their attention was directed not so much at what people might do for society as at what society had done to people and how that might be changed. Conceptions of citizenship centred on duties gave way to ones centred on rights. The direction of the imaginative link between citizens and the state was thus reversed from one in which the state was created from the actions, decisions and capacities of its citizens to one in which the citizen was mainly conceived as a bearer of rights and entitlements bestowed by the state. No longer did citizens come together to create the state; rather the state recognised and protected the rights of its citizens.

Not that the new social movements used the term 'citizenship' a great deal. They were more likely to talk of civil rights and to conceptualise these within the growing discourse of human rights that grew out of the United Nations Declaration of Human Rights. Australian Liberals' moral conception of citizenship gradually faded, and when interest in the concept revived in the 1980s it was seen as a purely political concept, often with a very narrow focus on the formal status of nationality. A 1995 parliamentary discussion paper on national citizenship indicators reported that very few of the submissions it received mentioned duties at all.[54] And when talk of duties was revived it was in the changed context of coercive attempts by governments to wind back their services and withdraw entitlements from people, as in the concept of mutual obligation which governments were using to renegotiate various welfare entitlements.

Keynesianism, Affluence and the Expansion of Credit

The third pillar of Australian Liberals in the first half of the twentieth century, the ideas and habits of sound finance, had also disappeared almost entirely by the end of the second half. It survived residually among the elderly, or as a chosen personal financial style for the cautious and risk averse, but was no longer a set of habits and ideas binding the private financial practices of individual citizens to those of the nation. In fact it often seemed just the opposite, as any voluntary restraint of consumption threatened to undermine the continuing buoyant levels of demand on which the nation's economic health depended. In the wake of the terrorist attack on the twin towers of the World Trade Center on 11 September 2001, Americans were urged to show their patriotism by continuing to spend, in sharp contrast with the patriotic thrift campaigns of the two world wars. Australians at the end of the century were carrying record levels of personal debt, and household savings were low. Two separate though related historical processes are at work in this transformation of the relationship between the virtuous household and the financial practices of the nation. The first is the development of Keynesian economics, the second postwar affluence and the expansion of consumer credit.

Keynes' argument that when recession threatened and demand began to fall, governments should expand credit and spend, and that when the good times were rolling they should tighten their belts was an argument that national governments should respond to economic situations in quite the opposite way to individual businesses and households. According to Keynesianism the management of the national economy was governed by a different logic from the economic enterprises of civil society. The financial experience built up in the management of a business, farm or household, was thus no longer any guide to the management of the national economy which became the province of expert economists wielding increasingly technical tools. Ordinary people – even those skilled in the handling of money – were shut out from any easy understanding of the nation's financial management, as the link between individual decisions and the capacity of the national economy to deliver prosperity was broken. It was only in the 1980s, after Keynesianism's collapse in the face of stagflation, that analogies between the financial management of the household and small business and the national economy started to reappear in public discourse.

As nations learned the benefits of credit and deficit budgets, so too did individuals, and the availability of hire purchase – or instalment credit – revolutionised people's patterns of saving and spending. Hire purchase had been available in Australia since the 1920s, but was little used. After the war it took off, as pent-up demand combined with the expansion of hire purchase facilities and a range of more affordable consumer goods to fuel a spectacular rise in hire purchase debt. In 1945 hire purchase debt was less than £6 million, by mid-1952 it was £100 million, by the end of 1955 £200 million, and by 1967 $2000 million (approximately equal to £1000 million).[55] The bulk of the credit was for private consumption. In 1959, 70 per cent of the loans were for motor vehicles, 25 per cent for household goods, and only 5 per cent for plant and machinery for productive use, prompting the contemporary observation 'that the obvious gap between the funds going into producer as against consumer goods is rather startling'.[56]

The responses to the enthusiasm with which Australians took to purchasing on credit were mixed. Enid Lyons' remark that by the 1960s the whole world had gone fiduciary, 'from the Smiths on the basic wage with their fiduciary TV set and washing machine to the young man with his fiduciary sports car' points to the way it unsettled social hierarchies of class and age, and weakened the link between effort and reward. It became much harder to use the range and type of material goods a household or individual possessed as a reliable marker of social distinction, and the young could afford pleasures they had barely earned. One effect was to contribute to the lowering of the average marriage age. Where once a couple had to save for the necessary household goods before they could 'afford' to marry, now they could acquire them on credit with the wife working for several years to pay them off before having children.[57]

The disturbance hire purchase brought to the middle-class social world is clearly registered in the trade journal of one of the purveyors of goods of middle-class social distinction – The *Commonwealth Jeweller and Watchmaker* – as it debated whether or not retail jewellers should adopt instalment selling to protect their market share from the competition for people's spending on consumer durables such as cars and white goods.[58] Jewellery, with its symbolism of enduring value, watches as rewards for loyal, long service to the firm, fountain pens to sign cheques, mantel clocks, cutlery sets and silver trays to furnish the home, the goods sold by retail jewellers and watchmakers all carried rich symbolic loads (and low use value), which made them particularly vulnerable to disturbances in the retail culture. Would these symbolic meanings be compromised if the goods were purchased with instalment credit?

One correspondent, J. B. Lyons, argued that hire purchase would lower the prestige of the watchmaker and jeweller in the eyes of the public, bringing them down to the common level of businesses 'selling anything from hardware to refrigerators and what have you'. As well there were practical worries: what were the watchmaker's obligations to repair a watch still being paid for? And how would establishments keep track of clients who shifted address, with the increased attendant risk of bad debts?

> Provision would have to be made for bad debts, especially in regard to the floating population of New Australians who, we find, are enquiring for this type of business more than any other section of the community. Imagine the difficulty of trying to keep trace (sic) of this particular type of client, the spelling of the names of these people alone constitutes a nightmare.

The assumption is that the capacity to purchase the goods of the retail jeweller and watchmaker is a consequence of achieved social stability, evidenced at least by a permanent address. Registered here too is the disturbance to traditional social knowledge of the new immigrants whose social standing was all but impossible for this correspondent to read. He concludes:

> let us continue to trade along the same sound, traditional lines upon which our businesses were founded and established and which have proved themselves over the years ... having weathered two world wars and a depression. In other words let us not throw away the substance of a well and fully proved system for the shadows of a dubious and unproved one.[59]

As in the debates of the 1930s, credit is associated with shadow and illusion, in contrast to the solidity of traditional methods, anchored in the experience of the past.

But there were vigorous voices promoting the advantages of the extension of hire purchase, both among the jewellers and more broadly. Another correspondent to the *Commonwealth Jeweller*, Mark Barnett, saw credit selling as a modern merchandising trend, successfully practised in 'that very amazing and most progressive country, America'; and he argued that credit selling would contribute to a general raising of standards of taste as people became able to buy merchandise 'of a class and category far above what they could afford' if they had to pay cash.[60] Barnett is unperturbed by the effect this might have on systems of social signification and couches his arguments in terms of individual consumers and their aspirations. This is in keeping with the general promotion of hire purchase as a system of selling appropriate to a forward-looking, democratic society, 'a convenient means to the ownership that expresses the fundamental instincts in the peoples of democratic countries with expanding economies'.[61]

Supporters of hire purchase were quick to point out its similarities with the old virtues of prudent saving and pride of ownership. Sir Arthur

Warner, Liberal member of the Victorian Parliament and a tireless advocate of hire purchase, described hire purchase as 'the defence of the appliance and motor industry against the daily temptation of the public to spend on drink, smoking, gambling and other transitory attractions upon which money can be spent without future benefit'.[62] Hire purchase spending by contrast was on assets not consumption, 'the capital equipment' of the household, and repayment imposed 'a form of budgetary discipline'.[63] 'Hire purchase produces a nation of savers – not spendthrifts' and it was directed towards the ownership of property and the enhancement of the family: 'We can pat ourselves on the back when we point to the family group gathered round the TV set, much more often together in the home than they were a few years ago'.[64] By the end of the 1950s hire purchase was clearly respectable: 1930s champions of sound finance and the need to live within one's means, J. B. Were & Son, advised their clients that 'no Australian equity portfolio is really representative if it does not include a proportion of hire-purchase company shares'.[65]

The expansion of hire purchase was but one aspect of postwar affluence and rising standards of living. Security of employment and rising wages gave people the financial confidence to incur debt, and the proliferation of affordable consumer goods for the modern family home gave them the motivation. After the fears of inflation in the early 1950s passed, the economy settled into a period of continuous, stable growth: unemployment was negligible and average weekly earnings increased by about 4 per cent per annum.[66] The expansion of home ownership was accompanied by a generally rising standard of living for the vast majority of the Australian population. The sharp material boundaries that had separated the prewar middle and working classes gradually dissolved into the shared capacity to enjoy 'the Australian way of life': a comfortably furnished home with most mod cons, a motor car, a steady job and an annual holiday, preferably at the beach.

As well, the engine of economic growth was continuing the shift from production to consumption. It was not just productive work on which the prosperity of the nation depended, but spending power and buoyant demand. 'Thrift would have ruined Australia' observed Donald Horne in the mid-1960s.[67] The citizen consumer became as important as the citizen producer in the imagining and management of the national economy, and with this the relationship between the government of the nation and the character of its citizens was changed profoundly. Nicholas Brown has written of the anxieties of Australian policy-makers in the 1950s as they learned to govern affluence rather than manage scarcity. They had to shift from 'managing a national population' conceived as a potential, evolving unity which could be managed from above to 'governing prosperity'.[68]

As one of the advocates of hire purchase wrote in 1964: 'The shaping of our society is accomplished day by day in untold millions of decisions on the part of individual consumers'.[69] Government had a role to play in the regulation of these interactions – and there were frequent calls for greater government regulation of the hire purchase industry – but the democracy of the market set the agenda.

To conceive society as a market shaped by millions of individual decisions was very different from conceiving it as a nation, and it had very different implications for the imagined relationship between the individuals who composed the nation and the government. Frederic Eggleston worried that 'good citizenship' was being replaced by 'organised selfishness'.[70] Eggleston's formulation went to the heart of the effect of the changes in the postwar period for Australian Liberals' conception of citizenship, with its belief that good government and a strong nation were firmly based in a virtuous citizenry. Selfishness, to put the interests of the self, or even of the part, before the interests of the whole, was the key vice of the bad citizen. But this was just the behaviour on which the rationality and smooth functioning of the market relied. The 'organised selfishness' of the market might produce outcomes of general benefit, but they did so independent of any intention of individuals to direct their actions to the common good, or even give it a passing thought, and so independent of their character and moral qualities. The virtues or otherwise of the citizenry were quite irrelevant to the proper functioning of the market. Like the logic of Keynesianism, the logic of the market undermined the causal links between the virtues of individuals and their households and the strength and prosperity of nations on which Australian Liberals' ideas of citizenship had depended. Keynesianism had disconnected the financial practices of the household from those of the nation, and the growing power of a consumer-driven market compounded the process. Decisions about spending and saving retained their moral drama for many people and they were still important for their long-term prosperity, but they were losing their overt political meaning. By the end of the century when policy-makers started to worry that the population was failing to save sufficient for its old age, their exhortations fell on ears attuned only to warnings about falling individual living standards.

The New Middle Class

Increased affluence and increased attentiveness to individual rights were two processes disaggregating the prewar class-based social formations, and with them the nation itself, into assemblages of individuals. Processes of government were also changing in ways that undermined Liberal conceptions of citizenship. The capacities of the Australian national government expanded enormously between 1939 and 1945 as it took powers from the states and expanded its administrative capacities in order to fight the war. The Uniform Taxation Act of 1942 gave the Commonwealth a virtual monopoly of income-taxing power and established its financial dominance over the states. The Commonwealth public service grew rapidly; between 1939 and 1951 the number of Commonwealth public servants increased by 300 per cent, and then by a steady 4 per cent per year until by 1967 it was 7.5 per cent of the workforce. Canberra's growth was similarly spectacular: from 17 000 in 1947 to 50 000 in 1959 to 120 000 in 1962.[71] In comparison with the rather ramshackle, prewar state-based bureaucracies the postwar Commonwealth public service was increasingly professional, the province of the expert and specialised knowledges of university graduates.

The effect of the expansion of the powers of the Commonwealth government on the relationship between the virtuous middle class and the state was twofold. The growing reliance on expert knowledge increased the distance between government administration and policy formation on the one hand and commonsense social knowledge on the other. We have already seen how Keynesian economics drove a wedge between commonsense financial knowledge and the government of the national economy. Similarly, the rise of social statistics and of the social scientific understandings of the determinants of behaviour competed with the voluntarist understandings of moral responsibility in everyday life. The sociological understandings of the individual later spread by the social movements were also becoming entrenched in government activities as the welfare state expanded to help society's less fortunate.

Secondly, a new section of the middle class was being formed, with views of its particular capacities and moral strengths somewhat at odds with that of the prewar moral middle class. Working for the *national* government, employed as *public servants*, they too understood their contribution to the nation in terms of service in the national interest, but there were subtle differences that were to become a rupture in their understanding of how this was to be achieved. For Australian Liberals the opposite of national was sectional; for the new Commonwealth public servants, the opposite of national were the state-based governments, and many were convinced of the creative possibilities of an expanded national government. They became a natural constituency for Labor's more expansive view of the possibilities of state action and its impatience with the constraints of federalism, if Labor were ever to become a credible reforming government. And where the old moral middle class offered the nation their virtuous characters constructed over a lifetime of self-discipline, members of the new middle class offered the expert knowledges and administrative capacities they had acquired through education.

The expanded expert and professional Commonwealth public service was mirrored in the private sector as job opportunities increased for professional and white collar workers. Professional and white collar employment grew from 25.3 per cent in 1947 to 29.4 per cent in 1966, and with 31.7 per cent by 1972 the growth was showing no signs of slowing.[72] Education was expanding too, to meet the growing demand for professional and technical workers. More children were staying at school for longer, and many more were participating in tertiary education. At the end of the war there were six universities in Australia; by 1972 there were eleven, along with newly developed colleges of advanced education. These were very different places from the preserves of the prewar middle class as the proportion of university students in the 17- to 22-year age group increased from 4.2 per cent to 9.5 per cent between 1955 and 1975. If we add those attending Council of Adult Education courses, 18.5 per cent of the age group were in tertiary institutions.[73] Many of these were the first members of their families to receive tertiary education.

The new, educated middle class, many of them employed in the public sector, depended for their social power on the control of knowledge rather than on their capital or their character. They were impatient with the slowness of political change as the 1950s gave way to the new ideas and movements of the 1960s. Donald Horne's *The Lucky Country*, published in 1964, expressed a widely felt growing frustration as the old prewar elites held on to power by Menzies' coat tails and it seemed as if the better educated, better informed postwar generation would never get a chance: 'Everywhere one goes in Australia among sensitive, intelligent people of the middle generation – once the conversation reaches a certain depth – one meets a sense of desperation'. Such people, Horne said, were losing faith in the future of their country as it seemed stalled in 'a perpetual state of Stand Easy', waiting for a generational change that may never come.[74] It was not just Menzies who was still there – so were many other old men, like Country Party leader John McEwan who was a minister for twenty-one years; and Labor Party leader Arthur Calwell had fought in the conscription battles of World War I.

While Menzies was still in place, the Liberals were able to ignore the impact of social change, his continuous presence confirming their conviction that they were the only party fit to govern Australia. Impatient, younger men simply had to bide their time. Menzies retired in January 1966 and was succeeded by Harold Holt. Holt certainly brought the feel of a generational change, as he was photographed in a wetsuit with his three bikini-clad step-daughters-in-law. The reputation of his government is overshadowed by the mounting protests against the Vietnam War and the Party's electoral dependence on the anti-communist DLP. On domestic issues however, there was more room to move, and as Horne and more recently Ian Hancock have argued, many of the reforms which later came to be associated with the Whitlam government were well underway by 1972.[75] The Holt government reformed immigration law to increase numbers of non-European immigrants; initiated the referendum giving the Commonwealth joint powers with the states in the area of Aboriginal policy; and began the rethinking of Australia's relations with Asia. It also continued Australia's involvement in the Vietnam War which had begun in 1965 when the first Australian troops were committed. Conscription had been introduced in 1964 to bolster Australia's military capacity for the war. It was done by a ballot of birthdays and in 1966 the first conscripts left Australia for Vietnam. Labor leader Arthur Calwell who remembered the fierce opposition to conscription in World War I led Labor to a massive defeat on the issue in the 1966 election. At this stage, majority public opinion was with the government.

Holt drowned after barely two years as Prime Minister. He was succeeded by John Gorton, a returned service man who had been in parliament since 1950. He was a compromise candidate, who was required to continue the government's prosecution of the war in the face of increasingly sceptical public opinion and mounting protest. By the late 1960s the anti-war movement staged regular protests and demonstrations and there was widespread civil disobedience of the government's conscription laws, with many young men refusing to register. The moratorium movement reached its peak in May 1970 when huge anti-war demonstrations filled the streets of the nation's capital cities. Mass street protests now have an accepted place in the repertoire of political actions available to Australian citizens, but in 1970 many saw them as dangerous breaches of law and order and the Gorton government was under pressure to clamp down on them. It was also under pressure to deal more decisively with the draft dodgers and conscientious objectors, but was reluctant to prosecute them all lest it publicise the extent of the civil disobedience.[76] At this point the expression 'small-l liberal' started to be used to distinguish political positions based on the classic nineteenth-century liberal arguments, associated with John Stuart Mill, from more conservative positions within the Liberal Party.[77] Its coining is an indication of the gap which had opened up during Menzies' final years between the values and experiences of the new middle class and the Liberal Party, a gap which was widened, particularly for the young, by the anti-war movement's challenge to the authority of the state.

Gorton was a nationalist, in terms both of elevating Australia's international status and of increasing the powers and capacities of the Commonwealth government in relation to the states. He expanded the Commonwealth government's support for the arts, raised doubts about the degree of foreign ownership of Australian resources, made the first moves in the decolonisation of Papua New Guinea (PNG), and began to flex the Commonwealth's muscles in relation to the states' management of the environment. However, Gorton lacked the political skills and authority to carry through such a major reversal in the party's commitment to states' rights, particularly in the face of powerful Liberal state premiers like Victoria's Henry Bolte. He fell victim to doubts about his moral capacities to hold office, and was succeeded by William McMahon, who continued Holt and Gorton's directions of reform. Australia's highly restrictive censorship regime was reformed, and McMahon confirmed the Commonwealth's commitment to new areas of responsibility by establishing the Department of Environment, Aborigines and the Arts. He continued the rethinking of Australia's foreign policy begun by Holt, softening the Liberals for the recognition of Communist China which was already an important trading partner, demanded a timetable for the independence of PNG, withdrew the combat troops from Vietnam and further diversified Australia's immigration program; he set up a poverty enquiry and announced an ambitious new framework for urban growth.[78] All of these directions of reform have come to be associated with Whitlam and the Labor Party.

The reforms undertaken by the Liberal governments in the seven years between the retirement of Menzies and the election of Whitlam in 1972 were substantial, but in electing McMahon the Liberals squandered their credit in the comic spectacle of a small man with big ears and a squeaky voice playing at power. Instead the credit went to Whitlam and the Labor Party, with consequences for the Liberals from which they have never really recovered. McMahon's political skills were even fewer than Gorton's so he had less chance of steering a nervous and fractious party through the reform process. And in selling the reforms to the public he was completely outclassed by Whitlam. The watershed between Menzies and the new Australia, the period when Australian politicians finally responded to the social changes of the 1960s, thus came to be seen as December 1972.

In *The Lucky Country* Horne described the educated middle generation's despair at the possibility of change. However, he ended the book on an optimistic note: 'all the same something is going to happen', a reformer with broad views of change was needed who would forget the present occupants of power and look to the future.[79] There is no suggestion that

Horne thought such a reformer would be found in the ranks of Labor; more likely he would be a dissident Liberal, someone like the Sydney businessman Gordon Barton who in 1966 formed the Liberal Reform Group (later the Australia Party) to oppose the government's position on Vietnam. The Australia Party was the familiar sort of splinter protest party on the Liberal side of politics, formed around principle by educated people of means, and it had some modest success for a few years.[80] At the end of the 1960s the political allegiance of the new middle class was up for grabs. They were a new segment of the professional and white collar workforce, formed by the previous twenty years of economic expansion, with new bases of social power. The younger among them were reaching voting age in an atmosphere of scepticism about the values and institutions of the past, when the Liberal Party was identified with the established order and the Labor Party still dominated by the trade unions. They seemed politically footloose, and might have provided the base for a new minor party or for a reform group within the Liberal Party. But instead they provided a base from which Whitlam could reform the Labor Party. Writing about this group a decade later, David Kemp thought that Labor's trade union connections would be a barrier to these people's identification with Labor.[81] What he missed was the identification with the reforming potential of the state by so many of its new tertiary-trained employees.

Whitlam

The ALP had always attracted some of the more radical members of the middle class but these had generally been either intellectual mavericks, like Maurice Blackburn, or successful sons of working and lower middle-class families, scholarship boys like Bert Evatt. Whitlam was neither of these but a child of the already-established professional middle class who saw the Labor Party as the vehicle for progressive social improvement. His father, Frederick Whitlam, was himself a lawyer, who worked in the Commonwealth Crown Solicitor's Office. He moved to the raw new capital of Canberra in 1928 when Whitlam was eleven, and in 1936 was appointed Commonwealth Crown Solicitor. Unlike Menzies who was the first of his family to attend university and appeared ill-at-ease and rather bumptious to contemporaries, Whitlam was at home in the middle class preserve of the prewar university where he studied law and classics. He was tall, clever and good-looking and should by rights have been an outstanding Australian Liberal. But he joined the Labor Party and became representative within it of sections of the new middle class.

Whitlam joined the ALP during the war, when the powers of the Commonwealth government were at their height, and when the party's trade union connections were muted by the war effort. He was galvanised into political life by Curtin's 1944 referendum which sought to extend some of the powers the Commonwealth government was exercising for wartime planning into peace. As the son of a Canberra-based Commonwealth public servant, Whitlam had little sympathy for the rights of the states and the irrationalities these introduced into national politics. He supported the referendum and was 'appalled by the spurious arguments' being put against them by 'the conservative elements in Australia'. To Whitlam the Labor Party was the vehicle for progressive national reform: 'My background in English terms would be that my parents would have been voting not Conservative or Labor [sic] but Liberal. In the Australian context they would vote Labor as the party of change and public responsibility.' No mention here of trade unions or the working class; no mention of the pledge or conference control of Labor parliamentarians. Whitlam redefines the Labor Party as the party of Deakinite liberalism and the natural home of good public servants like his father. He was, he said, the first Prime Minister of Australia who had lived in Canberra, 'the son of a great public servant, among whose colleagues were great public servants'. This early family experience gave Whitlam his faith in the constructive and benevolent role of government and in the capability and integrity of the public service and drew him to Labor as his natural political home.[82]

He entered federal politics at a by-election in 1952 as member for the outer Sydney seat of Werriwa and in 1963 was elected deputy leader of the federal Party. He succeeded Calwell as leader after Labor was routed at the 1966 election, which Calwell, for whom loyalty to the party's past was stronger than his vision of its future, had chosen to fight on the issue of conscription. Whitlam proceeded to give the party a future, wrenching control from its labourist trade union base and opening it to new middle-class reformers like himself. Whitlam believed passionately in the potential of Australia's national government to deliver more equitable and efficient government services than the states were managing to do in their traditional areas of health, education and urban planning; and he believed passionately in the need for Australia to develop a more independent foreign policy. Building his political support during the burgeoning social protest movements of the late 1960s and early 1970s, he came to believe too in the national government's capacities to meet many of these movements' demands. The Women's Movement, the sexual liberation movement, the environmental movement, the Aboriginal protest movement, all came to see a future Whitlam government as a step forward in achieving their goals, and all began alliances with Labor which have more or less endured. In all of these movements, except perhaps the Aboriginal movement, the reforming energy came predominantly from people Horne calls 'the concerned middle class'. Just like the prewar moral middle class, these people were used to making decisions, were articulate, confident of their opinions, and had ideas about how things could be improved: 'The protest movement was largely an alternative programme for how to run things, produced by middle class people who thought their way was better than that of the middle class people then in control'.[83]

Whitlam's impact on Labor was dramatic. Six years after he became leader Labor won federal government for the first time in twenty-three years, with an increase in its electoral support between 1966 and 1972 of 9.6 per cent.[84] The shifts in the class position of the two parties depended not so much on shifts in the class basis of their electoral support but on the interests and positions which came to be associated with them. Much has been written about the so-called middle-classing of the ALP: the influx of middle-class activists into the party branches and the gradual marginalisation of working-class members, the tensions between the goals of the social movements and the trade unions, the struggles of women members against the party's masculinist ethos. But Whitlam's impact was equally dramatic on the other side of politics as it was deserted by a new section of the moral middle class which was forming around new values and principles, spearheaded by a new, nationalist intelligentsia. Liberal politicians might continue to describe the ALP as class-based, to point to its connection with the trade union movement, and to argue that its policies were motivated by sectional self-interest, but the middle-class people who came to support Labor because of its policies on Aborigines, or multiculturalism, or women, or the arts, or attitudes to Asia, or the environment belied these descriptions. They supported Labor because it accorded with their principled beliefs about the policies that would advance the national interest.

Perhaps even more galling to Australian Liberals was that Whitlam came to be given the credit for many of the reforms they had already begun, and their seven years of government since Menzies' retirement sank into oblivion. As the changes which began in the 1960s became matters of pride and achievement, the Liberals tried to establish their precedence: they pioneered the new relationship with Asia; they effectively dismantled the White Australia policy; they opened the way for Commonwealth involvement in Aboriginal and environmental policy; they established the Australia Council for the Arts. All of this may be true, but in making their claims the Liberals find Whitlam already occupying the historical ground in popular memory, an occupation even more infuriating when they contemplate the chaotic three years which followed 1972. Why has Labor's three years of bungling and inexperienced government all but obliterated their previous seven years of cautious reform? Why is Whitlam remembered for Liberal achievements?

Politics is not just about legislation and administrative reform; it is not even just about good government. It is also about symbolic work, about explaining to people how their society is changing, about why new policies are needed and what they are, about recognising new groups and new needs, and giving people new images of themselves and their country. The Liberals may have removed most of the racially discriminatory regulations from Australia's immigration legislation, but they were nervous about proclaiming this too loudly lest it provoke a backlash, and anyway, they still clung imaginatively to the ideals of social homogeneity expressed in white Australia. They may have moved from assimilation to integration as the goal for Australia's non-English-speaking migrants, but they did not actively reach out to them as Whitlam did when he attended political meetings in the Italian or Greek communities. They may have established the power of the Commonwealth in Aboriginal policy, but they were slow to use it and completely inept at dealing with increasingly radical indigenous demands. And in foreign policy, despite their recognition of the need to rethink Australia's relations with Asia, they were hamstrung by two decades of anti-communism and their involvement in the Vietnam War. They may have done all those things, but they did them timidly, nervous of arousing opposition, of moving too fast, and without ever bringing them together as an agenda for change. Whitlam, by contrast, was supremely confident: he told Australia that it had changed and that it needed to change more; and he embraced the changes, making them seem to those swept along by his enthusiasms both exciting and inevitable. He was a superb public performer, and to watch footage of his 1972 election rallies is to be inspired again by his confidence and optimism. In 1972 Whitlam won the allegiance of a section of the middle class for Labor and they became some of its most loyal supporters. Horne's visionary reformer had arrived.

7
Fraser

The Dismissal

The Whitlam governments lasted scarcely three years. Australia's first Labor government since 1949, and its first modern social democratic government, was caught up in a series of crises caused by a combination of domestic and international factors. Domestically its failure to win control of the Senate was the key, as an Opposition, unwilling to accept Labor's legitimacy, held the new government hostage. Internationally, the long boom ended, and the Australian economy started to falter, as did every other economy in the western world. The appearance of 'stagflation', in which rising levels of unemployment are accompanied by rising inflation, showed that the usefulness of Keynesianism in managing national economies was over. The inexperienced Whitlam government became increasingly desperate and accident prone as the economy spun from its control, and at the end of 1975 the Opposition brought it down, as its belief in the new government's incompetence was given daily vindication by ministerial scandals and a deteriorating economy. The Liberal Party returned to government under a new leader, Malcolm Fraser, believing that now the right people were back in power, and that Whitlam had been revealed as arrogant and foolish and his government as an inexperienced rabble, all would be well. The economy would right itself, the Liberal Party would quickly re-establish the moral ascendancy it had held during Menzies' days, and it would be clear to all that the Whitlam government was nothing but an aberration.

But the Whitlam government was not simply an aberration. Two things had changed fundamentally for the Liberals since they lost in 1972. First, many of the new middle class who had voted for Whitlam in 1972 were now permanently out of their reach; second, the world economy had changed, as the end of the long boom gave way to a new phase of economic globalisation. National governments would no longer be able to understand their main economic task as the containment and resolution of domestic differences among the producer groups. As Australia's economic performance declined through the 1970s and 1980s it became clear that government had to restructure the economy.

One of the key players in the events which drove Labor from office, and their chief beneficiary, Fraser became a figure of bitterness and division. His actions ensured that many of the new middle-class supporters drawn to Labor by Whitlam stayed there, and his government was haunted by doubts about its legitimacy. At the time Fraser justified his actions by his promise to restore the economy to prosperity after the three dark years of Labor misrule, but he failed. When he was defeated in 1983 the economy was in worse shape than when he took office. Fraser approached the task of economic recovery through the Liberals' traditional precepts: reduce government spending and reduce wages. At the time his stern admonitions about government spending and the need for self-reliance sounded like the revived neo-liberal economics then starting to gain currency, and there were common elements. But in retrospect it is better to see Fraser's economic precepts as the last time the class-based model of the Australian economy seemed to offer a plausible framework for government economic management.

The Liberals' return to government was accompanied by the confident reassertion of the Liberals' view of the political virtues on which their claims to government were based: leadership, political experience and financial rectitude, all guided by commitment to an underlying political philosophy. In an influential article on the meaning of the 1972 defeat for the Liberal Party, David Kemp, then a political science academic at the University of Melbourne, had argued that the most obvious explanation was the failure of the party's leadership since Menzies' retirement. Kemp was writing for an internal party publication, and his focus was on the leadership of the party rather than the nation. 'In politics,' he argued, 'victory is the great legitimator'; and it has the added advantage of giving the leader patronage to bring dissidents into line. In opposition, authority is much harder to come by. Personal qualities are obviously important, but, cautions Kemp, these are not enough to bind a leader and his colleagues. Reiterating Edmund Burke's emphasis on shared principles in creating political unity in the parliament, he argued that 'The ultimate source of a leader's authority is his role as expounder of a philosophy or ideology which commands common consent and adherence in the party'.[1]

There is nothing to indicate that Kemp had Fraser in mind when he wrote 'A leader and a philosophy', but when Fraser defeated Snedden in March 1975 Kemp joined Fraser's staff as a speech writer and helped him develop his philosophical credentials. Fraser had already begun staking out the territory in January of that year in a speech to the Australian and New Zealand Association for the Advancement of Science (ANZAAS).

> There is an important difference between the socialist and the Liberal ... The Liberal seeks to maximise individual decisions. The socialist seeks to maximise central government decision making which at best is an arrogant assumption by a small group, at worst an endowment of the state with superior purposes and powers – the metaphysical justification.[2]

Little is new here, except perhaps the flourish about metaphysics. The socialists intent on expanding the power of the state were the same ones Menzies had battled, and Bruce and George Reid before that, although they were now a considerably smaller target. Since Labor had dropped the socialisation objective from its platform the term 'socialism' no longer evoked fears of nationalisation. The enemy now was social democracy – the ever-expanding capacities of government responding to ever-expanding popular expectations. And the culprit was Keynesianism, which, in delivering full employment, had given to the state 'the power of spending resources it did not have or own';[3] and had removed fear from the economy.

> Trade union leadership is no longer fearful of large scale and continuing unemployment ... [and] national governments have lost the art of restraint. Roads to political popularity have been to promise to spend people's money in ever increasing quantities. The Government now acts as though its resources are without limit.[4]

Fraser's 1975 speech is the first significant assault in Australian politics on the postwar Keynesian orthodoxy. He grants that Keynesianism made a contribution in its day, but that day is now over. According to Fraser's first biographer, John Edwards, the single most persistent theme in the development of Fraser's political ideas was the role of government spending and trade union wage demands in causing inflation in a full employment economy.[5] In his maiden speech Fraser criticised government spending for its contribution to inflation, as well as expressing doubts about the burgeoning personal consumption which was using resources that might otherwise go to investment.[6] But this was 1956, and few were then inclined to listen to such cautions. They sounded like the voice of the past, when people had to live with scarcity; in 1956 the task was to learn to live with affluence, to loosen the habits of restraint and enjoy spending.

Fraser had never been comfortable with Keynesianism's deficit financing and now that its flaws were evident, he slipped back easily into morally charged financial precepts reminiscent of the 1930s: governments shouldn't spend money they don't have; governments must reduce their expenditure; people must accustom themselves to restraint and sacrifice; 'Governments must again learn how to say "no"'; 'all the pump priming in the world will not cure unemployment'; and most famously 'life wasn't meant to be easy'. Now that inflation had reappeared as a major danger to economic and social cohesion, there is 'little time for the easy optimism and endless expectations of yesterday'.[7] Fraser's diagnosis of the causes of the economic problems of the mid-1970s revived earlier Liberal thinking about the relationship between personal virtue and national strength, and his remedies were equally familiar. The trade unions should learn to moderate their wage demands; and governments should reduce their expenditure.

In his 1975 campaign speech 'Turn on the lights' Fraser promised the return of 'sound and honest management of Australia's affairs', after Labor's three years of damage: 'There will be an end to Government extravagances and excesses'; 'there will be no international safaris by members of Parliament'; 'there will be no more jobs for the boys'. A handbill produced by the New South Wales branch asked electors if they approved of such actions as 'the exorbitantly expensive trips and sight seeing tours Whitlam and his large number of family, friends and others he took along for the ride, enjoyed at your expense? The expensive cars Whitlam ordered for himself with your money? The very lavish ALP conference at Florida Hotel, Terrigal, paid for by your money?'.[8] With the possible exception of the Curtin and Chifley governments, Liberals have levied accusations of extravagance, financial incompetence, cronyism and indulging in the perks of office against Labor governments since 1910. This was reassuring stuff, and there was enough evidence of it in Whitlam's last days to convince both the Liberals and the electors that this diagnosis of the causes of Australia's economic troubles was accurate. If the problem was Labor's extravagance and incompetence, then returning to government those experienced in sound and honest management would restore economic stability. To this day Fraser remains publicly unrepentant of his actions in forcing the Whitlam government from office. People have forgotten, he says, just how bad the Whitlam government was.[9] His priorities on returning to government were 'to re-establish a sense of stability to the government of Australia, re-establish a sense of financial stability ... and to explain to governments overseas that the Whitlam government had been nothing but an aberration'.[10]

Shame Fraser Shame!

But the Whitlam government was more than an aberration and despite its manifold disasters it permanently changed the political agenda. Many Labor supporters of a certain age still have badges proclaiming 'Shame Fraser Shame' lurking in the corners of their memorabilia. They wore them at the rallies and demonstrations of the 1975 campaign when they pledged with Whitlam to 'Maintain the Rage'. The Labor election campaign opened with a massive open-air rally in the Domain in Sydney followed by one in Festival Hall, Melbourne. Whitlam delivered a televised address to the nation, calling on the men and women of Australia to remember Remembrance Day 1975 as 'Mr Fraser's day of shame', and to rally to the defence of Australian parliamentary democracy. At the end of the meeting Whitlam was mobbed by emotional supporters, and the crowd sang the new national anthem, 'Advance Australia Fair', as well as 'Waltzing Matilda' and 'Click Go the Shears'.[11] To those present it was the greatest political rally they had ever witnessed, but the intensity of their passion was out of step with the mood of the electorate.

Whitlam campaigned on the outrage the actions of the Liberals had done to democracy, and on the illegitimacy of any gains they might make from it. Fraser campaigned on Labor's damage to the economy and the urgency of restoring good government. Both used a rhetoric of crisis, one constitutional and political, the other economic, and the Australian electorate, ever practical in their demands on the state, responded to the economic rhetoric with a uniform swing against Labor of 7.4 per cent. This was the largest swing since 1943.[12] It is an obvious fact that election results depend on the votes of everyone, and take no account of the conviction and knowledge with which they are cast. Generally this does not matter too much, although as we have seen Australian Liberals have always worried that there was more passion on Labor's side than theirs. In 1975 the imbalance of passion was colossal. Had Fraser waited till the next election was due he would have won easily, in a cooler political climate, without arousing the passions which bonded some of Labor's new supporters to it for life. An unintended consequence of the Liberals' actions in precipitating the constitutional crisis of 1975 was that many of the new middle class drawn to Labor by Whitlam stayed there to become some of its most loyal supporters. Anger at the unfairness of the dismissal prevented them from facing the sheer incompetence of much of Labor's term in office. It gave Labor an excuse, and the frustration and disappointment which might otherwise have been directed to a government that had failed to live up to expectations was transformed into contempt for Kerr and the Liberals.

Fraser clearly thought that the size of his electoral victory would establish his authority, and it may well have done so for the majority of Australians who think little about politics between elections. But two significant groups of Australians remained vocally and implacably hostile.

The first of these was the leadership of the trade union movement, the second a significant section of the middle-class intelligentsia. The reaction of the trade union movement was to be expected. Along with employer groups it has been the most consistent site for class-based action and understandings in Australian politics. Although it had not been particularly enamoured of the Whitlam government, the dismissal of the first elected federal Labor government in twenty-three years simply confirmed its beliefs in the existence and the ruthlessness of the Australian ruling class. And there was plenty of evidence. After some support for Labor in 1972 the capitalist press had reverted to form in a campaign of such blatant bias that the journalists at Rupert Murdoch's News Ltd had gone on strike.[13] Fraser was an Australian ruling-class leader straight from central casting. The son of a pastoral family, educated at Melbourne Grammar and Oxford, himself now a grazier in the Western District, he was a symbolic descendant of the pastoralists who had fought the shearers' strikes, and of the squatter on the thoroughbred who had hounded the swagman to suicide in a billabong.

Various parodic songs of the time exploited the parallels. For example, 'Shame on you, Fraser! Shame! Shame! Shame!' sung to the tune of 'Click Go the Shears'.

> The squatter's in the Lodge, he thinks he's got us beat,
> But he'll soon be in the cold and his Kerr will be on heat.
> For we're stopping work today and we're taking to the street
> He's smashed the constitution so we'll vote with our feet.
>
> ...
>
> Fraser the grazier, you tried with your lies
> But you can't pull the wool over twelve million eyes,
> Shoulder to shoulder the whole working class
> Is marching united to give you the arse.[14]

To see Fraser as the squatter mounted on his thoroughbred was so obvious that even the singing of 'Waltzing Matilda' reinforced his class stereotyping. John Edwards' 1976 biography had a photo of Fraser on horseback on the cover. Before the popular culture revival of Australia's nineteenth-century pioneering heritage in the 1980s, men on horseback were more likely to be associated with mounted police than the 'Man from Snowy River' and were easy symbols of ruling-class power.

Marxism was widely taught in Australian universities in the 1970s as a fruitful way of understanding the power relations of capitalist societies. To many students and academics, and to people radicalised by the opposition to the Vietnam War, the actions of the Liberals and John Kerr confirmed left-wing views of ruling-class power. At the extreme fringes of Labor's supporters stories circulated about conspiracies. The most popular one had Kerr conspiring with the CIA to get rid of Whitlam and Labor before they could stymie the renewal of the leases on US military installations.[15] Fanciful conspiracies aside, understanding the Whitlam government as a victim of ruling-class power had a plausibility both to some of Labor's new middle-class supporters and to its traditional working-class and trade union membership. It was a narrative which drew them together into the longer narrative of the Labor Party's political history, and gave them the basis for sharing a language to help them bridge the obvious differences in their experiences and aspirations. Whitlam, the middle-class lawyer, became a Labor hero, a martyr to ruling-class bloody mindedness and chicanery, not quite on the same scale as the original martyrs of the 1890s strikes, but with a neat historical symmetry in the role of the grazier class. And young middle-class supporters felt for themselves the implacable forces of reaction that had always been lined up against the working class and its progressive allies in Labor's mythologies.

The second group to refuse Fraser legitimacy was a broad section of the middle-class intelligentsia which included but was much wider than the radical left. There were plenty of Labor's new supporters who had little time for class-based explanations, conspiratorial or structural. For them the lesson of 1975 was the imperviousness of the Liberal Party to the pressures for change in Australian society; its seemingly permanent capture by the ideas of old British Australia; the threatened return of the stifling conservatism of Menzies' last days. Donald Horne was no veteran of the moratoria, but he wore a political badge for the first time in his life to a fund-raising dinner party after the Whitlam dismissal at the North Shore home of Sydney architect, Harry Seidler and his wife Penelope. Whitlam appealed to the Sydney movers and shakers at the Seidlers' because of his contemporaneity: 'He was not resisting the times: he was trying to understand them'. To Horne there was nothing particularly labourist about Whitlam's priorities. He was simply taking up ideas and attitudes which already existed and most of which 'might equally well have been taken up by a non-Labor party'.

> People forced towards the Labor Party by the conduct of the Liberals in their shabby frenetic stage imagined that, after Whitlam's 1972 win, the Liberals

would refurbish and come out fighting the 1975 election looking like a contemporary political party. They came out looking like 1949.[16]

Under Fraser the Liberals seemed to have become a party of reaction, and what had been a forced choice in 1972 became a more permanent political allegiance. Horne describes his attendance at the Seidlers' dinner as 'a coming out occasion, a declaration'. Other prominent artists and intellectuals also came out for Labor in November 1975. A rally at the Sydney Opera House was addressed by Patrick White, Manning Clark, David Williamson, Lloyd Rees, Kate Fitzpatrick, Les Murray and Frank Moorhouse.[17] Artists, actors, writers, academics, journalists, publishers and musicians were drawn to Whitlam's daring. There was some self-interest here. Whitlam had consolidated and expanded the system of government support for the arts begun by Gorton. A flourishing cultural life was part of his ambition for Australia, and under his governments federal government expenditure on the arts increased from $7 million to $24 million. But it was not just self-interest. Whitlam's willingness to experiment and his playful wit made politics seem more like cultural activity than the hard boring through hardboards it most often is. The point, argued Graham Little, was Whitlam's stature. He lent the nation at large his own self-confidence and sense of autonomy, opening up a space for new, risky ideas and expanding the sense of what was possible.[18] Patrick White expressed the newly felt sympathies between political and cultural work when he said: 'I am an artist. I think I can safely say that the creative arts can only survive in Australia if we are politically creative as well.'[19]

White appealed to people to support Labor with arguments that might have come from Menzies: 'Today I am not talking to artists, rather to those who are not creative themselves, thousands of thoughtful people throughout Australia for whom the life of the imagination – books, painting, music, theatre – plays a very important part, and without which existence would be very drab indeed'.[20] In 1942 Menzies had attributed to the 'Forgotten people' a similar interest in the higher things in life:

> the middle class [which] provides ... the intellectual life ... which finds room for literature, for the arts, for science, for medicine and the law ... The artist if he is to live must have a buyer, the writer an audience. He finds them among the frugal people to whom the margin above bare living means a chance to reach out a little towards that heaven which is always just beyond our grasp.[21]

Since the Whitlam government we have become used to thinking of artists, writers and intellectuals as part of Labor's natural constituency, but from a longer historical perspective it is remarkable that the party of the uneducated working class and the trade unions should have become the natural party of support for culture and the arts. Barry Humphries' monstrous creature of philistinism and appetite, Labor's Minister for the Yarts, Les Patterson, shows what the middle class used to think of Labor's cultural potential.

After the events of November and December 1975 White ruthlessly culled friends and acquaintances who welcomed the Fraser government and was himself snubbed in Sydney's eastern suburbs for his hostility to a man from his own class.[22] White's reaction may have been extreme, but it shows the depth of disenchantment with the Liberal Party among many who should have been its natural supporters. Advertisements sponsored by long lists of well-known names from academia and the arts became a regular feature of Labor campaigns, replacing the advertisements for Liberals once sponsored by leading clergy and businessmen. In one sense there was a continuity: leading members of the middle class were making use of their public prominence to attempt to influence their fellow citizens. But they had changed their allegiance.

Over the next few years the rightness of the actions of the Liberals and of John Kerr continued to be vigorously questioned by prominent academics, journalists, constitutional lawyers, historians and writers. There were also intellectuals who defended Kerr and the new government, but the issue refused to die as the Liberals had clearly thought it would. Kerr's actions reawakened the republican cause and issues of constitutional reform. Almost immediately after the dismissal, a group calling themselves Citizens for Democracy was formed to push for John Kerr's resignation and a more democratic constitution. The group used the traditional Australian Liberal description of itself as 'non-party', and its methods were the standard methods of Australian citizen groups – newspaper advertisements, petitions and public meetings, the passing of motions and resolutions, the establishment of branches to provoke local discussion and raise funds for the cause. In September 1976 it held a public meeting at the Sydney Town Hall which attracted a huge crowd. Donald Horne, Patrick White and Manning Clark were again prominent and Clark gave a rather heated speech about the dead hand of the past and predicted that if the Constitution were not reformed, blood might yet stain the wattle.[23]

Although Kerr was the immediate target of animosity, the atmosphere was generally hostile to Fraser and the Liberal Party. The amalgam of high culture and cultural nationalism in the program indicates the cultural coalition now opposing the Liberal Party. Works by Albinoni, Bach and Vivaldi were played as the audience arrived, and the meeting opened with everyone singing 'Advance Australia Fair'. (Fraser had restored 'God Save the Queen' as the national anthem as part of his immediate setting of the country to rights.) In one interlude between the speeches the folk singer Alex Hood sang 'Waltzing Matilda', and in another the actor John Gaden read 'bitterly apposite excerpts' from the 1853 debates on the New South Wales' Constitution in which liberal patriots defended the cause of representative government against an oligarchic upper house. 'A virtuous cause in the hands of a dauntless yet temperate people must triumph over monstrous misuse of power', the audience heard.[24] The whole proceedings were broadcast on the ABC's 'Lateline', provoking the first of the many accusations from the Liberal Party about the ABC's lack of balance.[25]

At the time the Liberals shrugged off the opposition of the intellectuals; they were, after all, only a small number of votes. Writing in 1979 Max Walsh could see clearly the damage an uncooperative trade union movement was doing to Fraser's government; he was less sure about the long-term effects of the alienation of the intelligentsia.[26] We now know. This was the beginning of the culture wars of the 1980s and 1990s fought across the gap Fraser had helped create between the Liberal Party and the cultural elites. The party, which for most of its history had been able to rely on a sympathy between its underlying values and those of the articulate and educated, could no longer do so. And worse than this, when another Labor government was elected, it became clear that they were now in Labor's camp.

Fraser in Government

Despite its economic and political incompetence, three years of Labor had changed the political agenda and on many of the new issues there was no going back. The challenge for Fraser and the Liberals was to develop their own response. Whitlam's foreign policy initiatives were not reversed, although Fraser was more responsive than Whitlam might have been to the revival of Cold War politics at the end of the 1970s. The biggest casualties were the expensive policies in Whitlam's program, such as Medibank and the Department of Urban and Regional Development, as the new government looked for ways to rein in government spending and to reassure the states. The raft of new demands thrown up by the social movements of the late 1960s and early 1970s fared a good deal better. Fraser's record on ethnic affairs and multiculturalism, on indigenous issues, on women and on the environment is good, particularly when compared with the government of John Howard, and he continued federal support for the arts.

Fraser was deeply opposed to racism, and committed himself to a more racially and ethnically tolerant Australia. His government passed the Aboriginal Land Rights Act (Northern Territory) which gave Aborigines title to Northern Territory reserves and established the Northern and Central Land Councils, although he was slowed down by his respect for states' rights and was not prepared to tackle the blatantly racist policies of the Queensland government. His achievements on multiculturalism were more substantial. The term had first been used by Whitlam's Minister for Immigration, Al Grassby, to project a new Australian identity which could accommodate non-British migrants and their children. The Fraser government turned this idea into a framework for policy. It commissioned the Galbally Report (Committee to Review Post-Arrival Programs and Services for Migrants) which made wide-ranging and generous recommendations on the Australian government's responsibilities for its non-English-speaking citizens and has been described as 'the high water mark of multiculturalism'.[27] In retrospect it is clear that Fraser's welcome to the Vietnamese boat people marked the practical end of White Australia. He accepted the challenge from second-wave feminism to build some consideration of women's affairs into the processes of government. Prominent Liberal women like Beryl Beaurepaire realised that the Liberals could not allow themselves to be painted into a reactionary corner by the women's movement, and she pushed hard for the government to develop a credible policy.[28] He also responded to the new environmental movement, effectively blocking the mining for sand on Fraser Island by refusing to issue export licences.

Fraser received little credit for most of this. He was unable to win the trust of the social movements or of the middle-class radicals loyal to Whitlam. His confrontational anti-Labor rhetoric led many political activists and journalists to assume he was driven by a doctrinaire commitment to undo everything associated with the Whitlam years, and he never managed to convince them otherwise.[29] As well, because of his government's reduction of government expenditure, there were always particular programs facing the axe to support the belief that Fraser was a destroyer of new ideas and initiatives rather than a builder. For much of this Fraser had himself to blame. Where Whitlam had encouraged people to hope, and to imagine ways in which Australia might be better, Fraser saw his task as to impose realism and restraint, to dampen expectations not to excite them, and to force people to take responsibility for themselves. It is not surprising that many people at the time took more notice of what Fraser said than what he did.

This included some members of his own party. When Fraser challenged Snedden for the leadership John Gorton commented, 'If Fraser got in it would be a disaster. He is extreme right wing. The Liberal Party can't be a right leaning affair.'³⁰ Gorton, of course, had personal reasons to distrust Fraser, but he was also expressing the view of those in the party who had hoped, with Donald Horne, that the defeat of 1972 would lead to a Liberal Party with a more contemporary feel. When Fraser formed his first Cabinet he did not include one of the more prominent liberal Liberals, Don Chipp. Chipp had been the minister responsible for modernising Australia's censorship laws in the Gorton and McMahon governments, and Shadow Minister for Social Security under Snedden. Relaxed, friendly and self-consciously contemporary he abhorred Fraser's authoritarian political style and was opposed to the dismantling of many of Labor's social welfare reforms. In 1977 Chipp resigned from the Liberal Party, expressing his disenchantment with party politics and the domination of the two major parties by 'vested interests' – Labor by the trade unions and the Liberal Party by big business. What of 'the medium and small-sized businessmen who form the backbone of our industrial sector' he asked? Might not the ordinary voter 'yearn for the emergence of a third political force, representing middle-of-the-road policies which would owe allegiance to no outside pressure group'?³¹

Chipp's complaints about the capture of the major urban non-labour party by vested interests recalled the last days of the UAP when it was fragmenting into splinter parties. The difference was that the UAP was weak. Chipp was attacking a party in government with a huge majority and a Prime Minister with a firm grip on power. Even so, he struck a chord among dissident Liberals, and his resignation became the catalyst for the formation of a new party, the Democrats, which challenged the Liberals for the votes of the moral middle class. The party's origins were in the 1960s and early 1970s with Gordon Barton's Australia Party, the Liberal and New Liberal Movement in South Australia, and the Centre Line Party in Western Australia. Although these had different origins in the politics of their originating states, they were all critical of the Liberal Party's unresponsive conservatism and shared a commitment to loosening the hold the two major parties had on available policy options. They drew on middle-class political activists uncomfortable with trade union power in the Labor Party. Although they were all but wiped out in the polarised political atmosphere of the 1975 election, they had an organisational infrastructure on which a new party could build and a core of political activists. Chipp's resignation provided a high profile leader to capture media interest and he was quickly convinced to lead a new party in time to contest the 1977 election. The new party's slogan for that campaign, 'Get Australia Together', expressed the Australian Liberals' faith in the harmonious middle, in contrast to the ruthless adversarialism which had engulfed Australian politics since Labor's win in 1972. The Democrats polled well, and two candidates, including Chipp, were elected to the Senate. In 1980 they won another three Senate seats and the Coalition lost its majority. Since then, no government has controlled the Senate.[32]

The electoral support base for the Democrats is indistinct, although it is lightly marked by higher education, urban residence and government employment.[33] The party has, however, been associated with many of the defining issues of the new class, such as environmentalism and equal opportunity. As the two major parties embraced economic rationalism, it voiced a continuing commitment to the ethical role of the state in working for social justice. Its participatory organisational structure made it attractive to political activists, and during the 1980s as Labor moved decisively to the right on social movement issues, disaffected Labor supporters joined. Its well-known slogan 'Keep the Bastards Honest' (first used by Chipp and then revived by Cheryl Kernot) connects it with the long-established ambivalence about party politics among Australian Liberals and the ambiguous morality of power politics. The formation and continuing existence of the Democrats has been another challenge, along with the post-Whitlam Labor Party, to the Liberals' claims to be the party of principle in Australian politics.

Fraser's major promise in 1975 was that returning the Liberals to power would restore the economy to prosperity, but by 1980 Fraser's record on economic management was not greatly superior to Whitlam's. Fraser's economic strategy was 'to fight inflation first'. If inflation were brought down, productive investment would increase and with it employment. The government was relatively successful in reducing inflation from the peaks of 1975, but the cost was borne by the unemployed who were between 6 per cent and 7 per cent of the workforce by 1980. One response was the government's anti-dole bludger campaigns. This was a blame-the-victim strategy which shifted attention from the failure of the economy to create jobs to the failure of individuals to try hard enough to find them.[34] Another was to place unrealistic faith in a mineral resources boom which would deliver an export-led economic bonanza. By mid-1981 the resources boom had collapsed and the economy was sliding into a deep recession, exacerbated by drought and by a general world recession. In 1983 unemployment peaked at 10.3 per cent.[35]

Throughout all of this Fraser's analysis of the ills afflicting the Australian economy never faltered. The problem was inflation and the chief cause of this was the trade union movement's continued pursuit of increased wages: 'In Australia's present situation there can be little doubt that excessive wage rises and damaging strikes are placing economic progress at serious risk'.[36]

High wages were contributing to unemployment, and any recourse to increased public spending to create jobs was out of the question as it would only add further fuel to inflation. Fraser was not so austere in his response to the Liberal Party's traditional support groups. He slowed Labor's program of tariff reductions for manufactured goods and restored the superphosphate bounty to farmers. And in the face of electoral disaster in 1983 he loosened the strings on government expenditure. The urgent need to reduce government spending was the other continuing theme in Fraser's economic rhetoric, and after a slow start he was meeting with some success. In the 1981/82 federal budget the deficit was a mere 0.4 per cent of GDP, down from 4.9 per cent in 1975/76. All of these gains were thrown away in the next budget when the deficit ballooned from $553 million to $4448 million, and made him look like just any other vote-buying politician.[37]

Fraser called a double dissolution election early in 1983. He hoped that by going to the polls early he would pre-empt both a worsening of the economy and the election of Bob Hawke as Labor leader. Hawke had been a very successful and high profile President of the Australian Council of Trade Unions (ACTU). He entered federal parliament at the 1980 election with the clear intention of becoming leader. Bill Hayden had succeeded Whitlam as leader after Labor lost the 1977 election, and he had led Labor to a very credible performance in 1980. But he could not withstand Hawke's determination, nor the conviction of the party that with Hawke as leader they would sweep the Liberals from office. Early in the morning of the day Fraser requested approval of the Governor-General to call the election, Hawke was elected leader of the Labor Party. Labor supporters relished the irony of the timing. Events were now playing into their hands as they had once played into Fraser's and there was a smell of revenge in the air.[38] Fraser focused on the economic irresponsibility of Labor and in a moment of misjudged hyperbole he warned electors that if Labor were elected people's savings would be safer under the bed than in a bank. Hawke responded: 'The man is getting desperate, isn't he ... They can't put their savings under the bed because that's where the Commies are.'[39] Fraser looked a fool as Hawke kicked the communist can into oblivion. Everything was running Labor's way and journalists, long frustrated with Fraser's pious, evasive answers, were merciless.[40] The Coalition lost the election in a 4 per cent swing to Labor and Fraser's eyes moistened as he conceded defeat and resigned as Liberal leader. For Labor supporters it represented a sort of closure.[41] For the country as a whole it promised relief from Fraser's politics of aggressive divisiveness. Hawke had established himself as a deal maker when he was President of the ACTU, one who could sit trade unions down at the table with big business, and he promised to bring this consensual approach to national economic management. As well, he had an easy rapport with ordinary Australians that Fraser could never achieve.

The Australian Prime Minister Fraser was most like was Bruce. Both were aloof, buttoned-up men of impeccable ruling-class credentials and experience, from the sources of their families' wealth (one mercantile money, the other pastoral), to their Oxbridge educations and their patrician views of their political responsibilities. Fraser on his horse was, in its day, as recognisably an image of ruling-class privilege as Bruce in plus-fours leaning against his latest motorcar. They were both elected after periods of turmoil with the promise of restoring order to the nation and gravitas to government, and both worked hard to deliver good government. But neither had the common touch, nor a broad-based experience of Australian society. When following the standard economic policy of their times failed, both blamed the unions: if only unions would moderate their demands, profitability would be restored, investment revive, and employment recover. The style was hectoring and, coming from such obviously wealthy men, not very convincing. The fading power of anti-communist rhetoric stopped Fraser from following Bruce in his pursuit of alien agitators, though his anti-Soviet foreign policy showed he still regarded communists as powerful enemies. Both were unimaginative men who approached the problems of their times within the already established solutions of their party's rhetoric, and both lost office when it was clear their solutions were not working. Fraser had a far greater will to power than Bruce and until 1983 his political career was marked by the ruthless use of principle in the service of ambition and control. Bruce always claimed he was drafted to the job and there is nothing to suggest he was dissembling. Once there, though, he too wanted control. The biggest difference between the careers of the two men is that Fraser was followed by the most successful Labor government of the century, and was turned on by his own party who accused him of wasting their time in government.

During his last three years of government Fraser lost the confidence of significant sections of the parliamentary Liberal Party, together with some members of the business and financial policy elites.[42] The palpable failure of Keynesian economics and the problems besetting western economies had led to a revival of neo-liberal economics: the state had got too big and flabby and was crowding out the productive private sector of the economy; people had grown lazy as welfare programs had sapped their initiative and nurtured a culture of entitlement; businesses had lost their entrepreneurial edge as they strangled in red tape or spent their energies on lobbying for subsidies. The solution was to open the economy to the cleansing, invigorating winds of competition by increasing the role of the market in the distribution of goods and services and reducing the role of state allocation. Competition would restore vigour and energy, weed out the weak, reward the strong, make people, businesses, nations, independent and prosperous.

This was not just a matter of reducing government spending but of radically rethinking the role of government in the economy. Policy intellectuals started formulating programs to undo government regulation of the economy and to transfer government functions to the private sector: floating the dollar, dismantling protection and subsidies, deregulating the labor market, and selling government-owned utilities. Economic reforms were linked to powerful political values of freedom and choice, and to the promise that they would restore the dynamic effects of competition to society and the economy to prosperity. The term the 'New Right' was used to describe these new ideas, and social democrats watched in horror as taxation and public provision were attacked and their arguments for equity and social justice pushed aside by advocates of excellence and the benefits of incentive. The tough, new thinking was being done in the United States and the United Kingdom where new approaches to social and economic policy were being dramatically enacted by British Prime Minister Margaret Thatcher and US President Ronald Reagan. In Australia networks were established among journalists, politicians, academics and policy intellectuals: dining clubs and think-tanks were formed and the pages of journals of opinion turned over to attacks on Keynesianism and the welfare state. During the 1980s these think-tanks emerged as powerful sites of policy formation.[43]

At the time Fraser's attacks on government spending were taken as a commitment to this radical rethinking, particularly by social democrats. In retrospect it is clear that they were nothing of the sort, but rather grew from familiar Liberal views about Labor's extravagance and financial incompetence and about the need to keep a close eye on taxpayers' money. His fixation with the union movement as a major cause of Australia's poor economic performance accorded with the emphasis on deregulation in neo-liberal thinking. Australian Liberals have always seen the compulsion associated with union membership as an attack on individuals' freedom of contract and as a problem for the efficient operations of the economy. There was thus a partial fit, but it was only partial. Within the government there was increasing frustration as Fraser baulked at more radical reform of the government's role in the economy. A report into financial deregulation, the Campbell Report, was commissioned, but its recommendations to float the dollar, and to relax controls on banking, languished. Treasury was opposed, the union movement was opposed, and Fraser carried the farmer's traditional suspicion of the banks.[44]

Similarly frustrating for the neo-liberal converts was Fraser's continuing support for tariffs. Since the late 1960s when Alf Rattigan became Chairman of the Tariff Board there had been calls for an overhaul of Australia's complicated system of industry protection. Whitlam had begun the process, but Fraser stopped it, unconvinced that the turmoil it would bring for both manufacturers and their workers was worth it. The Country Party also continued to support the policies so closely associated with its postwar leader John McEwan, despite the increased costs which flowed on to Australia's export-oriented rural and mining industries. But within the Liberal parliamentary party, among the think-tanks and financial journalists, and in the newly formed National Farmers' Federation, the conviction had formed that Australia's protective tariff wall had to go. Fraser was seen as weak and indecisive, still hobbled by doubts about his legitimacy and haunted by the passions of 1975. As became clear during the 1980s, this reading did Fraser a disservice. He did not press ahead with the dismantling of economic controls and the deregulation of the financial markets because he was not convinced about the benefits. His slowness to reform was based on lack of conviction, not weakness of will.

Fraser was a nation builder and his economy was one of farms, mines and factories operating inside a still bounded nation state. He talked about the diversification of the export base, but by this he meant that minerals had joined agricultural products as the mainstays of Australian exports. And he saw services as essentially unproductive: 'The government needs to remember that private enterprise employment is productive employment, government employment is service employment.'[45] Fraser wanted to strengthen the market economy, but his market was still essentially a market of goods, tangible products like bales of wool, machines, clothes and iron ore, not the fast growing post-modern market of services, images, experiences and intellectual property. A farmer shaped by the old economy, he could not see that the structure of the Australian economy which had delivered relative prosperity for most of the century was fast becoming unsustainable. It was Fraser's belief in the old economy rather than his reluctance to embrace neo-liberal economic solutions that was his greatest economic failing. He was not alone in this. When Labor took office in 1983 it too did not realise the extent of the task it faced.

When Fraser lost the 1983 election there was such glee at his going that it seemed his political career was over. For Labor supporters it was the final revenge for 1975; for Liberals it cleared the way for economic reform. But Fraser did not leave the political scene for long. He became a member of an Eminent Persons Group established by the 1985 Commonwealth Heads of Government to move South Africa towards a non-racially divided democracy. And he started to comment on the directions of Australia's economic reform, questioning the cost in human lives of policies which destroyed people's jobs. Fraser had always been divided between the patrician and the pugilist, between a controlling and conflictual style that seemed to thrive on aggression and the patrician stance of the statesman.[46] Lofty principles were always on hand to rationalise his more ruthless moves on power. Once out of the parliamentary contest Fraser was able to let the more adversarial aspects of his personality mellow as he settled into the consensual spaces to which Australian Liberals have always aspired. Australian Liberals have always vacillated between their view of themselves as the party of good government in the national interest and their partisan role as the chief opponent of Labor. In office Fraser was a ruthless opponent of Labor; out of office he could more comfortably inhabit the centre.

8
Neo-liberalism

Labor was in office from 1983 to 1996. This was the longest Labor had ever held power, and by 1990 as the Liberals lost their fourth election on the trot commentators were starting to think that Labor may have supplanted the Liberals as the natural party of government. The Liberals lost again in 1993, an election they thought was unlosable, after Paul Keating had ousted Hawke from the Prime Ministership. When the party Menzies had formed in 1944/45 celebrated its fiftieth birthday in 1995 it had been out of office for more than ten years. The Liberal Party responded to their lengthening period out of government with a rapid turnover of leaders: as each leader failed to topple Labor – or was thought to be about to fail – he was himself replaced in what became an almost farcical revolving door: Andrew Peacock, John Howard, Andrew Peacock, John Hewson, Alexander Downer and finally John Howard again.

Both Peacock and Howard were experienced politicians, though neither was experienced enough to moderate their rivalry and ideological differences for the sake of party unity. When they failed, the party turned to two untested newcomers. The first was John Hewson, an academic economist who had been an adviser to Howard when he was Treasurer in Fraser's governments and who was a passionate believer in neo-liberal economics. He proved too narrow, with little competence outside economics, and was easily portrayed as a dogmatic zealot. The second was Alexander Downer, a third-generation Liberal politician whose so-called blue-blood pedigree was meant to signal that the Liberals were returning to tradition. He and his deputy Peter Costello were called 'The Dream Team', which is what they turned out to be. The inexperienced Downer bumbled his way through a series of gaffes which left the Liberal Party with little option but to change leaders yet again, and give Howard his second chance. In 1996 Howard led the Liberals back into government and so secured his claim to leadership.

Liberal leadership problems provided plenty of political drama during Labor's thirteen years, and prompted predictions of the party's terminal decline. Such commentators, including myself, have had to eat their words as Howard has remade the party into a confident party of government and won three elections in a row. In the early years of the twenty-first century it is the Labor Party which is in disarray, lost for direction and without a leader able to challenge Howard's hold on the Australian electorate. The drama of elections and leadership challenges holds a continuing fascination, and is well told elsewhere.[1] But it is too close up and detailed to reveal the broader patterns shaping Australians' relationship with their governments in this period. Its focus on the adversarial party conflict ignores the larger forces affecting both sides of Australia's political divide.

The large story of the last two decades of the twentieth century was not about the comparative political fortunes of the two parties, but about the transformation of the Australian economy from a highly regulated and relatively protected economy to an open trading economy in an increasingly globalised world, and about an accompanying change in the relations between Australian citizens and their governments. Book titles from the early 1990s give images of dramatic change: *Reinventing Australia, Remaking Australia, Shutdown, A Nation Building State Changes Its Mind, The End of Certainty*.[2] This transformation was the result, not of pressures from below, of groups and interests working through the party system to influence government policy, but of an elite conversion to the belief that the Australian economy had to be restructured, whether the Australian people liked it or not. Political leaders, both Labor and Liberal, senior bureaucrats, financial and business leaders, looked at Australia's declining economic performance and concluded that the settled policies that had delivered economic prosperity and social stability to Australia for the past century were no longer working. They then imposed on the people a set of solutions based on the new neo-liberal orthodoxy which had replaced Keynesianism as the guide to the management of western economies. This was done in the name of long-term national interest, but it caused a radical rupture of Australian political processes which has weakened the bonds between ordinary Australians and all of the parties.

There are two aspects of this process: for each of the parties there is a particular story to be told about the impact of the policy changes on the traditional supporters and processes of that party. For Labor the focus is on the impact of dismantling tariffs on blue collar workers in the protected industries; for the Nationals it is on the impact of the government expenditure cuts and privatisation on services in the bush, and the end of the marketing schemes; for Liberals it is the transformation of selfishness and greed from vices to dynamic, entrepreneurial virtues, the transformation of citizens into consumers, and changed meanings to the concept of the individual. In keeping with academics' generally greater interest in the ALP than the Liberal Party, there are a number of books on the transformation of Labor during the 1980s and 1990s.[3] The National Party received attention in passing as commentators tried to explain the popularity of Pauline Hanson's One Nation Party in regional Australia. This chapter is primarily concerned with developing some arguments about the meaning of these decades for Australian Liberals, both for the party and for the arguments and values that once linked the party to its supporters in the moral middle class. But there is also a general story, about the way the policy process of the last two decades of the twentieth century eroded the traditions of all three major parties, leaving the Australian people as a whole feeling alienated from the political institutions which once connected them with their governments.

Economic Rationalism and the New Public Management

Economic policy dominated Australian politics for the first ten years of Labor's government.[4] The new Labor government was determined to establish its reputation for economic management quickly, to show that Labor had learnt from the debacle of the Whitlam governments. In December 1983 it acted on the key recommendations of the Campbell Report, floating the Australian dollar, abolishing exchange controls and opening the Australian financial system to foreign banks. Paul Kelly has argued that these decisions were the most important in the internationalising of the Australian economy for they subjected Australia's economic performance to instant judgements by capital markets.[5] Daily fluctuations in the value of the dollar were reported on the nightly news, just before the weather, like a barometric reading of Australia's international standing. The new government also tackled the wages explosion through the Accord, a corporatist-style agreement with the union movement to hold back on wage demands in return for a social wage, which included the re-introduction of a public medical insurance scheme.

Labor's economic performance was relatively successful in its first few years. With wages held back, inflation declined and employment started to grow again. But then, between January 1985 and August 1986, the Australian dollar declined by 38 per cent. The immediate cause was a sharp deterioration in the terms of trade, a ballooning current account deficit and growing foreign debt.[6] Paul Keating announced that Australia risked becoming 'a banana republic'. The message was clear: the structure of the Australian economy which had underpinned its population's relative prosperity for 150 years was no longer working. Australia was not earning enough from the export of its primary commodities to support its population in the manner to which it had grown accustomed, and its manufacturing sector was in no shape to compensate.[7] Restructuring of the Australian economy was the only option: Australia had to find new ways to earn foreign income.

Australia's historical competitive advantage was in the production of primary products, predominantly agricultural but also mineral. This made Australia a very wealthy country by world standards in the nineteenth century and into the twentieth. In 1960 Australia was still fourth in OECD countries in income per head, but after that it began to slip quickly and by 1987 was ranked 16 out of 24. What was happening? The answer in brief was that Australia was persisting with an export economy based almost entirely on primary commodities when the growth in world trade was in manufactures. In the nineteenth century when Australia's wealth was built, trade in primary commodities was two-thirds of world trade, in 1963 it was 45 per cent and by 1989 it had shrunk to 26 per cent, as global trade in consumer goods and manufactures had grown steadily since World War II. Australia's economy was thus deviating more and more from that of other OECD countries. In the 1980s commodities made up about 80 per cent of Australia's merchandise exports; whereas manufactures were more than 80 per cent of the merchandise exports of the world's powerful economies Germany, Japan, Britain, the United States. And to add to the problems of continuing to rely so heavily on commodity exports, their prices were both in steady decline and subject to severe fluctuations which could precipitate currency and balance of payment crises.[8] As the world moved into the 1990s the explosive growth in world trade was in services and in the cultural goods of the information economy, further marginalising commodities.

The other side of Australia's structural economic problem was its continuing reliance on tariffs to protect a manufacturing sector oriented primarily to production for the domestic market. That is, Australia developed something of a dual economy, with efficient, export-oriented agriculture and later mining industries, and a protected and on the whole inefficient manufacturing sector serving the domestic market. Protection began in colonial Victoria to provide jobs to the expanded population after the gold rushes, and it persisted as a favoured Australian job creation and protection strategy. High male wages were linked to tariff protection in Deakin's New Protection. After World War II when Australia wanted to expand its population, foreign investment behind protected tariff walls built the car and white goods factories to provide the new migrants with jobs. All of this depended on continuing high prices for export commodities. In the 1980s when Australia desperately needed export-oriented manufacturing industries to compensate for the declining price of its traditional commodity exports they were in no state to compete on world markets. Decades of protection had left them better at lobbying politicians and bureaucrats for the continuation of their tariffs than developing new markets and products.

As with the earlier collapse of confidence in the settled Keynesian policies, the collapse of confidence in the underlying structure of the Australian economy was responded to with solutions provided by neo-liberalism. There is an element of historical coincidence in the collapse of Australia's terms of trade at a time when neo-liberal economic policies had intellectual ascendancy in the Anglo-American democracies. But this coincidence determined the perceived solutions. If the Australian economy needed restructuring, then the way to do it was by opening it up to market forces. At other periods, a coordinated industry policy or state-led investment may have seemed to offer the solution. Resources, capital and labour, had to be forced to shift by exposing them to the chill realities of their marketworth in a world market. In 1988 the government announced plans for across-the-board phasing-out of tariffs, although with some leeway for the car, and the clothing, textile and footwear industries.[9] The manufacturing lobby was swept aside and with it many Australian businesses and jobs. Just as the establishment of a minimum wage based on the cost of living and protective tariffs had been a means of settling the competing demands of capital and labour in the first part of the century (the so-called Deakinite Settlement), so the alteration of the terms of economic survival of one led to irresistible pressure to change the conditions in which the other operated. Removal of manufacturing's protective tariff had to be followed by reform of the industrial relations system if Australian businesses and Australian jobs were to survive. It was psychologically and politically easier for a Labor government to tackle the business end of the historic settlement first, but by the end of the 1980s, as the international pressures on the economy became increasingly apparent, the Labor government began to reform Australia's industrial relations system and to link wage rises to improvements in productivity. There was also a desperate search for other ways to earn export income; for example, through the promotion of Australia as an international tourism destination, and the rapid expansion of fee-paying foreign students. Government spending was reduced and the 1987/8 budget delivered the first surplus in thirty years. A program of corporatisation and privatisation of government-owned enterprises was begun. Icons of government ownership have been progressively sold off, the Commonwealth Bank, which had been established by a Labor government in 1911, Qantas, 49 per cent of Telstra, and at the state level, public transport and gas and electricity utilities.

The party conflict continued its adversarial ways throughout this process of reform and restructure. The Liberals accused Labor of going too slow on labour market deregulation, Labor predicted that if the Liberals were returned there would be no protections left and we would have a dog-eat-dog society. At election times both the Labor and the Liberal parties relied on their parties' traditional arguments and images to attack their opponents and to put forward their own case for government, even though there was, in fact, bi-partisan support for the general direction of change. The National Party, which might have been expected to offer some resistance, tagged compliantly along with its coalition partner. The policy measures were part of a worldwide trend, encouraged by international organisations like the OECD and the World Bank and policed by the financial markets. National governments of varying complexions moved in similar directions in the name of greater international competitiveness and the need to boost exports. The result has been a rapid intensification of the internationalisation of economic activity in which obstacles to the free movement of money, goods and labour have been progressively removed (financial deregulation, trade liberalisation, labour deregulation) in a new phase of globalisation.

Perhaps even more unsettling for ordinary Australians because less visible was a revolution in the understanding of government's role as a service provider. Accompanying the rise of neo-liberalism as a guide to managing national economies was a new paradigm for managing public sector service delivery, known as 'New Public Management'.[10] Just as national economies were to be transformed and revitalised by opening them up to competition and the entrepreneurial spirit, so too should the lumbering government bureaucracies which had developed to deliver the welfare state. Again the sources of inspiration for this were external to Australian political traditions and thinking. The bible was David Osborne and Ted Gaebler's *Reinventing Government: How the Entrepreneurial Spirit is Transforming the Public Sector* (1993).[11] This was the source of the much-used distinction between steering and rowing. It was government's job to steer, to set the general policy direction, but the rowing, the actual delivery of the services, they argued, was better done by private providers who would compete with each other to win government contracts. A range of providers would replace the one-size-fits-all model of the bureaucratic welfare state with the choice and flexibility required by a diverse population. Members of the public became customers and clients entitled to services tailormade to their needs. And competition between the providers would ensure that services were provided with maximum efficiency. One commentator has described this as the creation of a market bureaucracy in which the social democratic culture of service and equity was replaced by a market culture of competition and consumer choice.¹²

Such thinking was encapsulated in the National Competition Policy negotiated between the Commonwealth and the state Premiers in 1995, which required all governments to ensure that their legislation did not restrict competition. It was behind the Victorian Kennett government's drive to contract out a wide range of government activities to competitive tendering, and the Howard government's abolition of the Commonwealth Employment Service and its replacement by Joblink. More generally, private sector management techniques were introduced into public sector management, and workplaces centred on ideas of equity and service were remade into ones centred on rewards for quantifiable individual performances. And although this was all done in the name of reducing the size of government, it was accompanied by an increase in the exercise of direct political control over sectors that had once been more autonomous. The higher education sector is a case in point. Where once universities were left relatively free to manage their budgets, since the late 1980s and the so-called Dawkins reforms, federal governments have been devising ever new ways to distribute funds according to closely monitored performance measures. Universities are forced to reorganise their internal practices to enable their 'output' to be visible to government measurement.

Economic rationalism emerged as a catchall phrase in Australian public debate to describe the whole gamut of neo-liberal economic reforms designed to increase competition in the economy, from the large-scale economic restructuring of tariff reform to the contracting out of public sector services. It was a powerful term of abuse, of Australian origins, capturing something of the puzzlement felt by most Australians as their familiar political and economic landscape was changed, seemingly overnight and despite their wishes. It expressed the sense that much that was valuable in Australian political experience was being swept aside in the name of slogans of dubious wisdom, that the economists had got hold of the reins and were driving us towards a utopia which would turn out to be as misguided and flawed as all past utopias; that having survived the ideological certainties of the communists we were in the hands of a new bunch of zealots.[13]

From Citizens to Consumers

The new policy regime was particularly damaging to the way the middle class had understood its political role. The core of the political position of the moral middle class was the connection they believed existed between their character and the way they lived and the state of the nation. Educating and caring for their children, they were educating future citizens and contributing to a healthy population; working hard, buying their homes or building up their businesses they were developing the resources of the nation; paying their taxes they were contributing to a more equal and civilised society; working in professions and for institutions with embedded ethics of service they were contributing to the national good; exercising their political choices they were endorsing principles they thought would best serve the national interest. That is, although the members of the middle class pursued their individual self-interest, they did so within the framework of the nation in which their actions were not wholly self-directed. We have already seen how the changes of the postwar period, in particular the widely experienced increasing affluence and the advent of Keynesian economics, had weakened people's sense of connection between their own financial practices and those of the nation. During the 1980s and 1990s as Australian politicians struggled with managing the Australian economy in a rapidly changing world economy, this sense of connection weakened further.

The cynical realism of neo-liberalism's model of human behaviour was a direct affront to the role of principle and value in public life, and so to what this book has been arguing is one of Australian Liberals' core beliefs. The dominance of national policy by economic policy was accompanied by the dominance of the economist's model of human nature as motivated by a rather crude material self-interest. Public choice theory put forward a model of the relationship between politicians and pressure groups in which politicians eager for re-election gave pressure groups what they asked for, a mutually reinforcing dynamic of self-interest which explained why government expenditure kept increasing. Lobby and pressure groups have always held an ambiguous position in liberal democratic politics; on the one hand they push the case of the part or the section, on the other they represent interests which need to be considered by government as they formulate policy in the national interest. Public choice theory minimised the contribution of pressure groups to policy-making, casting them as so many selfish and greedy snouts in the trough. There was, it seemed, no interest that wasn't vested, and government consultation was reduced to deal-making. As John Hewson said of the Labor government: 'Behind every one of this Government's so called reforms lies a deal with some pressure group'.[14]

The organisational behaviour of the public bureaucracies was similarly seen as primarily motivated by self-interest and survival. Terms like 'the welfare industry', 'the land rights industry' and 'the industrial relations club' appeared, with the implication that those working in them were far more concerned with their own material interests, or with the expansion of their own power and status, than with any of the overt goals they were purportedly serving. The alliance of welfare state user groups with service providers concerned to maximise the budget allocations was regarded as a particularly insidious combination.[15] The danger for governments intent on reducing expenditure was capture by special interests, and almost any organised grouping of people could be a special interest. Keith Hancock's 1930 picture of the Australian state attacked by 'swarms of petty appetites' could well have been written by an advocate of the new public management, had their prose style survived their MBAs: 'A multitude of fragmented interests assail the common interest. Defence is difficult because there is no exact measure of financial failure; a host of scattered insolvencies can be hidden in the general solvency of the State.'[16] Hence the need for program budgeting, made even more urgent by the growing state debt which raised legitimate doubts about the state's long-term solvency. The only way of keeping the self-interested individuals in the public sector honest was to subject their pursuit of private gain to competition.

All of this was deeply insulting to the professional workforce, particularly those who were employed in the public sector. It was a rejection of the ethical practices embedded in their historical traditions and internalised in their professional identities. The term 'service' no longer made any sense in a model of human behaviour with no place for other-directed activity. It seemed that economic rationalism was rejecting the very possibility of ethical action and internalised norms in its belief that all claims to serve the public good were at base self-interested. Many of the men and women forced out of the public sector during the 1980s and 1990s by various downsizings felt justifiably bitter at the rejection of the meaning of their life's work and the contribution they felt they had made to the common good.

The reform of the public sector had twin motivations: the desire to reduce government expenditure – most simply done by shedding staff; and the development of more flexible models of service provision to accommodate a more diverse and individualised population. The second of these had long been a goal of left-democratic professionals concerned to empower client groups, but it was now pursued through creating markets in service delivery to be driven by consumer choice. This made the most vulnerable individuals even more exposed, as they were left to bear the costs of their ignorance and poor choice, and was a further blow to the helping professions' understanding of their social role. More generally it dissolved the public into a multitude of self-interested individuals. Public transport companies started addressing passengers as customers, and people seeking help to find jobs were no longer citizens enjoying their entitlements but clients seeking services. As much as possible the language of private, market-based contracts was used to re-describe the relations of public provision, though there was and still is resistance. University students were unwilling to be described as customers, and it is hard to describe an accident victim at a public hospital emergency unit as a freely choosing consumer.

These changes in language were significant. Anna Yeatman has argued that economic rationalism, and its fellow traveller the new public management, were attempts to change the mode of governance for liberal democracies.[17] In classical liberal social contract theory society is understood as the result of a contract between freely choosing individuals; in contracting into society they form the polity, giving up parts of their innate rights and freedoms and taking on obligations to the social whole. They are the citizens on whom the power of the state is based; it is their individual and continuing acts of consent which legitimises the state's domination and it is from their virtues that the state draws its strength. For Australian Liberals, the vertical bonds between the citizen and the state were accompanied by equally strong horizontal bonds between the citizens. The strength of these bonds, the recognition of mutual responsibility and shared fate were, as I argued earlier, as important for Australian Liberals' ideas and practices of citizenship as were the direct bonds with the state.

The new contractualism has no place for the horizontal bonds which link citizens together. In fact, it prefers not to talk of citizens at all, as it sees talk of citizenship as primarily about claims to entitlements, and is similarly wary of the concept of the public. In Australia the idea of 'the public' has been a key bearer of people's ideas about mutuality and common fate, and it has carried the social democrats' belief that public provision serves the common good better than private provision. The new contractualism disaggregates the public of citizens into self-interested individuals who become clients and customers of government. For all its talk of the freedom of individuals, the new contractualism is fundamentally statist, with the very top levels of government (where the steerers dwell) harbouring the only people empowered to act in the interests of the whole. They alone seem to be beyond self-interested behaviour as they impose disciplinary strictures on the rest of the citizenry whose claims to act in a public-minded way are dismissed as so many self-serving illusions.

The economist's model of people as acting only in response to material sanctions and incentives was deeply unsettling for commonsense understandings of society. The incentives were to be distributed by increasing the role of competition in economic life, through mechanisms such as bonuses and performance-related pay, as if people could not be expected to do a good job unless there was something in it for them. And, of course, losing too much money to the taxman was an obvious disincentive. The spread of economic rationalism was accompanied by a libertarian elevation of the value of personal liberty, particularly in regard to how one spent one's income. Incentives and competition were supposed to bring dynamism and energy. John Howard in his first stint as Liberal Party leader launched a policy program based on 'incentivation', a clumsy coining which was laughed off the stage, but which showed the direction of Liberal thinking.[18]

From Independence to Choice

The rights and freedoms of the individual have always been central to the Liberal Party's philosophy, and the values it used to distinguish itself from Labor. For most of the century the contrast centred on the degree of government social and economic planning, with the Labor Party's commitment to socialism a convenient foil for the Liberals' commitment to the individual and free enterprise. But with Labor having dropped its socialist objective and now embracing deregulatory economic reforms the Liberal Party was pushed further right, until it started to sound as extreme as Labor's socialist commitments once had, and as disconnected from commonsense. Also pushing the Liberal Party to the right were the think-tanks formed in the late 1970s and early 1980s, such as the Australian Institute of Public Policy (Western Australia) and the Centre for Independent Studies (Victoria) and a reinvigorated Institute of Public Affairs. As their name implies, think-tanks were concentrations of the intellectually trained. They brought together a formidable group of economists, politicians, journalists and academics, and produced a steady stream of publications in which neo-liberal ideas were applied to a wide range of policy issues. Employer groups too were moving to the right, as they became more committed to labour market de-regulation, and in 1986 the H. R. Nicholls Society was established to fight 'the industrial relations club'.[19] These groups, which were putting forward views well to the right of public opinion, challenged the Liberal Party's capacities to aggregate and represent non-labour opinion and interests.

Inside the party a battle was waged after 1983 over economic policy and its relation to general social policy. The two sides were called the 'wets' and the 'dries', after the factions in Mrs Thatcher's cabinet; the wets still believed in government intervention, the dries were converts to hard-headed economics which was teaching people lessons in independence and self-reliance. It was a metaphor which favoured the dries, representing them as hard and decisive while the wets were mired in sentimental, feminine indecision. During the 1980s and into the 1990s the dries, many of whom were active in various think-tanks, gradually won, and prominent wets left the parliamentary party – Fred Chaney, Ian Mc Phee, Chris Puplick.[20] This substantially compounded the Liberal Party's electoral problems, in particular its capacity to present itself to the electorate as a party capable of governing for all Australians.

Australian Liberals' commitment to individualism had only ever been a partial commitment, as the Labor Party's commitment to collectivist solutions had also only ever been partial. In the modern world social and political thought has to give an account both of how people are individuals and of how it is possible for them to live together and to cooperate for shared endeavours. Because liberalism starts with the individual, social unity seems the more problematic, something to be constructed from the interaction of individuals, or held in place by overarching symbolic structures. For collectivist political philosophies, the same underlying problem presents itself in the reverse, beginning with the collectivity, the needs and demands of individuals become problematic. For most of the century, certainly until the 1970s, Australian Liberals' commitment to individual freedom was contained and limited by widely shared understandings of the basis of Australia's social unity. Race, crown and nation all provided plausible representations of what Australians shared, and an ethic of service balanced talk of rights with that of duty and obligation. An earlier chapter discussed the melting of the symbolic glue of race and crown in the decades immediately following World War II. Nation was still powerful, though its meanings were confused by the 1980s as Labor redefined Australia as a multicultural nation, and as Aboriginal groups pushed claims to various forms of sovereignty. And the Liberals' core concept, the individual, carried very different associations in 1990 from those it had carried in the middle of the century.

In 1950 the dominant associations to individualism were independence, self-reliance and responsibility as they had been for at least the previous century. Two of its important contemporary associations, freedom and choice, were relatively minor. The word 'choice' did not appear at all in Menzies' speech to the forgotten people and the word 'freedom' only once: 'The greatest element in a strong people is a fierce independence of spirit. This is the only *real* freedom and it has as its corollary a brave acceptance of unclouded individual responsibility'. Freedom here means freestanding and individualism was understood predominantly in terms of independence. On this conception of the individual, the recognition and acceptance of responsibility was an expression of individual independence rather than a constraint on an individual's freedoms.

The second half of the twentieth century has seen enormous changes in the way people in western societies experience themselves and organise their lives. In basing their political philosophy on the concept of the individual Australian Liberals drive their foundations into the shifting sands of individual subjectivity, all the while believing they are on a bedrock of solid bluestone foundations. Consumerism and its supporting language of advertising made the expansion of individual choice its central legitimation, and postwar affluence taught thrifty individuals the pleasures of spending. By the 1980s the alliance of advertising with an ever more pervasive and technologically sophisticated media was saturating people's lives with images of commodified pleasure. Children learned to choose and to spend before they learned to work and earn the wherewithal to spend. The meaning of the good life changed from one of earnest endeavour to one of pleasurable, easygoing consumption. And as previous generations' understanding of life as the accommodation of fate was replaced with one centred on the exercise of choice, people began to describe themselves as having a lifestyle rather than a life. Consumerism was not the only force at work disaggregating earlier social forms into collections of individuals. The social movements of the 1960s had revived the romantics' quest for individual authenticity, and this was continuing to influence cultural forms. As well, the long peace had enabled people to focus on private pleasures and meanings as the obligations of wartime national duty and sacrifice became a thing of the past. Unlike the 1930s, the young men of the 1980s did not expect to be called on to fight, and would have been enormously shocked if their lives had been interrupted by the bugles of war.

When neo-classical economics was revived in the 1980s, it easily attached the competitive self-interested individual who drove its market mechanisms to the freely choosing individual of consumerism, and so further marginalised the earlier associations of the concept of the individual with independence and social responsibility. It also tried to revive the independence and dynamic energy of the entrepreneur, and talked a lot about rewards for excellence and the dismantling of the regulatory frameworks which stifled talent and sapped energy. The social value of this, however, was significantly undermined by the economic excesses of the 1980s unleashed by financial deregulation. As banks competed to lend, greed was no longer checked by restrictions on credit. Spectacular fortunes were made in an asset boom the government had little means of controlling, and the media was filled with stories of fabulously wealthy business men like Alan Bond, John Elliot and Robert Holmes à Court. The wealth of the businessmen of the 1980s did not come from making things but from financial manipulation and asset stripping, activities which had little to do with expanding the productive base of the country. The stock market crash of October 1987 delivered a temporary blow to the belief that greed was inevitably rewarded. By 1990 interest rates were approaching 20 per cent as the government used the one lever left to it to control the availability of credit. However, it pressed it too hard and precipitated a recession – the recession we 'had to have' as Keating tactlessly put it.

John Hewson and the 1993 Election

To ordinary Australians brought up to eschew selfishness and greed as socially destructive, the world seemed to be turning topsy-turvy. And the economy's roller-coaster ride through the 1980s in which private fortunes were being made as the public sector was squeezed undermined their confidence that Australian politicians really knew what they were doing. The highpoint of anxiety about a society based on competition between self-interested individuals was the 1993 election in which the Liberals were led by the economist John Hewson to a disastrous defeat. Hewson, who had only joined the party in 1985, became leader after Peacock lost the 1990 election. He produced an ambitious policy blueprint, 'Fightback!', which included the introduction of a consumption tax, an across-the-board 10 per cent cut in government expenditure, and a tightening of unemployment benefits. He also committed himself to zero tariffs in contrast to the modest levels Labor was retaining. Hawke was starting to flounder and after he failed to make much impression on Hewson he was defeated by Paul Keating in a leadership challenge.

One year out from an election Australia had a new and untried Prime Minister, and one who was associated not just with the economic transformation of the 1980s but with the recession we had to have. The next election should have been a pushover for the Liberals: but it wasn't. Labor skilfully out-politicked Hewson by deflecting the electorate's anger about the direction of its economic policy on to the Liberal Party. Because Hewson promised to go further and faster down the free market road, Keating was able to present Labor as the party of caution and compassion, and resurrect something of social democracy's language of fairness and compassion in contrast to the dog-eat-dog society he attributed to the Liberals.

The politically inexperienced Hewson was reluctant to talk about anything other than economic policy, and even then was unable to connect Fightback's policy prescriptions with commonsense economic experience. In a deeply damaging exchange he could not explain to Mike Willesee of Channel 9's 'A Current Affair' how the goods and services tax (GST) would affect the price of a birthday cake.[21] Hewson lacked the deep internalisation of the party's political traditions which a leader needs to produce convincing political rhetoric under pressure, and on which Howard was to draw so successfully in his second stint as leader. He did try, but he got it wrong. At the official launch of the campaign, with Dame Pattie Menzies in the audience, he introduced 'five of today's forgotten people – unnecessary victims of an unnecessary recession'.[22] A hairdresser, a housewife, a pensioner, a farmer and a single mother; they were a disparate bunch, joined in shared victimhood to an uncaring government but without the deeply shared values and social experiences which shaped Menzies' forgotten people. And there was another crucial difference. When Menzies addressed the forgotten people – the professionals, farmers, small businessmen, salaried white collar workers and housewives – he did so as one of them, as a professional man who shared their values and spoke to them in a language they shared. Hewson's experience by contrast was quite unlike that of any of his forgotten people. A trained economist, a policy expert, only recently in parliament after a stint as a political adviser, he came into parliament from the side as it were, without deep, lived connections to the people he was representing.

In this he was representative of a new breed of professional politicians among Australia's parliamentarians, increasing numbers of whom were winning pre-selection after working as policy advisers, party or trade union officials. By the 1996 parliament over 15 per cent of parliamentarians were employed in this category immediately prior to their entry into parliament. Hewson was also representative of an even more marked shift in parliamentary membership which was the takeover of parliament by the professional middle class. People like to see in parliament people with whom they can identify, whom they recognise as in some way like themselves, bringing to the business of government values and experiences not too different from their own. Not only do they feel more confident that their life experiences and aspirations will be understood and so taken into account in policy formation, but it makes them feel more deeply connected with the processes of government. This is the argument used for the increased representation of women in parliament, or of people from non-English-speaking backgrounds. While in the case of gender and ethnic background there has been some increase in the representativeness of parliamentarians since the 1970s, in one important dimension there has been a decline. Parliament has become much more middle-class and so decreasingly representative of the range of work and more generally of life experiences of contemporary Australians. In the 1996 parliament, 55 per cent were employed as professionals immediately prior to entering parliament, compared with 25 per cent in 1950. Primary producers were 12 per cent compared with 22 per cent in 1950, and the representation of tradesmen and workers had declined from 7 per cent to 1 per cent.[23]

At the 1993 election, Hewson became something of a scapegoat for the process of policy formation of the past decade in which the intellectually trained policy elites had imposed policy solutions on the electorate that had very little tangible public support. Martyn Painter has argued that the rapid victory of neo-liberalism over one hundred years of settled policy is because it offered governments, confused by the collapse of Keynesianism and then by Australia's rapidly deteriorating terms of trade, a way to re-establish a framework for policy-making.[24] These ideas, however, did not come primarily from the traditional ideologies of either party, though some did resonate with enduring Liberal economic precepts. Nor did they come from sectional or interest group mobilisation. In fact, as we have seen, they were largely directed against traditional interest groups which were redescribed as 'vested interests'. That is, they were not based in the experiences or the ideologies of any particular section of the Australian society but were the product of technical experts with few connections with people's commonsense economic understandings. In many cases they ran counter. Opinion polls during the 1980s showed that Australians on the whole were economic nationalists who supported a high degree of government intervention.[25] Why would a government reduce tariffs when it was obvious businesses would collapse and people would lose their jobs? Why would a government privatise a huge enterprise like Telstra when it was making a profit? Why would a government sell off buildings it owned and then rent them back at a higher price? It didn't make sense to anyone outside a fairly narrow range of policy elites. The embrace of neo-liberalism by both major parties put a huge strain on their relations with both their traditional interest groups and their traditional supporters in the electorate. The Liberals were attacking manufacturers, and Labor the jobs of blue collar workers. Party membership dropped across the board. The Liberals estimated that their membership fell from 127 000 in 1967 to 73 500 in 1990. This was part of a long-term decline which accelerated during the 1990s. The Labor Party which had a national membership of around 370 000 in the 1930s and 1940s had around 52 000 in the 1990s when the population was three times as big.[26] Newspaper estimates were even lower, one report putting national memberships of the two major parties as low as 40 000 each in 1994.[27]

Keating won the 1993 election in good part because he was much more skilled in Labor's traditional political rhetoric than Hewson was in the Liberals, and so was able to deflect much of the electorate's anxiety about neo-liberalism on to the opposition. After the Liberals lost, the party undertook a public soul searching. How had they lost the unlosable election to a Prime Minister who was responsible for the worst recession since the war? There were of course the standard reasons based on the underhand tactics of Labor.[28] And there was the GST and the associated complex package of taxation reform – it was always going to be hard to win government while promising a new tax; there were deficiencies in the campaign; Hewson was inexperienced, and so on.[29] But the most popular explanation was that the Liberals failed to convey to the electorate a vision of Australia's future. John Hyde believed that the party did have a social vision but that the leadership had failed to communicate it. They needed memorable expressions. He suggested they put away the economic textbooks for a while and read some good biographies and political speeches, some heroic poetry even.[30] John Hewson, whose communicative competence was found so wanting in 1993, was well aware of his inadequacy. In 1990 he had lamented that 'Our Party has long suffered from want of an evocative phrase such as Chifley's splendid "light on the hill".'[31] Here was yet another form of the Liberal's sense of their handicap in relation to Labor. Labor, it seemed, could master the language in ways none of them, except for Menzies, was able to do. Malcolm Fraser was blunter about the reasons for the Liberals' election debacle. The problem was the message not the messenger. The Liberal Party had become too ideological. It owed its past success to pragmatism and commonsense and needed to return to both.[32]

In the wings as this debate took place was John Howard. There was still another leader to go before he would get his second chance. But when he did he proceeded, slowly and skilfully, to rebuild the Liberals' capacity to represent the nation as a whole after more than a decade of radical economic liberalism.

9
John Howard, Race and Nation

For All of Us

John Howard became leader of the Liberal Party in January 1995 after Hewson's successor, Alexander Downer, resigned. Hewson had hung on for fifteen months or so after the March 1993 election, but his leadership was fatally wounded. As the election post-mortems had argued, he did not have the depth of political skills needed to rebuild the party's electoral plausibility. His successor, Alexander Downer was, if anything, worse and he collapsed under the merciless pressures of the job into embarrassing gaffes and displays of ignorance. Howard was drafted into the job by a desperate party, and fourteen months later, on 2 March 1996, he led it back into government. He has since won two more elections, in 1998 and again in 2001.

Early in 1995 it was clear that Labor under Paul Keating was in trouble. A by-election in the ACT electorate of Canberra delivered a massive 16.2 per cent swing against the government, and in May the popular Queensland Labor government had its majority reduced from twenty-one seats to one.[1] Keating's second period of government, the one he had won in his own right, was dominated by cultural issues. With good reason, Keating believed that the economic reforms of the 1980s were starting to bear fruit. Now that he was Prime Minister he turned his attention away from the economy to what he called 'big picture issues' about Australia's position in history and the region: relations between settler and indigenous Australians, Australia's position in Asia, and the republic. This made him enormously popular among intellectuals. At last it seemed they had a Prime Minister to succeed Whitlam, to grapple with the big questions about Australia's cultural and national identity, and to make Australia part of global conversations about the place of race and ethnicity in the post-colonial world and Australia in the region. On indigenous issues, at least, fate played into his hands. In June 1992 the High Court overturned the doctrine of *terra nullius* in the Mabo decision, finding that at the time of British settlement indigenous Australians did possess native title, and that in some cases this may have survived. The court's decision required a legislative response, which finally came in the Native Title Act (1993). But Keating went further than this, and used the need to respond to the Mabo decision as an opportunity for a more general renegotiation of settler–indigenous relations.²

Keating's big picture was grandiose. It pushed all other pictures about Australia's past and future out of the frame as he claimed for Labor all the reforming energy in Australia's political life and presented the Liberals as yesterday's men, cap-doffers to Australia's British past, mooning after Menzies' 1950s, cautious little men without the intellectual capacity to imagine the future.³ Under Hewson's leadership, and even more spectacularly under Downer's, the Liberal Party was disabled by Keating's big picture issues. It was divided over the issue of Australia becoming a republic and at sixes and sevens on indigenous issues: some of Downer's worse gaffes were in this area. Expertise on social issues had belonged to the wets, and with people like Fred Chaney and Ian McPhee gone, the parliamentary Liberals seemed ignorant and directionless. When Howard replaced Downer Keating faced a very different opponent. Howard was not disabled by Keating's cultural issues, he disagreed with them profoundly and drew on the party's traditions to develop a strategy to counter them.

In the eight years since he became leader Howard has emerged as the most creative Australian Liberal since Menzies, as he has reworked the images, themes and arguments of Liberal Party philosophy to respond to the social and economic changes in Australia since Menzies' retirement, and to a changed Labor Party. Howard is steeped not just in Australian Liberal rhetoric, but in the experiences he speaks of: families and small businesses centred on work and neighbourhood, bounded by a relatively taken-for-granted nationalism. Howard's critics have mocked him as a suburban man pushing Australia back into the conformity of the 1950s.⁴ This is grist for the satirist's mill, but it is not good history. Howard is not going back. Because Australian Liberals lack political memory, and because the party was re-formed in 1944, Menzies is seen as the originator of the values and arguments Howard espouses. He is not. Menzies too was adapting an inherited political language. Howard is Menzies' successor not because he has gone back to him, to mine his words and images to oversee a return to 1950s Australia, but because like him he has been able to adapt the language and thinking carried in his party's political traditions to the circumstances of his political present. When Howard became leader in 1995 he faced the task of recreating a language of social unity and cohesion for the Liberals after their thirteen-year association with economic liberalism and the language of competitive, market-based individualism.

The first detailed account of Howard's thinking is in *Future Directions*, the policy document developed during his first period as leader from

September 1985 to May 1989. This was a clumsy document. Its prose was ponderous and impersonal, and its cover image of a blonde wife, a suited husband and two neat, clean children in front of a white picket fence was a cliche waiting for ridicule. But it did show that Howard realised that economic policy was not enough, and that the party needed convincing positions on a range of social questions, including multiculturalism, indigenous issues and support for families. It showed Howard trying to flesh out his combination of economic liberalism and social conservatism.[5]

The document is a mixture of dry economic policies, such as the need for smaller government and deregulation, particularly of labour practices, and social policies based on support for families and an assimilationist nationalism. The cover image, and the argument that Australia needs to return to and strengthen traditional family values, invites obvious comparison with the homes Menzies placed at the centre of national life in 'The Forgotten People' speech. But there were big differences. In 1942 the home was a consensual symbol of domestic life and Menzies was using it to argue against Labor's construction of social identity in the relations of work and the economy. He was not defending the traditional home against other sorts of homes, inhabited by gay couples, single mothers or blended families. Nor was he presenting the home as fragile and threatened by family breakdown, crime, social decay. The homes of Menzies' middle class were solid castles of privacy and individual freedom whose only threat was too much government interference. In the 1980s championing the home was more fraught when only about 20 per cent of households were single-breadwinner, married couples with children. Homes and family life did not provide the same easy pickings for consensual politics in the 1980s and 1990s as they did in the 1940s and 1950s.

The second social theme of *Future Directions* is its assimilationist nationalism. Policies on multiculturalism and indigenous Australians are brought together under the heading of 'Building One Australia': 'We want a united Australia proud of its distinctive identity and history in which all Australians, irrespective of social background, ethnic heritage, religion or nationality have an equal opportunity to achieve what they might want for themselves and their families'.[6]

Future Directions was launched to a theme song about a plain man, played to a country beat and with the repeated refrain 'Son, you're Australian, That's enough for anyone to be'.[7] The most significant point about this refrain is not its obvious appeal to nationalism but its dismissal of affiliations to social groups and identities larger than the family and smaller than the nation – class, religion, ethnicity, region, gender, race. Thus *Future Directions* rejects 'so-called multicultural programmes which simply ensnare individuals in ethnic communities denying them the opportunity to fully participate in Australian society', and 'treaties with Aboriginal Australians which would permanently recognise them as citizens apart, unable to participate in the mainstream of Australian life, even where they wished to do so. Where communities are kept separate from Australian society there is no equality of opportunity.'[8] Family and nation are enough for anyone. Other bases of social identity risk limiting individuals' freedoms and dividing the nation.

A divisive debate on race and immigration rumbled through the 1980s, started by historian Geoffrey Blainey's comments that the rate of immigration from Asia posed a threat to Australia's social cohesion. It flared again in 1988 after the government-commissioned Fitzgerald Report found low levels of popular support for the current immigration program. In the subsequent public debate Howard was backed into a corner in which he refused to rule out the possibility of an Australian government imposing some form of racial restriction on immigration intake. He did not advocate this, but he stubbornly stood his ground on a government's right to consider all the options, and in doing so prolonged the debate. Howard's stance was deeply damaging to his credibility as a leader, both among sections of the Liberal Party and among broad elite opinion.[9] By the next election in 1990 he had been replaced by Peacock. Shortly before he became leader for a second time Howard gave an interview to *Australian* journalist Greg Sheridan which could be read as a public recanting of his 'clumsy' remarks on race and immigration in 1988.[10] This showed that as well as his stubbornness, Howard did have the capacity to learn from experience.

Throughout its period in government Labor made minority issues work for it. It built on and renewed the alliance between Labor and the new middle-class issues of the 1970s based around sexual tolerance, gender equity, the environment, and racial and ethnic diversity; and it strengthened the alliance with non-British Australians. Whether or not indigenous issues ever worked for Labor at the electoral level is a moot point, but Labor gave them attention as part of the progressive agenda inherited from Whitlam. There is a continuity between the Labor Party's commitment to class politics and its embrace of the new issues of the 1970s in the attention to the social conditions which shape and limit people's life chances, and to the possibilities of state action for reforming these. Like class, differences in gender, sexuality, race and ethnic background created inequalities of power, resources and life chances and were amenable to reform by state action.

Just as Labor drew on its origins in responding to the demands of identity politics, so under John Howard has the Liberal Party. In the 1996 election campaign Howard turned the tables on Labor by presenting it as captive to minority interests and thus out of touch with mainstream Australia. In this reversal Howard was repeating Australian Liberals' formative move against the Labor challenge but adapting it to a new range of opponents. As was argued in chapter two, Australian Liberals' claim to govern on behalf of the whole rather than the part was first made in response to the class-based politics of the labour movement. Unlike Labor, Liberals would govern in the interests of *all* Australians, of the nation as a whole. As Howard claimed in his 1996 Menzies lecture, 'The Liberal Party has never been a party of privilege or sectional interests or narrow prejudice … Liberalism has focused on *national* interests rather than *sectional* interests.'[11] How the whole is described has varied: the nation, the national interest, the Australian way of life, ordinary Australians, middle Australia, the mainstream. Also changed are the parts or sections Labor is supposed to represent. Although anti-union rhetoric remains a continuing part of the Liberal Party's armoury, since the 1970s class and the unions have been joined in the Labor camp by other representatives of the part – feminists, environmentalists, the ethnic lobby, multiculturalists, the Aboriginal industry – sometimes all simply lumped together as 'noisy minority groups' or vested interests. In his first 'Headland' speech in 1995 Howard skilfully adapted the opposition of part and whole to take in Labor's alliance with the new middle class and their faith in bureaucratic political action:

> There is a frustrated mainstream in Australia today which sees government decisions as increasingly driven by the self-interested claims of powerful vested interests with scant regard for the national interest … This bureaucracy of the new class is a world away from the myriad of spontaneous, community based organisations which have been part of the Australian mainstream for decades.[12]

The Liberal Party's 1996 campaign slogan, 'For all of us', and Howard's explicit appeal to mainstream Australia was a reworking of the Liberals' standard move against Labor, with a sharpened edge of grievance after thirteen years of Labor governments. According to Liberal campaign director, Andrew Robb,

> [it] was aimed predominantly at middle Australia … to reach people who legitimately felt betrayed. What we were saying was that in governing, we would not just consider the wellbeing of a select few, but we would consider the broad national interest. We would govern not just for some, but *for all of us*.[13]

The Liberal Party's 1996 campaign was also a response to perceived shifts in the patterns of social and economic advantage since 1983. In a reversal of the traditional patterns of party-class identification, Labor was represented as governing in the interests of the rich as its base now included 'the social progressive, often highly educated, affluent end of middle Australia'.[14] As Barry Jones commented after the election defeat, Labor had been seen as cultivating 'the big end of town'.[15] The rich could be inserted as an elite minority interest for those who wished to hear it, and for Labor's traditional supporters it added to their sense of desertion.

The campaign pitch was overwhelmingly successful. A Liberal exit poll identified a shift to the coalition of a significant section of Labor's blue-collar male base. Andrew Robb gloated that this 'significantly broadened the coalition's voting base within middle Australia. And this movement overwhelmingly comes from workers and their families – Howard's battlers'.[16] The term 'Howard's battlers' was quickly taken up by journalists and pundits to explain the election results. This was a decisive rhetorical victory for the Liberals. Howard had begun appealing to battlers in 1995:

> Powerful vested interests seem to win the day when it comes to duchessing the government and access to public funding. The losers have been the men and women of mainstream Australia whose political voice is too often muffled or ignored – the families battling to give their children a break, hardworking employees battling to get ahead, small businesses battling to survive, young Australians battling to get a decent start in their working lives, older Australians battling to preserve their dignity and security, community organisations battling the seemingly ever-expanding role of intrusive central government.[17]

Like the forgotten people, battlers were unorganised individuals, their identity located in family and local community, their enemies well-organised interests and an intrusive central government. But there were subtle and important differences. Where Menzies' forgotten people included the professions, they were more clearly identified with small business, and the sense of powerlessness and grievance was stronger. And they were explicitly identified as workers.

When I was working on the emotional and rhetorical patterns of 'The Forgotten People' speech, I was struck by the absence of the symbol of work from the speech. This was surprising. Work, after all, was central to the middle-class's belief in its economic virtue. In place of work, Menzies gave inordinate emphasis to thrift and savings. The reason for this, I surmised, was the successful hold the labour movement then had on the symbol of work. Workers wore blue singlets, not grocers' aprons and certainly not suits. Since the 1940s, not only has the nature of work changed, but the Labor Party, in widening its base to include sections of the middle class, has given less emphasis to its labourist traditions. And as Labor governments under Hawke and Keating restructured the national economy in the name of the long-term national interest, they destroyed thousands of jobs in the traditional protected manufacturing industries. The cry 'What about the workers?' ceased to be a rallying cry for Labor supporters and became an accusation of betrayal. Labor's central symbol of work was left to drift, vulnerable to a takeover by the other side. Like Menzies' transformation of the forgotten class into the forgotten people, Howard's battlers transcend class identities and include both the employed and the self-employed as they struggle to raise a family and make ends meet.[18] With the widespread acceptance of the term 'Howard's battlers' Australian Liberals won a historic victory over Labor, from which Labor has not yet recovered. It not only claimed to represent the mainstream, or the whole, but did so in a way that directly challenged Labor's core historic identity. It also showed that class had all but disappeared as a basis of ordinary Australians' political identity and understanding.

There are two classic explanatory frameworks in western political thinking: liberal individualism which explains social and economic relations as the outcomes of individual actions, values and beliefs; and Marxism which understands society and people's positions in it in terms of the underlying relations of the economy.[19] Both have an explanatory range from the higher reaches of social theory and political history through the ideologies of political parties to the commonsense understandings of everyday life. They are only powerful as frameworks for political action and understanding, however, when they connect with the lived experiences of people's daily lives, when they provide them with explanations of their place in the world which make sense. When Menzies opposed the forgotten people's formation in the private sphere of the home and individual action with their formation in the workplace, he was opposing an articulate and strong class-based politics carried by the Labor Party and the union movement and confirmed in the organisation of people's everyday lives: their experience of work, the spatial organisation of the cities and suburbs, differences in institutional access and in schooling, styles of dress, speech and manners. A host of markers of difference in everyday life divided Australian society into opposing class camps. Of course this was always a contested view of Australian society, but the point is there was a contest. Class-based understandings had a grip.

By 1996 this grip had all but gone. Class understandings no longer framed people's day-to-day lives nor their understandings of political action and possibilities. The spread of suburbia and increased levels of home ownership, the increased mobility given by the motorcar, the general increase in living standards, and spread of consumerist, home-centred lifestyles, described in an earlier chapter, had made the politics of class difference seem largely irrelevant. And since Whitlam, the Labor Party's class identity had been confused. It still talked the language of class conflict with its trade union wing, in private as it were; in public and to its new middle-class supporters it talked the much milder language of social democratic inclusiveness. The larger story behind Howard's renovation of the Liberal Party's claim to the mainstream and his takeover of the symbol of work from the Labor Party was the decline of the persuasiveness of class-based models of understanding. Inequality, deprivation, injustices and oppression had not gone, but class differences no longer seemed to most people a plausible way of understanding them, and class-based actions no longer a viable way of remedying them.

The decline of class-based explanations left the way clear for social explanations based on individuals' qualities and actions. One of the themes of this book is the Australian history of the belief that the strengths and virtues of the state are based on the strengths and virtues of individual citizens. When these citizens are feeling strong and optimistic, such a belief can inspire action and responsibility, but it carries a shadow, a propensity to see social problems as the result of individuals' weaknesses and moral failings, and so to pursue a politics of blame and recrimination. Liberal individualism's resentful fellow-traveller is sometimes called petit bourgeois ideology. Its natural home is among small shopkeepers and traders whose livelihood depends on small margins and relentless hard work. Even as they praise and practise the virtues of self-reliance and independence, such people are in fact extremely vulnerable to the vicissitudes of the economy and to larger more organised interests – organised labour on the one side and organised capital on the other. And when times get very tough they are vulnerable to paranoid explanations of their troubles based on larger forces acting against worthy but vulnerable individuals.

The Australian Liberal Party and its predecessors have always included a strong strand of this lower middle-class ideology in its broad church. It was one of the strands in Menzies' speech to the forgotten people, but it was only one. That speech also appealed to the middle-class's view of itself as the bearer of cultural and spiritual values in the face of an ill-educated and philistine working class, and as the natural supporter of the institutions of higher learning. And as Menzies and Australia settled into the affluence of the 1950s and 1960s, Liberals were happy to leave the politics of grievance, envy and paranoia to Labor. But there has always been an ambiguity in the Liberal Party's commitment to the whole that makes the revival of its petit bourgeois strand a permanent possibility: is it the interests and welfare of the whole, the national interest; or is it majority opinion, the views and values of the mainstream? The one is in keeping with the Liberals' belief that it is the party of responsible government; the other is populism, with its new, powerful tools of opinion polls and focus groups to take regular soundings of the public's views, and talkback radio to broadcast them. On economic policy the Howard governments cannot be accused of populism. They have pursued unpopular taxation reform and remain committed to the full privatisation of Telstra despite public opinion polls. They have listened to economic experts and drawn on academic knowledge. In social and cultural policy, however, it is a different story. Those who present well-informed and argued views of the long-term national interest which differ from the government's have been marginalised, treated as mouthpieces of minorities intent on imposing their views on the mainstream, and so unable to contribute to the formation of national policies as they think is their due. It is symptomatic of the ease with which the Liberal government under Howard has collapsed the idea of the national interest into that of the mainstream that the Liberal Party's official quarterly magazine is now called *The Mainstream*.[20]

Pauline Hanson

During the 1996 election campaign the Liberals presented a very small target. The campaign was directed to Labor's failings. Howard argued for the need to restore a sense of cohesion and common purpose, after the divisiveness of Labor, but apart from his long-familiar appeals to the family, to small business and an undefined Australian mainstream the common ground he was claiming against Labor had little worked-up content. Exactly how his government would pursue the national interest, as against the majority vote, was left vague. The result was that, for the first term at least, it lost control of the political agenda to Pauline Hanson, the new Independent member for Ipswich.

Pauline Hanson's election was a fluke, but she quickly became a lightning rod for all the grievances that had built up over the previous thirteen years of Labor government and for a widespread sense of alienation from the established major parties. She was pre-selected for a safe Labor seat which the Liberals thought they had no chance of winning, and so was never properly screened as suitable for political office. From the perspective of the political classes she soon proved her unsuitability, writing to her local paper accusing the government of showering Aborigines with money at the expense of other, more deserving Australians. She was disendorsed, but too late for her name to be removed from the Liberal how-to-vote cards. And she received a huge amount of local publicity. She stood as an independent and won the seat with a first preference anti-Labor swing of 21 per cent, the greatest voter defection from a major party in more than half a century.[21] Her maiden speech in September turned her from an electoral anomaly into a national figure.

Into the consensual middle ground Howard had prepared, Hanson poured the grievances of old White Australia against the economic and social changes of the past thirty years. The overwhelming grievance was one of neglect. While the government had been attending to various minorities, she and others like her had been suffering. In particular, unemployment had been mounting and she put forward a range of policy suggestions to tackle this. Her economic policy drew on 150 years of Australia's economic nationalism and showed just how far neo-liberal economic policies had diverged from ordinary Australians' commonsense economics. 'I may be only a fish and chip shop lady', she said, 'but some of these economists need to get their head out of the sand and get a job in the real world. I wouldn't even let one of them handle my grocery shopping!' She advocated more protection for Australian industry, job creation schemes to combat unemployment, infrastructure building projects which were once the mainstay of a nation-building state, and twelve months of national service for school leavers. She opposed the selling of government-owned enterprises like Telstra and wanted immigration halted 'so that our dole queues are not added to'.[22]

These were the commonsense economic nationalist precepts you could hear in any pub, taxi or lounge room. Labor governments had ignored them and there was every indication that Howard intended to ignore them too. However, Hanson's speech had another major preoccupation – the need for Australia to be one nation and for governments to represent all Australians. She attacked multiculturalism and called for a halt to immigration, but the area to which she gave most attention was Aboriginal policy. Attacks on Labor's indigenous policies occupied about one-third of her speech:

> We now have a situation where a type of reverse racism is applied to mainstream Australia by those who promote political correctness and those who control the various taxpayer funded 'industries' that flourish in our society, servicing Aboriginal, multiculturalists and a host of other minority groups ... Present governments are encouraging separatism in Australia by providing opportunities, land, monies and facilities, only available to Aboriginals.

By contrast Hanson called for 'equality for all Australians'. The Liberals' promise to govern 'for all of us' had become a siren song to accumulated grievances, including the extreme and paranoid versions which are always lurking at the fringes. And it had tapped a vein of resentment and confusion about Labor's attempt to change relations between indigenous and non-indigenous Australians.

Hanson's speech was met with a deluge of criticism from the media, and a surge of support from people who responded to her gutsy determination to have her say. Within months she had become the catalyst for the formation of a new party, the One Nation Party. Branches were formed across the country, with especially strong support in her home state of Queensland. At the 1998 federal election it received 8.4 per cent – or about a million – first preference votes, with 14.4 per cent in Queensland.[23] However, like many minor parties before it, it was unable to translate this electoral support into parliamentary representation. Hanson failed to win the newly created seat of Blair, and the seat of Oxley returned to Labor. One Nation did win one Senate seat in Queensland, but its candidate was disqualified for having failed to renounce her British citizenship.[24] Since then it has disintegrated in a welter of acrimonious organisational disputes. During its brief moment on the political stage it attracted an enormous amount of scholarly and journalistic attention as the educated, city-based elites tried to fathom its meaning, and was widely taken to indicate the continued racism of many ordinary Australians. Race became a central issue in Australian politics, and in the wake of Hanson's success Howard became embroiled in a rearguard action against accusations that he too was racist.

In part, this was Howard's own fault. He was slow to respond to Hanson's maiden speech, to distance himself and his government from the more outlandish of her claims and to use the authority of his Prime Ministership to reassure Asian nations and Australia's non-European citizens that his government had no truck with racism. Instead in a bad misjudgement and without mentioning her name, in a speech to the Queensland Liberal Party he welcomed the freer, more open climate of debate which his government had created, the lifting of 'the pall of censorship on certain issues': 'People can now talk about certain things without living in fear of being branded as a bigot or a racist'.[25] Finally, after enduring much criticism both in the Australian and in the Asian media for his failure to respond to Hanson directly, Howard made a statement to parliament. He reaffirmed his commitment to Australia's non-discriminatory immigration policy, and to racial equality and racial tolerance, but he also reiterated his familiar complaints about the repression of debate under the previous government, describing it as a 'sort of McCarthyism'.[26]

Even without Pauline Hanson's election, the momentum of indigenous politics would have made race an issue during Howard's first term of government. But her presence, and the uncertainty about the bases and extent of her support, greatly complicated Howard's responses. On my reading of Howard's speeches and statements prior to the 1996 election there is nothing in them to indicate that he was attempting to stir up racist feeling, either against Australia's non-European immigrants or against indigenous Australians. He was, as I have argued, opening up a space for grievance, but he was also restating the Australian Liberals' commitment to individuals' freedoms and opportunities. These conflicted with the more sociological understandings of identity formation that had been the basis of Labor policy. They led to a rejection of the multicultural nationalism associated with Labor and to very different policies on indigenous issues. Howard has continually argued that he is not racist. We can only understand Howard's positions on multiculturalism and immigration and on indigenous issues if we take this self-description seriously and attempt to understand it in its own terms. His positions are not the result of his racism but of his liberal individualism. We also need to consider his position on immigration and multiculturalism separately from his position on indigenous issues. Although both have strong historic links to the nation's commitment to White Australia, indigenous issues raise far more intractable problems for Australian Liberals.

Asian Immigration and Multiculturalism

Non-European immigration is easily accommodated within Liberal individualist paradigms. When John Howard finally did speak at length on the issues raised by Pauline Hanson's maiden speech he praised Asian migrants in terms of his core values of family, hard work and small business:

> People of the Asian communities have contributed very greatly to the enrichment of our life. They have brought their values of the extended family, they have brought their values of hard work, they have brought their values of commitment to small business and entrepreneurial flair and their infectious vigour in so many other areas to our shores.[27]

He has repeatedly expressed his opposition to 'any form of discrimination ... based on ethnic background, nationality, race, colour of skin, religious or political conviction' and to bigotry and intolerance.[28] So long as people can be seen as individuals, they can be embraced by Australian Liberals.

Howard's position on multiculturalism is more complex. In his first term it became known as 'the "m" word' – the word Howard wouldn't mention as he tried to put his own stamp on the nation's agenda. To his opponents this refusal was taken as evidence that Howard was uncomfortable with Australia's ethnic and racial diversity and soft on the idea of racially selective immigration, and that he hankered after the culturally and racially homogenous society of his childhood. I disagree that Howard's reluctance to use the term betrays latent racism or xenophobia. Instead it is the result of his views about the role of secondary associations in the lives of individuals and of governments in the lives of nations. Liberalism is wary of supporting particularist institutions that might impose group-based obligations on individuals which constrain their freedom of choice and action. So Howard rejects policies that 'simply ensnare individuals in ethnic communities'.

However, Howard's unease with multiculturalism is not only based on his reservations about ethnicity as the basis of social identity. It is also based on his views of the proper role of the state. The term 'multiculturalism' is used loosely in political debate to cover a wide range of policy in relation to Australia's non-European population. Its core is that government policy development, particularly in areas of government service delivery, needs to accommodate the linguistic and cultural diversity of Australian citizens and permanent residents. But during Labor's period in office it came to be associated with much larger claims about the basis of Australia's distinctive national identity and seemed to be promoting a cultural relativism that would make Australia's British cultural heritage simply one fragment, albeit a large one, in the rich mosaic of Australia's rich cultural diversity. This was never official policy under Labor, but Labor's enthusiastic endorsement of the benefits of diversity could easily seem like a rejection of Australia's cultural past.[29] And some of multiculturalism's more enthusiastic proponents seemed to suggest that before mass migration Australia had no culture at all.

When Howard avoided using the word 'multiculturalism' it was the larger claims about the basis of national identity he was rejecting, not the more limited claims about the rights of Australians of non-English speaking background. As he told Gerard Henderson in 1989:

> The objection I have to multiculturalism is that multiculturalism is in effect saying that it is impossible to have an Australian ethos, that it is impossible to have a common Australian culture. So we have to pretend that we are a federation of cultures and that we've got a bit from every part of the world.[30]

In his first term of office Howard was still to show his skill in evoking that common Australian culture, but already clear was his belief that the state is the expression of the unity of the nation but certainly not its creator. In his 1997 Australia Day speech Howard reflected on the sources of Australia's national identity:

> The symbols we hold dear as Australians and the beliefs that we have about what it is to be an Australian are not things that can ever be imposed from above by political leaders of any persuasion. They are not things that can be generated by [a] self-appointed, cultural elite who seek to tell us what our identity ought to be. Rather they are feelings and attitudes that grow out of the spirit of the people.

Howard posited two sources for these: great traumatic events, such as Gallipoli; and 'long usage and custom', such as our tradition of 'informal mateship and egalitarianism'.[31]

Both of John Howard's bases for nation-building, traumatic events and long usage, are problematic in relation to recent immigrants. This is clearly not intended, but it is evidence of the unexamined assumptions that kept exposing Howard to criticism on issues of nationalism, immigration and multiculturalism. Howard's main polemical point, however, was that national feeling cannot be imposed from above by cultural elites, and his target was Paul Keating and the association of his Prime Ministership with controversial interpretations of the future directions of Australian nationalism. But alongside the polemic, Howard is making a more enduring point that restates the individualism of Australian Liberals: society, and the characteristics and qualities of its members, comes before the state. He is thus attacking not just the arrogance of Keating but Labor's view of the state as an agent of cultural change, and multiculturalism as an official ideology imposed from above.

Indigenous Politics and the Limits of Liberalism

Non-European immigrants have come to Australia as the result of acts of choice, pursuing individual and family goals and can be smoothly incorporated into Australian Liberals' understanding of the Australian nation. The situation of Australia's indigenous people is very different. Descendants of people who suffered an invasion, they live inside political and social institutions to which they and their forebears have never formally consented.

There was no treaty, no formal ceding of sovereignty, and when the new nation of Australia was formed in 1901 the native population was left to the care of the ex-colonial state governments. It wasn't until the 1960s that serious moves were made to incorporate indigenous people into the national citizenry. They gained equal voting rights in the early 1960s, and in the 1967 referendum the clause preventing the Commonwealth government from making policy on indigenous issues was removed from the Constitution. In 1975 the Whitlam government passed the Racial Discrimination Act which forced the states to remove racially-discriminatory legislation, and which could be used by indigenous people to challenge exclusions based on social prejudice.

But even as they were gaining equal citizenship indigenous Australians began pursuing a quite different political agenda based on demands which flowed from their prior occupancy and their continuing status as an oppressed, colonised people. This agenda includes land rights, recognition of sovereignty through some form of treaty, the creation of forms of self-government, compensation for dispossession and subsequent suffering, and recognition of indigenous legal systems. Where the demand for citizenship was a demand for equality and inclusion, the new claims are based on the difference between indigenous and other Australians – on their status as a dispossessed and colonised people, and on their subsequent suffering at the hands of the colonising state. This second set of demands present Australian Liberals with intractable problems. While they are now quite comfortable with the demands for equal citizenship, with demands for separate treatment they reach their intellectual limits.

Howard's first term of government was dominated by indigenous issues not of his choosing. Reforming the tax system and industrial relations were his urgent goals. But the momentum of change in relations between indigenous and non-indigenous Australians that had been running since the Mabo decision continued throughout 1996 and 1997, and Howard was forced to respond. In December 1996 the High Court handed down a second landmark decision on native title in the Wik case. The Court found, contrary to widely held beliefs, that the granting of pastoral leases had not automatically extinguished native title. As with the Labor government in response to Mabo, the government had to formulate a legislative response. After wide consultation and furious lobbying from all sides, the government formulated a '10–Point Plan' to amend Labor's *Native Title Act 1993*, but as the government did not control the Senate, the passage of its Bill was tortuous and the lobbying continued. The passage of the Bill took twelve months and was twice rejected by the Senate, until finally passed in July

1998 on the vote of the Independent, Senator Brian Harradine, who held the balance of power. Some compromises were made to indigenous concerns, but overall native title rights were weakened.[32]

The second indigenous political issue in Howard's first term was reconciliation. In May 1997 a Reconciliation Convention was held to celebrate the thirtieth anniversary of the passing of the 1967 referendum on Commonwealth powers over Aboriginal affairs. Only days before, the Human Rights and Equal Opportunity Commission had released a report *Bringing them Home*, on the separation of Aboriginal and Torres Strait Islanders from their families. This had been commissioned by the Labor government. One of its recommendations was that all Australian parliaments officially acknowledge the responsibility of their predecessors for the laws, policies and practices of forcible removal and apologise to the individuals, families and communities involved.[33] Following the report's release the media was filled with terrible stories of grief, loss, anger and helplessness, and there was an outpouring of grief and sympathy from many non-indigenous Australians. The pressure was on Howard to use the opening of the Reconciliation Convention to make an official apology. Instead he made a weak personal apology: 'Personally I feel a deep sorrow for those of my fellow Australians who suffered injustices under the practices of past generations towards indigenous people. Equally I am sorry for the hurt and trauma many people here today may continue to feel as a consequence of these practices.' And he made a clear statement of his view of the reconciliation process as primarily concerned with practical outcomes in areas like health, education, housing, and employment, in contrast to 'symbolic gestures and overblown promises'.[34] Howard's speech was widely condemned as cold and mean-spirited. A reconciliation movement sprung up in the wake of his failure, culminating in huge marches across Australia at the end of 2000.

Throughout its first term the government struggled to articulate a coherent position on indigenous issues. On the one side were angry farmers and pastoralists dismayed by the Wik decision, miners nervous of any increase in native title rights over exploration and mining access, people offended by indigenous claims to special rights and defensive about accusations based on the wrongs of the past; on the other were indigenous people struggling for native title and grieving for their broken families, and non-indigenous people filled with shame and dismay at the history of Australia's race relations and looking for a meaningful way to repair the wrongs of the past. As with most political issues there were material interests at stake; but also at stake were emotional and psychological issues and moral credibility.

Moral credibility is important to Liberals, yet in the area of indigenous policy they have been unable to formulate policies and positions morally acceptable to indigenous and to many non-indigenous Australians. Much discussion of the reason for this has focused on race – as in Andrew Markus' book on the Howard government.[35] But the difficulties are deeper than this. In their own terms the Liberals are not racist, and to insist that they are simply reinforces their sense of misunderstood self-righteousness. The core issue is that indigenous Australians' relationship with the state cannot be fully encompassed by liberal concepts of citizenship.

Australian Liberals understand racism as the belief that a racially defined group of people is inherently inferior and hence that it is legitimate for another group, which regards itself as inherently superior, to deny them equal rights. They do not subscribe to such a position. Since the 1960s Australian Liberals have accommodated the demand for non-racially discriminatory citizenship both for immigrants and for indigenous Australians. They have embraced the formal gaining of political citizenship since the 1960s as well as the legitimacy of indigenous demands for equal social citizenship, although recognising that this is still a long way from being achieved. Faced with the political demand for reconciliation, Howard moved the achieving of equal social rights to the centre of the Liberal Party's indigenous policy and made the overcoming of the material and social disadvantages suffered by indigenous Australians the core of Liberals' commitment to reconciliation. This was an adaptation to the new political demand for reconciliation of the position already set out in *Future Directions*:

> '*As with other disadvantaged Australians* what is needed is a sensitive commitment to eliminate those impediments which prevent Aborigines from enjoying the equality of opportunity to fulfil their own personal goals and choose their own life style that has been enjoyed by all Australians' (my italics).[36]

The characteristic Howard most often attributes to indigenous Australians is disadvantage. This allows him to justify the government spending money on targeted programs in areas like health, housing and employment, while making clear that the basis for this is no different from that of programs designed to help other disadvantaged Australians.

Citizenship is a fraternal concept. From the perspective of Australian Liberals' commitment to non-racially discriminatory citizenship, indigenous Australians are Australians like everyone else. Since multiculturalism became accepted it has been easier to recognise their distinctive cultural heritage, but it does not follow from this that they should have any different rights or treatment. From this perspective indigenous Australians are members of the one Australian nation and should be treated the same as all other Australians. To do otherwise, they argue, is to reintroduce racially based policies. John Howard has repeatedly opposed calls for a treaty with indigenous Australians on this basis: 'It is an absurd proposition that a nation should make a treaty with its own citizens. It also denies that Aboriginal people have full citizenship rights now.'[37] A form of land title which can be enjoyed by only one group of Australians, recognition of customary law, talk of treaties and sovereignty all offend against Australian Liberals' commonsense understandings of equality. They are seen as divisive, setting one group of Australians against another. The limits of Australian Liberalism is reached when claims are made that go beyond non-discrimination and equal citizenship to a recognition of indigenous rights.

These limits are intellectual as well as political. Citizenship is a political rather than a sociological concept. In relying on a concept of citizenship to frame its indigenous policy Australian Liberals severely limit their intellectual resources. As I argued in the discussion of the assimilationist nationalism of *Future Directions*, the nation state, the family and the individual are the three key social formations of Australian Liberalism and there is no clear place for secondary associations. As the plain man sang at the launch of *Future Directions*: 'Son, you're an Australian, that's enough for anyone to be'. And it should be enough for indigenous Australians too. It is thus not surprising that Australian Liberals are unable to recognise the urgency of indigenous people's desire to maintain their traditional social structures and traditions. Liberalism is the political thinking associated with the broad historical process whereby people were driven or attracted away from various traditional, group-based identities and social formations and reconstituted as individuals bearing certain rights and obligations, and with the capacity to choose aspects of their life circumstances. Its historic mission was to free individuals from the obligations and superstitious practices of traditional society, in order that they and their land might participate in the rational markets of capitalist society. Faced with traditional social formations the Liberals' natural response is to see them as holding people back, rather than as sources of strength for people and a necessary base for their identity formation. This pre-sociological conception of the person blocks the capacity of Australian Liberals to understand the role of culture in the formation and maintenance of indigenous people's identity and sense of self-worth, and the integral links of that culture to the land.

The Liberal imagination relegates group-based identities to a premodern past, at the same time blocking any understanding of its own historical formation as an ideology of modernity. This has particular force in

Australian liberalism. Liberalism is an optimistic creed that sets its face resolutely to the future and the benefits of progress. It developed in the Old World in which the past was all around people, and in which a deep-rooted conservatism had rival ways of connecting the past with the present and future. Transported to a new country, a country without history as far as the colonisers were concerned, liberalism's arguments for the rights of the future became the country's commonsense and flourished unchallenged for the first 180 years of European settlement. Faced with contemporary indigenous Australians' political demands for a degree of separateness and autonomy, it is very difficult for contemporary Australian Liberals not to see premodern traditions as holding people back. If we add to this the axiomatic belief in the virtues of material progress that characterised the liberalism of the British settler societies, we see another level of difficulty for Australian Liberals in responding to indigenous political demands.

As the commonsense of the nineteenth-century nation builders, Australian Liberalism has a material, practical bent, with little interest in issues of subjectivity. Howard contrasts his governments' commitment to practical reconciliation with Labor's pursuit of symbolic gestures, such as a treaty, or an official apology to the stolen children and their families which are dismissed as so many empty gestures. The setting up of the opposition between practical and symbolic reconciliation has done great disservice to the general cause of reconciliation which requires both practical and symbolic work. By 2000 Howard was giving lip-service to the spiritual component, and could acknowledge that indigenous people were not just a problem for Australia but made a contribution – but these had made no discernible impact on the government's policy.[38] Practical reconciliation remained the cornerstone and even in this achievements were minimal.

The Howard government's insistence that reconciliation is simply a matter of practical improvement in indigenous living standards is in part the result of an inability to engage with new knowledge about indigenous Australia. Since the early 1970s there has been a revolution in knowledge about indigenous Australia. Archaeology has put the length of occupancy as somewhere between 40 000 and 60 000 years, and so revealed millennia of adaptation and survival. Anthropology has shown the groundedness of indigenous society and identity in relations to the land. Environmental history has revealed the sophistication of indigenous people's management of the harsh and varied Australian environment. Oral history has given voices and faces to individual Aboriginal people. And perhaps most importantly as far as the moral claims of settler Australia, historians have revisited the colonial period to reveal not just the triumphal progress of nation building but a protracted and bloody conflict on the frontiers of settlement that lasted into the twentieth century. Since Henry Reynolds wrote *The Other Side of the Frontier*,[39] it has been hard for educated Australians to avoid knowing that the process of settlement was also a violent invasion in which land was seized, people were killed and societies destroyed. And subsequent work has shown that the law and the state continued the processes of social destruction well into the twentieth century. Howard and his ministers have simply refused to acknowledge the changed state of knowledge, and have formulated policy as if they were still in the 1960s and the only problem was one of ensuring equal citizenship for all Australians.

Claiming the Australian Legend

Soon after he became Prime Minister Howard threw his hat into the ring of historical debate, claiming that there had been an attempt 'to rewrite Australian history in the service of a partisan cause'. Some of this was about the reputation of Robert Menzies, and was straightforward partisan polemic.[40] By the time of the Reconciliation Convention in 1997, however, Howard had extended his historical critique to reject the portrayal of Australia's history since 1788 'as little more than a disgraceful record of imperialism, exploitation and racism'. He acknowledged that there were 'blemishes', but 'the overall story' was 'of great Australian achievement'.[41] 'I am fed up with the defensiveness and self-flagellation' he said, when we have an overall record of achieving 'a tolerant, open, harmonious society'.[42] As Prime Minister, Howard prefers to praise rather than blame the Australian people, to make them feel good about themselves, 'relaxed and comfortable'. There is much to be said for this, particularly after the hectoring they received from both Malcolm Fraser ('Life wasn't meant to be easy') and from Paul Keating telling Australians to get their heads out of the sand, but in relation to the history of Australia's relations with Aborigines it involves a large amount of denial. Historical knowledge is always relative, in part dependent on the values of those who produce it, but even so it has rules of evidence. Howard's refusal to accept the evidence of historical scholarship has been a serious limitation on his government's indigenous policy. As an editorial in the *Sydney Morning Herald* stated: 'The antidote to political correctness is not historical incorrectness'.[43]

In his first term Howard's forays into history were shrill and reactive as he struggled to gain control of the political agenda. The consensual space he had opened with the campaign slogan 'For all of us' had filled up with grievances about various 'Them' who were preventing a self-declared mainstream 'Us' from receiving their fair share of both resources and recognition. The problems that beset him in his first term were partly the result of the success of his negative campaign against Labor, and the debt he owed to grievance. But one cannot govern for long on the basis of grievance and negativity, and Howard soon began to give a positive definition to his consensual centre of Australian life. To do this he raided the 'Australian Legend' for the Liberal Party.

The 'Australian Legend' was the term coined by radical historian Russel Ward in the 1950s to describe a set of distinctive Australian character traits forged from the nineteenth-century worker's experience of the land: egalitarianism, practical improvisation, scepticism towards authority, larrikinism, loyalty to mates, generosity. Ward claimed that the Australian tradition was inherently radical and that ordinary Australians were naturally left-wing. The itinerant rural labourers who formed the first labour parties bore its virtues, as did the Australian diggers of World War I, and it captured aspects of Australian working-class culture and its collectivist political traditions.[44] Until Howard, Australian Liberals had left the legend to Labor. Labor was the party of 'mates', committed to egalitarianism, the fair go and an assertive Australian nationalism. Liberals spoke the language of respectability, deference to Britain and support for the institutions of the state. Neither Menzies nor Fraser made any attempt to wield the imagery of the legend, and Gorton's larrikinism made him unfit to hold high office in the eyes of Liberal Party powerbrokers. But, as John Hirst pointed out, the Australian Legend was never as inherently radical as Ward had argued, and had a conservative version, the 'Pioneer Legend' of land-holding rural Australia.[45]

During the 1980s the Australian legend experienced a revival in Australian popular culture as globalisation and growing international tourism focused Australians' attention on the uniqueness of the country's natural environment and on the people who lived outside the cities. This revival can be seen in the popularity of films such as *The Man From Snowy River*, the transformation of rural work-clothes like Drizabones, Akubras and riding boots into fashion items, the confidence of Australian country music, the explosion of domestic outback tourism.[46] Labor benefited from aspects of this revival. Republican anti-Britishness was used against the Liberal and National Parties' support for the monarchy. But its rural provenance presented Labor with difficulties: the men from Snowy River and the heroes of the outback were probably racists. And the Australian legend clearly had stronger roots in Australian working-class than middle-class experience. Its revival thus added an overlay of obvious cultural difference to the tensions between the ALP's historic labourist working-class base and its new urban middle-class supporters excited by contemporary

Australia's cosmopolitan possibilities. The legend seemed about Australia's past, with little to offer its multicultural present and future. So, as with the symbol of the worker, Labor in government loosened its grip on the egalitarian imagery of the Australian legend and Howard claimed it to fill out his picture of the consensual mainstream of Australian life.

Howard's speeches are filled with characterisations of what he variously calls the 'Australian way', 'Australian values', the 'Australian identity' and the 'Australian character'. Here are a few examples:

> Our society is underpinned by those uniquely Australian concepts of a fair go and practical mateship.[47]

> Being Australian means doing the decent thing in a pragmatic and respectable society which lives up to its creed of practical mateship ... Australians are a down-to-earth people. It is part of our virtue. Rooted deep in our psyche is a sense of fair play and a strong egalitarian streak.[48]

> Being Australian embodies real notions of decency and pragmatism in a classless society which lives up to its creed of practical mateship.[49]

> The openness and unpretentious character of Australians has given us a well-deserved reputation for tolerance and hospitality.[50]

In his speeches since he became Prime Minister Howard has been reworking Australian Liberals' understanding of the virtues on which the nation is built. He doesn't completely drop the older moral middle-class rhetoric of service and leadership but he attaches it to the more broadly popular forms of the Australian legend. Thus he praises the surgeon hero of Changi, Edward 'Weary' Dunlop, for his laconicism and his mateship, as well as for 'his commitment to his country and his selfless service to his men'.[51] Like many Australian men, Howard is fascinated by the lessons of war, both for individuals and nations. Both his father and his grandfather fought in World War I and as Prime Minister Howard has been able to visit the sites of their wartime experiences. In many speeches he has embraced the national myth of Gallipoli 'where our nation's spirit was born'.[52] The death of the last veteran of that campaign, Tasmanian Alec Campbell, became an occasion of national mourning, with Howard himself delivering a eulogy at the state funeral in which he presented Campbell's life as 'contain[ing] the richness of our nation's history'.[53] Campbell had spent six weeks at Gallipoli as an under-age boy soldier. Most of his life he was a radical trade unionist and office bearer, and so to Liberal eyes a bearer of the various vices of militant unionism.[54] Howard passes lightly over

Campbell's radical politics as his life becomes an exemplar of the virtues of the legend. The death of sporting hero Sir Donald Bradman the previous year provided Howard with another occasion to reflect on the history of Australia's national spirit. Bradman's phenomenal cricketing success in the Test Matches against Britain in the 1930s and 1940s, claimed Howard, 'reinforced the national spirit, which was born out of the Australian sacrifice during World War I and helped to display the independence and self-reliance of a young nation barely decades old.'[55] Bradman spent longer at the crease than Campbell did at the front, but he too had another life, as an Adelaide stockbroker and company director, and as a long-serving cricket administrator. Throwing the lives of these two men, the radical trade unionist and the stockbroker-cricketer, into the powerful solvent of the Australian legend, their class differences are dissolved and they are reborn as nation-building comrades in arms, decent Australians and equally plausible representatives of a national mainstream.

Howard has also raided the Australian legend to restate Australian Liberals' long-standing belief that they belong to the party which best expresses Australians' civic identities. He has revived the concept of the volunteer to express the Liberals' foundational belief that society is based on the actions and qualities of individuals. In 1954 the Liberal Party asserted that 'We Believe in the spirit of the Volunteer ... the greatest community efforts can be made only when voluntary cooperation and self-sacrifice come in aid of and lend character to the performance of legal duties'.[56] Howard now describes Australia as 'the greatest volunteer society in the world'. With the language of citizenship now captured by statist meanings and ideas of entitlement, the concept of the volunteer reclaims active civic involvement as a core Liberal value. Describing volunteers as the people who 'when the chips are down hold our society and our community together' is a fresh and convincing restatement of the moral middle class's now rather clichéd claim to be the backbone of the nation. Volunteering is a flexible description of people's engagement with civic activities, from fire brigades to helping out at the local football club or school to the great 'volunteer army' of World War I. And in yet another brilliant move, Howard then links volunteering to the Australian legend by describing it as an expression of mateship: 'The great Australian capacity to work together in adversity – I call it mateship.'[57] So citizens have become volunteers have become mates, and Howard has planted the Liberals' flag firmly in Labor's territory of vernacular egalitarianism.

Howard has been astonishingly successful in linking contemporary Australian Liberalism to the Australian legend. It has given him a flexible language of social cohesion that is distinctively Australian and which enables him to generate a convincing contemporary rhetoric. It enables him to talk to rural Australia, where aspects of the legend still inform people's daily lives, as well as to families in the suburbs where it connects with a deeply held commitment to ordinariness. And it can be turned, for state occasions, into a modest national story. His moving of the volunteer from the relative invisibility of local community good works into the centre of national life has restored a meaningful civic identity to Liberal rhetoric which, under the influence of economic liberalism, seemed to have reduced people's social membership to participation in the competition of the market and the private pleasures of consumption.

Howard's opponents have been misled by his own description of himself as a social conservative and so missed his takeover of the symbolic repertoire of Australia's radical nationalist past to reconnect Australian Liberalism with ordinary Australian experience. His critics, many of them people who value skill with words, have been fooled by his rhetorical dullness. Howard is not a great orator, his language is plain and repetitive. There are no striking metaphors, no rolling cadences, no flights of fancy. Once he has hit on a form of words – like practical mateship – he repeats it, without embellishment, in speech after speech. This may be dull, boring even, but it does not mean Howard does not have a vision, nor that he is unable to strike chords from aspects of Australian experience.

There are still obvious tensions between Howard's commitment to radical economic policies which bring change and anxiety into people's lives, and his professed social conservatism. The trade unionists whose rights he attacks with industrial relations reform, the small business owners struggling to implement the GST or sent broke by extended trading hours, the young people working all hours in the deregulated service industry, also have families and want security. But there is nothing new in this. Politicians in capitalist democracies have always allowed big business and financial interests considerable room to move against people's established entitlements and ways of living. This after all was progress. The problem for the Liberals before Howard was that they had no plausible way of talking about anything other than economics. Now they do.

Border Control

But not everyone is convinced by Howard's renewed Australian nationalism. Under Howard the gap that opened up in the 1970s between the Liberals and Australia's intellectual and cultural elites has become a yawning gulf.

There are right-wing commentators aplenty on the 'op ed' pages of the newspapers and in journals of opinion, but they are eccentric, trading on exaggerated personalities and maverick opinions, rather than representatives of more generally held views or of an identifiable section of people. They feel embattled and complain regularly of the left bias in the country's cultural and intellectual institutions. There are no successors on the Liberal side of politics to Walter Murdoch. With his 'commonplace sort of mind, [and] knack for putting into words what other commonplace people have thought but never said', he connected Australian Liberals' values with the experiences of the educated middle class.[58] If he has a contemporary successor it is journalist and broadcaster Philip Adams. In 1997, accusing the Australian Broadcasting Corporation (ABC) of 'too narrow a spectrum of views' on political and social issues, Howard said: 'It is one of my criticisms of the ABC that it doesn't have a right-wing Philip Adams'.[59] But the problem is that a right-wing Philip Adams, someone with his capacity to talk intelligently on such a breadth of topics, is not easily imaginable in contemporary Australia.

The ABC has become a symbol to the Liberals of their loss of a constituency which was once their own. Ever since the intelligentsia defected to Labor with the coming of Whitlam, Liberals have viewed the ABC with suspicion. It came under such attack for bias during Fraser's governments that a defence association was formed, 'Friends of the ABC'. The Friends were mostly women, white collar and over forty-five, the sorts of people who were once the backbone of the Liberal Party's moral middle-class support. Now they were rallying to 'Save the ABC'.[60] After the Liberals defeated Labor in 1996, the attacks on the ABC began again and have continued. The ABC is seen as providing 'middle-class welfare', and arguments for the contribution of an independent public broadcaster to broadly defined public goods are simply dismissed out of hand.[61] Menzies' middle class that provided 'more than perhaps any other the intellectual life which marks us off from the beast', and which filled 'the higher schools and universities' and fed 'the lamps of learning', has become 'the chattering classes' and 'the chardonnay set', self-interested minorities and cosmopolitan elites. The progressive middle class is now more likely to oppose the Liberal Party than support it; the commonplace people who share Howard's views are more likely to be listening to the shock-jocks of talk-back radio than to the ABC. This is not necessarily an electoral problem, but it is a marked shift in the Liberal Party's historical position. Menzies would never have said, as Howard did shortly before the 2001 election, 'I am scorned by the elites and held in such disdain'.[62]

Since 2001 this scorn has settled on the Howard government's refugee policy. This is one of a series of issues about the treatment of marginalised non-white groups that has drawn moral condemnation to the Howard government. The Howard government inherited a harsh policy towards asylum seekers from the Labor government. In contrast to many western nations, people who arrive in Australia seeking asylum are detained in detention centres while their claims are investigated rather than being released into the community. These detention centres are cruel places full of desperate and unhappy people. They have been subjected to continuous criticism in the broadsheet press, on the ABC, and from various community action groups. In the tabloids and on talk-back radio, however, there has been far less sympathy. Asylum seekers are generally seen as illegal immigrants first and refugees second. In the second half of 2001 the number of asylum seekers coming by boat from Indonesia to Australia began to increase. Most were from the Middle East – Afghanistan, Iran, Iraq – and came via Pakistan using people smugglers. In August 2001 a Norwegian container ship, the *Tampa*, picked up 438 people from a sinking Indonesian wooden ferry headed for Australia. The government refused to let the ship enter Australian waters, which would trigger the provisions of the Migration Act and allow asylum seekers to pursue their claims on shore. After a lengthy stand-off, involving the ship's captain, the Norwegian government, the Indonesian government, the Australian military and navy, and a confused and divided Australian public, the asylum seekers were taken to locations in the Pacific while their claims were examined. It was a messy and protracted piece of policy-making on the run in which the government eventually got its way, and it greatly raised the political stakes around the issue of asylum seekers. For the government, the core issue was the protection of Australia's borders in the face of organised people smuggling. For the government's opponents, the issue was Australia's compassion as a wealthy, developed country towards desperate people and its reputation as an international good citizen.[63]

The September 11 attacks on the World Trade Center diverted attention from the *Tampa*, but increased public concern with issues of national security. A federal election was due at the end of the year. Given world events, the campaign was dominated by issues of security. Howard slid between the need to respond to terrorism and the need to protect our borders, arguing both that 'National security is ... about a proper response to terrorism' and that 'we will decide who comes to this country and the circumstances in which they come'.[64] The Labor campaign was thrown off track by the turn in world events. Six months out from the election public opinion polls indicated that Labor under Kim Beazley would win easily. There was continuing anger at the GST among small business people, and in April the Liberals lost the blue-ribbon seat of Ryan at a by-election.[65] Imitating Howard's strategy in 1996, Beazley was doing little to project Labor's alternative policies as he waited for Howard's unpopularity to deliver him victory. He was thus unable to project Labor as a convincing alternative government during a campaign focused on issues of national security and Labor and Beazley were comfortably defeated.

The asylum seeker issue has not gone away, however. The government has been accused of cynically exploiting it during the election campaign, in particular by allowing a story about refugees throwing their children overboard to run when it was known to be false. Howard's critics trace a line from his policy on immigration and multiculturalism, through his stance on native title and reconciliation, to his hard line on the mostly non-European asylum seekers to claim that he is racist.[66] And if he is not actually a racist or a bigot himself, then as Philip Adams claims, he is something worse – a cynical opportunist 'willing to manipulate and exploit bigotry for political advantage'.[67] So he refused to condemn Pauline Hanson outright, and practised what some have described as 'dog-whistle politics', in which he sent coded messages to those who wished to hear them while using forms of words which were publicly defensible.[68]

The moral condemnation of Howard moves from his treatment of one marginalised non-white group to the next. This continues a line of division apparent in opinion polls since the early 1970s on issues of race and migration according to levels of education. The tertiary educated are consistently more positive about multiculturalism and support higher levels of migration.[69] And they were the group least likely to support Pauline Hanson's One Nation Party.[70] Katherine Betts has argued that attitudes to race and to cultural difference have been central to the new class's identity formation, providing markers of social status which distinguish them from the small-minded xenophobia and crass materialism of working- and lower middle-class Australia. The new tertiary-educated professionals 'have built their claims to honour and prestige by painting a negative picture of parochial Australians and distancing themselves from that picture'.[71] They see Howard as a representative of the small-minded, smug Australia they have learned to loathe. Guy Rundle's and Max Gillies' portrayal of Howard as Barry Humphries' Sandy Stone epitomises this view of him as a suburban man running Australia with the commonsense of the lounge room and garage.[72] The last time a small suburban man was Prime Minister, Joe Lyons in the 1930s, the educated elites viewed him with condescension but were grateful for his capacity to hold Australia together. Today they view his leadership with dismay.

Betts draws attention to the way the social formation of the post-1960s tertiary-educated professionals has set them apart from less-educated Australians. The key here is the way tertiary education, particularly in the social sciences and humanities, trains people in processes of abstract and critical thinking that are reflexive, abstract and problematising. It teaches them to justify positions through argument and evidence rather than by appeals to authority, and it devalues the role of experience in favour of forms of knowledge and argument that are relatively situation-free. All of this makes them confident with the new, and excited by the possibility of alternatives, able to reach out for new ideas inside open-ended systems of meaning and to locate their ideas and experiences inside more universal systems of thought. These may be various technical expert knowledges, or they may simply be a well-developed general knowledge of world history and the breadth and complexity of possible human experience, the sort of qualities valued by an old-fashioned liberal education.[73]

The styles of knowing associated with intellectual training set them apart from those who learn their skills and knowledge in the university of life through hard knocks, practical experience and submission to authority. They learn a knowledge that is densely particular and situation-specific, tied to the local, known world, and of little use with the new and different. These two styles of knowing are associated with another pair of distinctions, that between cosmopolitans and locals, between those for whom the world is their oyster and those who know in their bones that home and its ways are best. The distinction between cosmopolitans and locals was first made by American sociologist Robert Merton to describe the difference in social and political orientation among the inhabitants of a small American town in the 1940s. Cosmopolitans lived their lives within the structure of the nation, compared with locals whose focus was the small world of their town.[74] In the contemporary world cosmopolitans are oriented to global culture and society, while those whose horizons of interest and identification are still bounded by the national seem like small-minded locals. Cosmopolitans have the social skills and attitudes that enable them to move among people of different cultures with confidence and purpose, whereas locals, even when they travel, are more attuned to the familiar than the different. For Australian cosmopolitans, it is their interest in and skills with cultural difference that most distinguish them from their parochial compatriots.

Cosmopolitans' and locals' different styles of knowing are associated with different projected moral communities. One aspect of globalisation is the development of human rights as a universal language which creates a universal human moral community co-extensive with the cosmopolitan's potential field of knowledge. Locals still live inside much smaller moral communities – of family, friends and neighbourhood, less and less of class, perhaps of ethnic group or religious congregation. So, of course, do cosmopolitans, but they are far more ready to acknowledge the legitimacy of universal claims. The historical function of the nation state was to draw locals within territorial units into the moral community of the nation, inside whose boundaries they would recognise reciprocal rights and obligations. The language of citizenship was a universal language of equality that operated across regional, religious and ethnic differences to create moral and political national communities. It operated, however, within territorially-based states, whose boundaries were created by particular historical processes which privileged those inside the territory against those outside. Sometimes, as with settler Australia's relations with indigenous Australians, it privileged particular groups within the state over others, on the basis of racial and cultural difference, generally by defining the nation in ways that excluded them. But this was a distortion of the equality implicit in the language of citizenship and since the 1960s it has been generalised to include all those legitimately within Australia's borders.

The language of citizenship is now being pushed beyond the boundaries of nation states to encompass the world as a political community, with no boundaries other than that of the globe itself. So cosmopolitans will describe themselves as 'citizens of the world' and be uncomfortable with and even hostile to the traditional languages of national political communities. Globalisation has turned national patriots into locals, and cosmopolitans often treat them with the contempt nationalists once directed at small-town folk. In Australia the intellectuals' traditional scorn for suburbia has slipped easily into a scorn for Australian nationalists. Nationalists for their part still value territorial sovereignty, and place their obligations to their fellow nationals much higher than to those outside the boundaries of the nation.

Howard is an unashamed Australian patriot, who has captured much Australian vernacular nationalism for the Liberals and in doing so created a workable language of national unity. He can claim, without even a nod to relativity of perspectives, that 'We all know Australia is the best country in the world in which to live'.[75] This is the voice of the local not the cosmopolitan, of the person who bases their judgements and views on the world they know. Just as Howard believes the national character of the people is built from the experience of the people, both in the high moments of national experience like Anzac and in the habits of daily life, so he too has built his knowledge and ideas from his experience. His speeches are full of references to his personal experiences, to encounters with people, to his own beliefs and feelings. This is the real meaning of his references to his childhood in the 1950s. It is not that he wants to go back, but that he legitimates his beliefs, both to himself and to others, in terms of his own experience rather than in terms of more abstract systems of cultural and social knowledge. It is why he has revelled in the chance being Prime Minister has given him to visit the sites of both his family's and the country's past – the battlefields of World War I, the streets of London and the halls of Westminster. This is not an exercise in nostalgia so much as an exercise in practical learning, in seeing with his own eyes the places from which the man he is and the country he leads have come. And it is why he has such rapport with that other local in charge of a nation, George W. Bush.

Conclusion

When Deakin launched the Commonwealth Liberal Party at the Melbourne Town Hall in 1909 he stood in front of a map of Australia to help his audience imagine the vastness of 'the 3 000 000 square miles of territory which is your possession – for whose present and future you and you alone are responsible'. Deakin was not using the map to draw attention to Australia's long coastline, nor to its isolation from Britain, but to its internal differences and divisions. Within the vastness were eight or nine distinct centres, 'each speaking with its own voice to its own surroundings', but the men and women in his audience needed to keep their eyes on the map to remember that the proposals they were about to hear were to be applied right across it.[1]

Deakin and his Liberals were nation-builders attempting to develop policies that would transcend local and geographically based loyalties and draw Australians into a heightened awareness of themselves as citizens of a national polity. Theirs was the language of citizenship, of independent men and women bound together by their recognition of reciprocal rights and obligations and their loyalty to the symbols and institutions of the state. But in the decade since Federation a new way of imagining the divisions of Australia had been gaining ground – one which saw Australians as divided not by state and regional loyalties but by differences of class and economic interest. Class differences too transcended geographically based experiences and they provided a powerful, rival way of imagining the nation. In place of the Liberals' polity of independent citizens, Labor presented the nation as divided by conflicts of interest and experience into workers and bosses, labour and capital, working class and middle class.

After the 1910 election, the Liberals had no choice but to accept the bi-polar division of Australian politics and to attempt to reorganise themselves accordingly to match Labor's superior discipline and organisation. However, they continued to refuse to accept that this was a true reflection of Australian society and to oppose Labor's language of class interest with appeals to citizens' obligations to the nation as a whole. When it was clear, after the 1910 election, that the majority of the working class were responding to Labor, the Liberals became the party of the rest – the residuum as

Eggleston described it – those people left over after Labor had captured the working class. Australian Liberals thus carried a dual identity. Labor's political mobilisation of the working class forced the middle class to recognise itself as having distinctive, separate interests. At the same time it deeply resented being forced into such recognition, and refused to accept the legitimacy of class-based models for understanding the national polity or developing national policy. To the Liberals the nation was composed of individuals, not of interests or classes, and they continued to wield the language of nineteenth-century individualism against the large bureaucratic institutions and the sociological understandings of twentieth-century modernity. It was on the qualities, actions and efforts of people that the strength of the nation was based, and it was to people as individuals that they continued to pitch their appeal.

For the first two-thirds of the twentieth century these two ways of constructing the national polity competed with each other. They were generated and contained within the boundaries of the Australian nation state and played out in the theatre of its national politics. Both addressed themselves to different aspects of Australians' lived experience in ways that embraced economic, social and cultural differences. Protestantism, liberal ideas of citizenship and the financial practices of responsible households all grounded Liberal political beliefs in the self-understandings and practices of everyday life. In the 1970s, as Labor incorporated other bases of social division into its construction of Australian society, Liberals continued to pitch their appeal to a nation of individuals. This often made Liberals seem unsympathetic to the demands of new groups, and it has been a continuing handicap in the formation of their policy towards indigenous Australians. But by the end of the twentieth century the tide of social change seemed to be again running the Liberals' way and its championing of the individual was taking on renewed plausibility.

A whole range of social processes was causing people to experience their lives as individual projects rather than as lived-out fates: continuing consumerism, the decline of lifetime jobs, the culture of authenticity and self-expression, changing practices of family formation, to name the most central. The bureaucratic institutions of modernity were being redesigned to deliver choice and flexibility to a society conceived of in terms of individual difference rather than uniform entitlement. At the same time, under the impact of continuing immigration from ever more diverse sources, Australia's population was becoming infinitely more ethnically, racially and culturally complex. Any residual plausibility retained by class-based understandings was becoming so criss-crossed with differences that Australia seemed more like a mosaic on the point of fragmentation than a society divided into two large conflicting class blocks. In the face of this complexity there is an appealing commonsense simplicity in championing the individual and the family as the bedrock of people's social identities and the consensual basis of the Australian nation, particularly in a nation of immigrants where the institutions and culture of the host society have shallow historical roots. The most apparent problems for Australian Liberals at the beginning of the twenty-first century were at the boundaries of the nation. Their language of individualism was unable to incorporate the political demands of indigenous Australians for recognition of community-based rights and obligations. And the contradiction in liberalism between its implicit universalism and its particularist application inside territorial states was making it difficult to sustain with moral integrity and good faith the belief that the moral and political community of citizens stops at the borders.

Inside the nation state the clear lines of division that once organised the differences between the parties and linked them to visible features of the society and the economy are now blurred almost beyond recognition. The result is that the parties are starting to float free in a way they have not done since the nineteenth century. As Australian society has grown more complex, it has become harder and harder for the major parties to represent the range of people's political views and activities. The parties' declining levels of membership and the disintegration of their stable patterns of identification are the result of these broad patterns of social change rather than of failings on the part of the parties themselves.[2] The parties are being reduced to rival teams of middle-class men and women who compete for political office, but whose experiential connection with their electorates is weak. In political science jargon these professional electoral organisations look more like the cadre parties of the nineteenth century than the mass-based parties of the twentieth, albeit with the main arena of competition shifted from the Houses of Parliament to the electorate.[3]

As people change their vote between one federal election and the next, between the House of Representatives and the Senate, between state and federal elections, purely political issues such as leadership, organisational unity and skills in building coalitions of supporters become more important. After Howard's third election victory the federal ALP looked very like the federal Liberal Party did in the late 1980s, floundering, pursuing me-too, catch-up politics, struggling with organisational problems. Given the parties' different histories and organisational traditions these problems were slightly different. Where leadership problems dominated the Liberal Party, the ALP was preoccupied with the appropriate role of the trade unions, though it too has leadership issues. There is an uncanny similarity as a party out of office looks to its traditional sources of cohesion and finds them wanting, and a party in government seems, despite mistakes, bad policies and ministerial scandals, to become more secure as each year passes. Government office itself now seems the main source of party cohesion, giving it effectiveness, media presence, ministerial offices for its ambitious members, and a leader who carries the symbolic weight of the state. Labor Premiers in the states seem to have a hold on office as hard to shake as Howard's on the Prime Ministership.

For the Liberal Party the return of politics is a vindication of its belief that it is not the instrument of non-political interests but an organisation based on shared values putting itself forward to govern in the interests of the whole. But, as I have argued in this book, the social experiences which underpinned this belief for the first half of the twentieth century have all but disappeared. The moral middle class, which began to shift to Labor with Whitlam, is now progressive left rather than concerned Liberal, although there are signs that its support for Labor is weakening as the Greens become the specialist party of disinterested concern. The Liberals, however, still have a convincing grip on the representation of the interests of the whole. By the end of the century John Howard had captured the language of nationalism for the Liberals, and this provided them with a powerful language of unity to contain the individual rights and freedoms to which they are also committed. Howard has made the Liberals the national party again, able to talk the language of the many ordinary Australians for whom the nation is still their taken-for-granted political community. This capture may well be the result of Howard's personal skills and representative capacities and so would not survive a Liberal leadership change nor the emergence of a Labor leader equally fluent in Australia's vernacular nationalism.

The other problem for the Liberals is deeper, and it also faces Labor or any other party that aspires to win office through the old language of national unity. It is that the nation itself is weakening as the primary cultural framework for people's lives. This is seen in the gap between Howard and vocal sections of moral middle-class opinion who are appalled by the apparent disregard for human rights in the Howard government's policies towards people seeking asylum. In this case, supporters of asylum seekers are embracing a language of human rights and expanding their sense of moral community. But the weakening of the framework of the nation may equally lead to the contracting of people's sense of obligation and interdependence, their transformation from concerned citizens into self-interested individuals with both the desire and the capacity to pursue their lives globally rather than nationally. As such they can escape the reach of all morally based political appeals, national or otherwise. This is not new in itself. Christopher Skase had plenty of predecessors. Cosmopolitans may be the new, globally concerned citizens of the world, but they may also be footloose individuals pursuing their lives and fortunes on a global stage.

I wrote in the introduction that I was taking the twentieth century as the frame for this history of Australian Liberals in the belief that the deep patterns of politics reveal themselves over longish stretches of time. The closer I came to the present, however, the less confident I became that I was tracing deep patterns rather than surface disturbances. We still do not know the long-term impact of the institutional transformations of the 1980s and 1990s on Australians' self-understandings; nor where globalisation is heading. It will undoubtedly create new global social formations within which people will form new understandings of political and moral interdependence and obligation. But the relationship between these emerging social formations and nationally based political parties is not yet clear – or at least not to me.

Notes

Abbreviations

AA Australian Archives
ADB Australian Dictionary of Biography
CPD Commonwealth Parliamentary Debates
ML Mitchell Library
NLA National Library of Australia
SLV State Library of Victoria

1 Australian Liberals

1. Address to the Melbourne Press Club, 22 November 2000.
2. Address to the 'Australia unlimited roundtable', 4 May 1999.
3. Hancock, *Australia*, p. 227.
4. Ingham, 'Political Parties in the Victorian Legislative Assembly, 1880–1900', p. 256.
5. Menzies' opening speech to the Albury Conference, 14 October 1944, cited in Starr, *The Liberal Party*, p. 90.
6. Edmund Burke, 'Thoughts on the Causes of the Present Discontents' (1770), in Robert A. Smith (ed.) *Edmund Burke on Revolution*, p. 40.
7. Deakin, 'The Liberal Party', p. 7, NLA MS 1924/18/51.
8. 'The Liberal tradition: The beliefs and values which guide the Federal Government', 1996 Sir Robert Menzies Lecture, 18 November 1996 in Gregory (ed.), *The Menzies Lectures*, p. 322.
9. Report of Interstate Conference of Liberal Organisations, 28–30 November 1911, Brookes papers, NLA MS 1924/18/1298.
10. Menzies, *Afternoon Light*, p. 286.
11. *The Liberal*, 1/1, July 1911, p. 15.
12. W.H. Anderson, 'Liberal Lead to an Expanding Nation', 1956 Federal Presidential Address, Liberal Party Secretariat.
13. See Ian Hancock, *National and Permanent? The Federal Organisation of the Liberal Party of Australia, 1944–1965*, pp. 156–60, 229.
14. See Peter Tiver, *The Liberal Party: Principles and Performance*, pp. 3–6 for a more extensive development of this position.
15. Crisp, *Australian National Government*, p. 227.
16. *The Liberal*, 2/5, 2 December 1912, p. 114.
17. Rickard, 'The middle class: What is to be done?'.
18. Lake, *Getting Equal: The History of Australian Feminism*.

19 McCalman, *Journeyings: The Biography of a Middle-Class Generation, 1920–1990*.
20 Brett, *Robert Menzies' Forgotten People*. Menzies' radio broadcast was made on 22 May 1942. It was originally published as a pamphlet by Robertson & Mullens, 1942, and again with other of Menzies' essays in *The Forgotten People and other Studies in Democracy*, Angus & Robertson, Sydney, 1943.
21 Commonwealth Bureau of Census and Statistics, Monthly Bulletin of Employment, February 1928, cited in Encel, *Equality and Authority: A Study of Class, Status and Power in Australia*, pp. 116–17.
22 Stuart Macintyre, *Oxford History of Australia*, vol. 4, 1901–1942, pp. 220–1.
23 Davison, *The Rise and Fall of Marvellous Melbourne*, pp. 175–6.
24 Kemeny, *The Great Australian Nightmare: A Critique of the Home Ownership Ideology*, p. 7.
25 See Clem Macintyre, *Political Australia: A Handbook of Facts*, pp. 1–13.
26 Brett, *Robert Menzies' Forgotten People*, pp. 31–73.
27 Interview with Jennifer Cashmore, *Australian Society*, April 1988, p. 41.
28 Himmelfarb, *The De-moralisation of Society: From Victorian Virtues to Modern Values*, p. 12.
29 McCalman, *Journeyings*, ch. 3.
30 Cited in Aimer, *Politics, Power and Persuasion: The Liberals in Victoria*, p. 11.
31 See Foucault 'Governmentality', pp. 87–8.
32 John Stuart Mill, 'On representative government', in Robson (ed.), *Collected Works of John Stuart Mill*, vol. 19, p. 389.
33 Cited in Collini, *Public Moralists: Political Thought and Intellectual Life in Britain, 1850–1930*, p. 94.

2 Organisation and the Meaning of Fusion

1 Duverger, *Political Parties: Their Organisation and Activity in the Modern State*, pp. xv–xvi.
2 Menzies' address to the Canberra Conference, 15 October 1944. Cited in Starr, *The Liberal Party*, pp. 74–5.
3 Loveday, Martin & Parker (eds), *The Emergence of the Australian Party System*, pp. 12–16; Kingston, *Oxford History of Australia*, vol. 3, 1860–1900, p. 251.
4 Report of the Conference of the Liberal Leagues, *The Liberal*, 1/6, 30 December 1911.
5 McMullin, *The Light on the Hill: The Australian Labor Party 1891–1911*, p. 15.
6 Hughes and Graham, *Handbook of Australian Government and Politics, 1890–1964*, p. 467.
7 Crisp, *The Australian Federal Labour Party 1901–1951*, p. 5.
8 McMullin, *Light on the Hill*, p. 12.
9 Childe, *How Labor Governs: A Study of Workers' Representation in Australia*, p. 16.
10 McMullin, *Light on the Hill*, p. 15; Childe, *How Labour Governs*, p. 17.
11 Bongiorno, 'The Origins of Caucus 1856–1901', p. 8.
12 Childe, *How Labour Governs*, p. 18.
13 ibid., p. 19.
14 McMullin, *The Light on the Hill*, pp. 45–6.
15 Clem McIntyre, *Political Australia: A Handbook of Facts*, pp. 1–2.

16 *Age,* 2 February 1904.
17 Webb, 'The Australian party system', p. 325.
18 CPD, vol. 49, pp. 1156–7, (14 July 1949).
19 Stuart Macintyre, *Oxford History of Australia,* p. 93.
20 Hume Cook, 'The History of the movement: report of meeting on 25 and 26 May 1909', Hume Cook papers, NLA MS 601/3/63.
21 Hume Cook papers, NLA MS 601/12/1–3.
22 Stuart Macintyre, *Colonial Liberalism: The Lost World of Three Victorian Visionaries,* p. 112.
23 Rickard, *Class and Politics,* p. 44.
24 ibid., pp. 88–93.
25 *The Liberal,* 1 July 1911, pp. 5–6.
26 Kelly, *The End of Certainty,* Introduction to 1992 edn.
27 Scrapbook of George Meudell, SLV MS 9558, Box 1143/1; Rickard, *Class and Politics,* pp. 177–81.
28 Scrapbook of George Meudell.
29 Loveday et al., *The Emergence of the Australian Party System,* pp. 412ff.
30 'Protection and Practical Legislation or Anti Socialism', Ballarat, 24 March 1906, p. 14, NLA.
31 'The Liberal Party and its Liberal Programme', Adelaide, 29 March 1906, pp. 6–7, NLA.
32 ibid., p. 15.
33 ibid., p. 7.
34 ibid., p. 7.
35 Webb, 'The Australian party system', p. 325.
36 Deakin, 'The Liberal Party', p. 16, Brookes Papers, NLA MS 1924/18/51.
37 Memorandum of understanding between Deakin and Reid, 18 May 1904, Hume Cook papers, NLA 601/316.
38 Cited in Crisp, *The Federal Australian Labor Party,* p. 164.
39 'History of the Liberal movement', 1909, Hume Cook papers, NLA MS 601/3/63.
40 La Nauze, *Alfred Deakin: A Biography,* vol. 2, pp. 548–9; Liberal Party Minute Book, Brookes papers, NLA 1924/18.
41 Deakin, 'The Liberal Party', pp. 13–16, Brookes Papers, NLA MS 1924/18/51.
42 Prime Minister at Ballarat, 1910 policy speech, (7 February), pp. 4, 22, NLA.
43 Ostrogorski, *Democracy and the Organisation of Political Parties,* vol. 1, p. 120; vol. 2, pp. 3–5.
44 ibid., vol. 1, pp. 181–2.
45 *The Woman,* 1 June 1913, p. 394.
46 Leaflet, Deakin papers, NLA 1540/16/1418.
47 *Australian Women's Weekly,* 3 August 1946, p. 24, cited in Lee, *Nothing to Offer but Fear?*
48 Deakin, 'The Liberal Party'.
49 ibid., p. 14.
50 *The Liberal,* 1, August 1911, p. 1.
51 Speech reprinted in Brett, *Robert Menzies' Forgotten People,* p. 6.
52 Lloyd, *The formation and development of the United Australia Party: 1929–1937,* pp. 17 ff; also *ADB,* vol. 11, pp. 142–3.

53 J. A. Carruthers to A. Parkhill, 22 May 1904, Parkhill papers, NLA MS 4742, folder 1.
54 Scrapbook of newspaper cuttings, Parkhill papers, folio 1, NLA MS 4742; Lloyd, *The formation and development*, pp. 17–18.
55 *The Liberal*, 1/1, July 1911, p. 11.
56 E. P. Simpson to Herbert Brookes, Brookes papers, NLA MS 1924/18/34; Minute Book Women's Central Committee CLP, 4 May 1910, Brookes papers, NLA MS 1924/18/1284.
57 J. McKay to Alfred Deakin 13 May 1912, Deakin papers, NLA MS 1540/16/1283.
58 Rivett, *Australian Citizen, Herbert Brookes 1867–1963*, p. 44.
59 *The Liberal*, 1/5, 30 November 1911, p. 102.
60 ibid., 1/11, 1 June 1912, p. 246.
61 Mrs Akinsall to Ivy Brookes, 1 July 1914, Brookes Papers, NLA MS 1924/18/710; see also 1924/18/682.
62 *The Woman*, 1 March 1930, p. 3.
63 Harold Holt, 'The Political Situation 4 February 1957', cited in Ian Hancock, *National and Permanent? The Federal Organisation of the Liberal Party of Australia, 1944–1965*, p. 169.
64 Ian Hancock, *National and Permanent*, p. 160.
65 *The Liberal*, 2/7, 1 February 1913.
66 Henderson, *Menzies' Child: The Liberal Party of Australia 1944–1994*, p. 219.
67 Cited in Kelly, *The End of Certainty*, p. 42 as part of a very perceptive discussion of the impact of neoliberal ideas on the Liberal Party.
68 Puplick, *Is the Party Over? The Future of the Liberals*, pp. 38–42.
69 ibid., pp. 34–7.
70 'Rule change victory boosts Downer', *Australian*, 31 October 1994, p. 4.
71 Frederic Eggleston, *Reflections of an Australian Liberal*, p. 125 ff.

3 Protestants

1 Cramer, *Pioneer, Politics and People: A Political Memoir*, pp. 100–2; see also Henderson, *Menzies' Child: The Liberal Party of Australia*.
2 Hamilton, 'Irish Catholics of New South Wales and the Labor Party, 1890–1910', p. 265.
3 Spann, 'The Catholic vote in Australia', p. 115.
4 Rydon, *A Federal Legislature: The Australian Commonwealth Parliament, 1901–1980*, p. 139.
5 Bollen, *Protestantism and Social Reform in New South Wales, 1890–1910*; Broome, *Treasure in Earthen Vessels: Protestant Christianity in New South Wales, 1900–1914*; Hogan, *The Sectarian Strand: Religion in Australian History*, ch. 6.
6 See Aitkin, *Stability and Change in Australian Politics*, Canberra, 1982, pp. 162–6 for this sort of account; or Alomes, 'Culture, ethnicity and class in Australia's dominion period, 1900–1939'.
7 Kemp, *Society and Electoral Behaviour in Australia: A Study of Three Decades*, p. 196.
8 Aitkin, *Stability and Change*, p. 162.
9 Hamilton, 'Irish-Catholics of New South Wales and the Labor Party, 1890–1910', pp. 254, 266.

10 Gilbert, 'Protestants, Catholics and loyalty: an aspect of the conscription controversy, 1916–17', p. 17.
11 Spann, 'The Catholic vote', p. 118.
12 MacDonagh, 'Emigration from Ireland to Australia: an overview'.
13 McConville, *Croppies, Celts and Catholics: The Irish in Australia*, pp. 86–8.
14 MacDonagh, 'Emigration from Ireland to Australia: an overview', p. 132.
15 Rydon, *A Federal Legislature*, pp. 141–3.
16 H. Moran, *Viewless Winds*, cited in Encel, *Equality and Authority: A Study of Class, Status and Power in Australia*, p. 178.
17 Broome, *Treasure in Earthen Vessels*, pp. xi–xiii.
18 Spann, 'The Catholic vote in Australia', pp. 127–8.
19 MacDonagh, 'The Irish in Victoria, 1851–91: A demographic essay'.
20 Rydon, *A Federal Legislature*, p. 140; Aitken, *Stability and Change in Australian Politics*, p. 165; O'Farrell, 'The History of the New South Wales Labour Movement, 1880–1910'.
21 Vincent, *The Formation of the Liberal Party 1857–1868*, Introduction.
22 All quotes from Bollen, *Protestantism and Social Reform*, pp. 76–7.
23 Gabay, *The Mystic Life of Alfred Deakin*.
24 Vincent, *The Formation of the Liberal Party*, p. xvii.
25 Rickard, *A Family Romance: The Deakins at Home*, pp. 59–70.
26 Gabay, *The Mystic Life*, p. 76.
27 ibid., pp. 178–9.
28 O'Brien, *Parnell and His Party, 1880–1890*, ch. 4; Kiernan, 'Home rule for Ireland and the Formation of the Australian Labor Party 1883–91', pp. 1–11. The connection was pointed out by Anthony St Ledger, in an article titled 'The machine: The curse and degradation of Australian Politics'. Ledger was himself a Catholic who deplored the increasing alliance between the Labor Party and the Catholic Church. *The Liberal*, 20 August 1914.
29 Rivett, *Australian Citizen: Herbert Brookes, 1867–1963*; Cochrane, 'How are the Egyptians Behaving? Herbert Brookes, British Australian'.
30 *The Liberal*, 30 November 1911.
31 *The Vigilant*, 23 September 1920, p. 3.
32 ibid., 14 September 1930, p. 3.
33 *Sydney Morning Herald*, 28 November 1962, cited in Encel, *Equality and Authority*, p. 178.
34 Firth & Hoorn, 'From Empire Day to Cracker Night'.
35 Colley, *Britons: The Forging of a Nation 1707–1837*, ch. 1.
36 Hogan, *The Sectarian Strand*, pp. 183, 103–9.
37 O'Farrell, *The Catholic Church and Community in Australia*, pp. 267–71.
38 Hogan, *The Sectarian Strand*, pp. 106–9.
39 Firth & Hoorn, 'From Empire Day to Cracker Night', p. 17.
40 Colley, *Britons*, pp. 350–60.
41 The meeting at the Town Hall at which Deakin inaugurated the Commonwealth Liberal Party ended with the organist playing 'Rule Britannia' and the audience joining 'fervently in the refrain'. 'The Liberal Party', Brookes Papers, NLA MS 1924/18/51, p. 18.
42 Firth & Hoorn, 'From Empire Day to Cracker Night', pp. 23–5.
43 Gilbert, 'Protestants, Catholics and loyalty', p. 16.
44 Cited by Gilbert, ibid.

41 H. L. Dwyer, chairing the inaugural meeting of the 'Middle Class Party', *Age*, 9 April 1943, cited in Aimer, *Politics, Power and Persuasion*, p. 11.
42 See, for example, Puregger, *Mr Chairman*, ch. 1.
43 Lord Campion cited in ibid., p. 9.
44 Bourinot, *Bourinot's Standing Orders*, p. x.
45 'M.P.', *The Young Man's Parliamentary Guide*, p. 5.
46 Cited by D. W. Rawson, 'Victoria' in P. Loveday et al., *The Emergence of the Australian Party System*, p. 60.
47 *Fighting Line*, 24 February 1921, p. 12.
48 Eggleston, *Reflections of an Australian Liberal*, p. 125.
49 Nationalist Party Federal Election pamphlets, 1922, ML.
50 *Fighting Line*, 20 April 1921, p. 11; political pamphlet for W. B. Simpson, candidate for Daley, Nationalist Party Federal Election pamphlets, 1922, ML.
51 'Vote for Captain S. M. Bruce', 1919 election pamphlet, AA, A1495.
52 Prime Minister's speech, delivered Bendigo 30 October 1919, Groom pamphlet collection, NLA.
53 *Nationalist Speakers' Handbook*, no. 1, The Campaign Council, Melbourne 1919, p. 2., Groom pamphlet collection, NLA.
54 *Fighting Line*, 20 April 1921, p. 21.
55 Amanda Gordon, 'The Conservative Press and the Russian Revolution', in Hazlehurst (ed.), *Australian Conservatism: Essays in Twentieth-Century Political History*, pp. 29–50.
56 *Nationalist Speakers' Handbook*, no. 1, 1919, p. 35.
57 Foley, *The Women's Movement in NSW and Victoria, 1918–1938*, pp. 57–63.
58 *Popular Politics*, the official organ of the National Federation of Victoria in the late 1920s, carried an article on Bolshevism, the Soviet Union or communism in most issues in 1926 and 1927.
59 *Australian National Review*, 25 September 1922, p. 9.
60 Nationalist Party, 1928 election pamphlets, NLA.
61 Crisp, *The Australian Federal Labor Party 1901–1951*, pp. 277–82.
62 Associated Chambers of Manufactures, President's address, Melbourne, 1918, extract in Connell & Irving, *Class Structure and Australian History: Documents, Narrative and Argument*, p. 267.
63 Lee, *Nothing to offer but fear? Non-labor federal electioneering in Australia 1914–1954*, p. 110.
64 *Nationalist Speakers' Handbook*, no. 1, 1919, p. 40.
65 *Australian Nationalist Review*, 25 August 1922. See my *Robert Menzies' Forgotten People*, pp. 85–98 for a fuller discussion of the logic of the construction of this sort of paranoid political view.
66 Loveday, 'Antipolitical political thought', p. 123; Moore, *The Right Road? A History of Right Wing Politics in Australia*, ch. 2.
67 Robson, *The First AIF: A Study of its Recruitment, 1914–1918*, pp. 202–3.
68 Moore, *The Right Road*, p. 29.
69 Stuart Macintyre, *Oxford History of Australia*, pp. 182–8.
70 W. M. Hughes, National Policy and Record, 19 October 1922, AA 5959/1 2400/1.
71 Eggleston, *Reflections of an Australian Liberal*, ch. 5, quote, p. 104.
72 Don Aitkin, 'Countrymindedness – The Spread of an Idea', pp. 50–7.

73 Potts, *A study of three nationalists in the Bruce–Page Government of 1923–1929*, pp. 42–8.
74 *Australasian Manufacturer*, 24 February 1923, cited in Potts, p. 48.
75 Cecil Edwards, *Bruce of Melbourne*, chs 2–4.
76 Norton (ed.), *The Conservative Party*, pp. 37–9; Blake, *The Conservative Party from Peel to Churchill*, p. 206.
77 Hudson and North (eds), *My Dear PM. R.G. Casey's Letters to S. M. Bruce*, p. xiv.
78 Menzies, *Afternoon Light: Some Memories of Men and Events*, pp. 96–101.
79 McKibbin, *Classes and Cultures in England, 1918–1951*, pp. 269–71.
80 Joseph Lyons, policy speech 1931 Federal Election, 2 December 1931, pp. 20–1, UAP pamphlet, NLA.
81 *Argus*, 24 April 1918, cited Potts, *A study of three nationalists*, p. 49.
82 Potts, *A study of three nationalists*, p. 40.
83 ibid., pp. 65–70.
84 Bruce, 'Prime Minister's Fighting Speech', Dandenong Town Hall, 5 October 1925, NLA, p. 7.
85 Schedvin, *Australia and the Great Depression: A Study of Economic Development and Policy in the 1920s and 1930s*, p. 3.
86 Stuart Macintyre, *Oxford History of Australia*, p. 242.
87 Prime Minister's Fighting Speech, pp. 3 and 36.
88 ibid., pp. 13–14.
89 Bruce, 'Bolshevism in Australia', Dandenong, 9 September 1925, p. 5, NLA.
90 ibid. The opening paragraphs are remarkably similar in their rhythm, tone and rhetorical devices to parts of Robert Menzies' speech to 'The Forgotten People'.
91 'Prime Minister's Home Coming', *Popular Politics*, 15 February 1917, pp. 29–30.
92 Edwards, *Bruce of Melbourne*, p. 133.
93 'What the government stands for', Prime Minister's policy speech, Dandenong, 8 October 1928, p. 51, NLA.
94 *Commonwealth Year Book*, no. 23, p. 400; Sawer, *Australian Federal Politics and Law 1901–1929*, p. 283.
95 Bruce, 'The government policy', Dandenong, 18 September 1929, NLA.
96 Potts, *A study of three nationalists*, ch. 9; Sawer, *Australian Federal Politics and Law 1901–1929*, chs 12 and 13.

5 Honest Finance

1 1922 Nationalist Party Federal Election Material, ML.
2 Faulkner, *The Commonwealth Bank of Australia: A Brief History of its Establishment, Development and Service to the People of Australia and the British Empire*, p. 102. Chapter 9 'Raising the war loans' was written by the Loan Organiser, Captain G. M. Dash. The account which follows is based on this chapter, which was also the major source for Ernest Scott's account in *Australia During the War*, pp. 499–502.
3 ibid., p. 138.
4 'The Commonwealth War Loan: £10 bonds and thrift', speech by T. J. Rothwell of the Central War Loans Committee, pamphlet, Brisbane, 1918, NLA, p. 7.
5 NLA Pictorial Plate no. 33778.
6 Commonwealth Treasury 1918: 'Are you doing your full share in winning the war?', NLA Pictorial Plate no. 27135.

7 NLA Poster collection.
8 Memo from Treasury to Secretary, Home and Territories Department, 18 September 1917, AA A361 DSG17/2236.
9 'About War Loan Bonds', 1918, NLA Poster collection.
10 NLA Poster collection.
11 Back cover of pamphlet, 'The Commonwealth War Loan: £10 bonds and thrift', Brisbane, 1918.
12 Women's Commonwealth Patriotic Association, *Thrift: The National Necessity*, Sydney 1917, ML.
13 See, for example, a series of pamphlets on thrift produced by the Women's Patriotic Association, which includes titles such as 'Thrift in dress', and 'Haybox cookery', Sydney, 1917, ML.
14 *Thrift During the War and After: An Appeal and a Suggestion to the Women and Girls of NSW from the League of Honour*, prepared and distributed by the Government Savings Bank of New South Wales, n.d [1917?], ML.
15 Foley, *The Women's Movement in NSW and Victoria, 1918–1938*, p. 111.
16 R. J. Hawkes, 'Thrift: a national duty'. An address delivered to Victoria League, Adelaide, 5 May 1916, NLA.
17 There is no index reference in McKernan's *The Australian People and the Great War* nor any discussion of the war loan in the relevant chapters in Beaumont (ed.), *Australia's War 1914–1918*.
18 Foley, *The Women's Movement*, pp. 114–31.
19 Jean Mitchell, 'Thrift Education in the US: Some reflections on its application to Australia', *Bank Notes*, October 1928, pp. 38–9. (*Bank Notes* is the staff magazine of the Commonwealth Bank of Australia.)
20 ibid., pp. 39–40.
21 *Australian National Review*, 26 August 1929, p. 24.
22 ibid., 24 June 1929, p. 8.
23 Cook, *The State Savings Bank of Victoria: Its Place in the History of Victoria*, p. 165.
24 Boris Schedvin, Foreword to Murray & White, *A Bank for the People: A History of the State Savings Bank of Victoria*.
25 Paul Johnson, *Saving and Spending: The Working Class in Britain, 1870–1939*, Conclusion.
26 Spearritt, *Sydney's Century: A History*, p. 34.
27 Collini, *Public Moralists: Political Thought and Intellectual Life in Britain 1850–1930*, pp. 96–9.
28 McKibbin, *The Ideologies of Class, Social Relations in Britain 1880–1950*, pp. 274–5.
29 For British figures see Paul Johnson, *Saving and Spending*, p. 103; for Australia, Encel, *Equality and Authority: A Study of Class, Status and Power in Australia*, p. 117.
30 McKibbin, *The Ideologies of Class*, p. 281.
31 Lyons, *So We Take Comfort*, p. 165.
32 Clem Lloyd and Philip Hart. Entry for Joseph Lyons in *ADB 1891–1939*, vol. 10, pp. 184–9.
33 Lyons, *So We Take Comfort*, p. 171.
34 For example, 1928 Nationalist pamphlet 'Under which Flag?', NLA.
35 Read by Sir George Pearce to the Senate, CPD, vol. 127, 13 November 1930, p. 238.
36 Sawer, *Australian Federal Politics and Law 1929–1949*, p. 313.
37 Schedvin, 'The long and short of depression origins' has a good summary of the econonomic and financial state of Australia during the depression.

38 Schedvin, *Australia and the Great Depression*, pp. 181–4.
39 David Clark, 'Was Lang Right?' in Radi & Spearritt (eds), *Jack Lang*.
40 Schedvin, *Australia and the Great Depression*, p. 9.
41 Memo, J. T. Heathershaw to Lyons, 11 September 1930, box 2, folder 14, NLA MS 4851.
42 Hart, *J. A. Lyons: a political biography*, p. 78.
43 CPD, vol. 27, 12 November 1930, p. 222.
44 Lyons' speech at Melbourne Town Hall, *Age*, 13 December 1930.
45 Treasury circular no 30/41, 20 November 1930, AA series A 786, AB 31/1.
46 Schedvin, *Australia and the Great Depression*, p. 202.
47 Hart, *J. A. Lyons*, pp. 87–90.
48 *Age*, 2 December 1930.
49 ibid., 16 December 1930.
50 ibid., 15 December 1930.
51 ibid.
52 *Sydney Morning Herald*, 12 December 1930 cited in Schedvin, *Australia and the Great Depression*, p. 202.
53 *Age*, 13 December 1930.
54 Schedvin, *Australia and the Great Depression*, p. 202.
55 *Age*, 18 December 1930.
56 *The Woman*, 3 March 1931, p. 3.
57 Schedvin, *Australia and the Great Depression*, p. 202.
58 *Advertiser*, 11 April 1931, Scrapbook, Lyons papers, box 4, NLA MS 4851; see also letters and telegrams of congratulations to Lyons on the success of the loan, Folder 1, correspondence for 1930, NLA MS 4851.
59 Cited in Lyons, *So We Take Comfort*, p. 167.
60 Lyons, *So We Take Comfort*, p. 170.
61 For a general account of these complex politics see Stuart Macintyre, *Oxford History of Australia*, pp. 261–4.
62 CPD, vol. 128, 13 March 1931, pp. 229–38.
63 Correspondence files, 1930, 1931, Lyons papers, NLA, MS 4851.
64 Head, 'Economic crisis and political legitimacy: the 1931 Federal election', pp. 14–15.
65 Loveday, 'Anti-political political thought'.
66 The following discussion draws on Lloyd, *The formation and development of the United Australia Party: 1929–1937*, pp. 63–8.
67 Richmond, 'Reaction to Radicalism: Non labour movements 1920–1929', pp. 56–8.
68 Minutes of inaugural meeting of the Citizens' League, 3 October 1930, cited in Lloyd, *The formation and development*, p. 68.
69 Lloyd, *The formation and development*, pp. 68–72; Geoff Hewitt, 'The All for Australia League in Melbourne'.
70 Lloyd, *The formation and development*, p. 70.
71 Matthews, 'The All for Australia League', p. 139.
72 Lloyd, *The formation and development*, pp. 59–60.
73 Ellis, *A History of the Australian Country Party*, p. 172.
74 Ellis, *The Country Party: A Political and Social History of the Party in New South Wales*, p. 138.
75 ibid., p. 141.

76 Minutes of the State Convention, 4 August 1931, Papers of Dominion League of Western Australia, Battye Library 431A.
77 E. D. Watt, Western Separation: *The History of the Secession Movement in Western Australia, 1918–1935.*
78 Lloyd, *The formation and development*, p. 71.
79 *News*, 9 April 1931, quoted in Lloyd, *The formation and development*, p. 105 who gives a general account of the Adelaide tour pp. 104–7; Lyons, *So We Take Comfort*, pp. 176–7.
80 Lloyd, *The formation and development*, p. 107.
81 Clem Lloyd gives a very good account of the complex politics of these events in 'The rise and fall of the United Australia Party' in Nethercote (ed.), *Liberalism and the Australian Federation*.
82 For example, Moore, *The Right Road: A History of Right-wing Politics in Australia*, ch. 3; Cathcart, *Defending the National Tuckshop: Australia's Secret Army Intrigues of 1931*.
83 Cited in Lyons, *So We Take Comfort*, p. 179.
84 *Adelaide Advertiser*, 10 April 1931, Scrapbook, Lyons papers, box 4, NLA MS 4851.
85 Charles Hawker to Jack Duncan-Hughes, 10 January 1932, cited in Needham, *Charles Hawker: Soldier – Pastoralist – Statesman*.
86 Humphries, *More Please*, p. 75.
87 CPD, vol. 128, 12 and 13 March 1931, p. 238.
88 Copland, *Australia in the World Crisis, 1929–1933*, pp. 28–9.
89 Lyons, *So We Take Comfort*, pp. 177, 178.
90 *Adelaide Advertiser*, 11 April 1931, Scrapbook, Lyons papers, box 4, NLA MS 4851.
91 Schedvin, *Australia and the Great Depression*, p. 249.
92 *Age*, 4 May 1931.
93 CPD, vol. 128, 12 and 13 March, p. 233.
94 Lyons' speech in Sydney Town Hall on Theodore's plan for credit expansion, *Sydney Morning Herald*, 25 April 1931.
95 Grenfell Price, *The Menace of Inflation*.
96 All quotes in this paragraph are from Grenfell Price, *The Menace of Inflation*.
97 Bruce at a reception at the Melbourne Town Hall after his return from abroad, reported in *The Woman*, 1 December 1930, p. 299.
98 CPD, vol. 127, 13 November 1930, p. 237.
99 Schedvin, *Australia and the Great Depression*, pp. 79–82.
100 UAP pamphlet for 1931 election, ML.
101 CPD, vol. 127, 13 November 1930, p. 237.
102 *Bulletin*, 18 November 1931, reproduced in UAP pamphlet 'Every Picture Tells a Story', no 1, Latham Papers, NLA MS 1009/50/103, 1009/50/107.
103 *Australian National Review*, 26 February 1931, p. 15.
104 NSW state election leaflets, ML 1932.
105 Latham papers, NLA 1009/50/327.
106 Latham papers, NLA 1009/50/88.
107 Lyons, *So We Take Comfort*, pp. 176–7.
108 Lyons papers, box 1, folder 8, NLA MS 4851.
109 These terms are from an analysis of the 1929 defeat by Massey Greene, cited in Lloyd, *The formation and development*, p. 31.
110 26 May 1931, newspaper clipping, Latham Papers, NLA MS 1009/49/74; 1009/49/108.

111 See Lex Watson, 'The United Australia Party and its sponsors' in Hazlehurst (ed.), *Australian Conservatism: Essays in Twentieth Century History*.
112 Hart, *J. A. Lyons*, pp. 161–6.
113 Lloyd, *The formation and development*, p. 230.
114 Hart, *J. A. Lyons*, pp. 174–5.
115 Martin, *Robert Menzies: A Life*, vol. 1, pp. 267–72.
116 ibid., p. 362.
117 Clem Lloyd, 'Rise and fall of the UAP'.
118 ibid., see also, Ian Hancock, *National and Permanent? The Federal Organisation of the Liberal Party of Australia, 1944–65*, pp. 10–23.

6 From Menzies' Forgotten People to the Whitlam Generation

1 Menzies' opening address to the Canberra Conference, 13 October 1944, cited in Starr, *The Liberal Party of Australia: A Documentary History*, p. 74.
2 Davies, 'Victorian Government and politics', p. 286.
3 Dame Elizabeth Couchman, History of the Australian Women's National League 1900–45, typescript, Australian Women's National League SLV MS 8713 Box 23/6(a).
4 Menzies' address to the Canberra Conference, 16 October 1944, cited in Starr, *The Liberal Party of Australia*, p. 95.
5 Ian Hancock gives a full account of the formation of the Liberal Party in chapters 1 and 2 of *National and Permanent? The Federal Organisation of the Liberal Party of Australia, 1944–1965*.
6 May, *The Battle for the Banks*, chs 3 and 8.
7 Eather, 'The Liberal Party of Australia and the Australian Women's Movement Against Socialisation 1947–1954', and '"Everywoman! This is your business": The Australian Women's Movement Against Socialisation'.
8 Menzies, *Afternoon Light: Some Memories of Men and Events*, p. 290.
9 *Sydney Morning Herald*, 8 December 1949, cited in Martin, *Robert Menzies: A Life*, vol. 2, p. 122.
10 Hancock, *National and Permanent?*, p. 107.
11 Alexandra Hasluck, *Portrait in a Mirror: An Autobiography*, p. 213.
12 Paul Hasluck, *Mucking About: An Autobiography*, p. 334.
13 Alexandra Hasluck, *Portrait in a Mirror*, p. 214.
14 Hancock, *National and Permanent*, p. 106.
15 ibid., p. 117.
16 John Murphy, *Imagining the Fifties: Private Settlement and Political Culture in Menzies' Australia*, ch. 8.
17 Hancock, *National and Permanent*, pp. 3, 156–9.
18 Davison, 'The past and future of the Australian suburb', in Louise Johnson (ed.), *Suburban Dreaming: An Interdisciplinary Approach to Australian Cities*, p. 100.
19 Davison, *Marvellous Melbourne*, p. 180.
20 Beverly Kingston, *Oxford History of Australia*, 1860–1900, p. 43.
21 Davison, *Marvellous Melbourne*, pp. 175–6.
22 Cited in ibid., p. 175.
23 Kingston, *Oxford History*, p. 313.
24 John Murphy, *Imagining the Fifties*, ch. 10.

25 Kemeny, *The Great Australian Nightmare: A Critique of the Home Ownership Ideology*, pp. 8–9. Figures based on calculations from the National Census.
26 John Murphy, *Imagining the Fifties*, p. 145.
27 Davison et al. (eds), Introduction, *The Cream Brick Frontier: Histories of Australian Suburbia*, p. 12.
28 John Murphy, *Imagining the Fifties*, p. 21.
29 See Kemeny, *The Great Australian Nightmare*.
30 Green, *From Orchard to Brick Veneer: Malcolm Street Blackburn and Environs, 1955–1985*.
31 John Murphy, *Imagining the Fifties*, p. 24.
32 Interview with Una Taylor, Nunawading, 1991.
33 Davison et al. (eds), *The Cream Brick Frontier*, p. 11.
34 Graeme and Barbara Davison, 'Suburban Pioneers', in Davison et al. (eds), *The Cream Brick Frontier*. For their description of the Pioneer Legend they draw on Hirst's 'The Pioneer Legend'.
35 See, for example, Connell & Irving, *Class Structure in Australian History*, pp. 299–300.
36 Brown, *Governing Prosperity: Social Change and Social Analysis in Australia in the 1950s*, p. 2.
37 Horne, *The Lucky Country: Australia in the Sixties*, pp. 179–80.
38 The classic account is Robert Murray, *The Split: Australian Labor in the Fifties*. See also Duncan, *Crusade or Conspiracy? Catholics and the Anticommunist Struggle in Australia*.
39 Murray, *The Split*, pp. 83–5.
40 The text of Evatt's press statement is in Murray, *The Split*, pp. 179–81.
41 Alford, *Party and Society: The Anglo-American Democracies*, pp. 191–2.
42 Warhurst, 'Catholics, Communism and the Australian party system: A study of the Menzies years', p. 240.
43 Hilliard, 'The religious crisis of the 1960s: the experience of the Australian churches', p. 216.
44 Breward, *A History of the Australian Churches*, pp. 160–87.
45 Hilliard, 'Church, family and sexuality in Australia in the 1950s', pp. 135–6.
46 McCalman, *Journeyings: The Biography of a Middle-Class Generation*, pp. 236–8.
47 Hilliard, 'Religious crisis', p. 220.
48 ibid., p. 221.
49 ibid., p. 223.
50 Bean, 'The forgotten cleavage? Religion and politics in Australia', pp. 551–69.
51 Henderson, *Menzies' Child: The Liberal Party of Australia, 1944–1994*, p. 107.
52 Marion Maddox, *For God and Country: Religious Dynamics in Australian Federal Politics*.
53 Putnam, *Bowling Alone: The Collapse and Revival of American Community*, p. 17.
54 Program of Nunawading YWCA Girl Citizens' Community Gathering, in author's possession.
55 Commonwealth of Australia, Senate Legal and Constitutional References Committee, Discussion Paper on a System of National Citizenship Indicators, May 1995, p. 64.
56 'Hire purchase', *Current Affairs Bulletin*, 11 May 1959, 24, p. 3; Runce, *The Economics of Instalment Credit*, p. 5 for the 1967 statistic.

57 'Hire Purchase', *Current Affairs Bulletin*, pp. 4–5.
58 I am very grateful to Humphrey McQueen for suggesting this source and lending me his file on hire purchase.
59 *The Commonwealth Jeweller and Watchmaker*, 10 October 1953, p. 98.
60 ibid., 19 August 1953, pp. 38–9.
61 Low, *The Philosophy of Hire Purchase*. Low was Chairman of the Victorian Division of the Australian Hire Purchase Confederation, which formed in 1958 as an advocacy body.
62 Sir Arthur Warner, Foreword to Maskell, *The Hire Purchase and Instalment Habit: Trends in Australia, New Zealand, Great Britain and the United States of America*.
63 Low, *The Philosophy of Hire Purchase*, pp. 40, 43.
64 Quoted in Editorial, *The Chartered Accountant of Australia*, September 1959, p. 134.
65 J. B. Were & Son, 'Hire-purchase – an equity investment', August 1958 (pamphlet, SLV)
66 Bolton, *Oxford History of Australia*, vol. 5, pp. 90–1.
67 Horne, *Time of Hope: Australia 1966–72*, p. 96.
68 Brown, *Governing Prosperity*, Introduction.
69 Roy Maskell, *The Hire Purchase and Instalment Habits*, p. ix.
70 Cited in Brown, *Governing Prosperity*, p. 11.
71 Encel, *Equality and Authority*, pp. 68–70, 288.
72 Kemp, *Society and Electoral Behaviour in Australia: A Study of Three Decades*, p. 47.
73 ibid., p. 313.
74 Horne, *The Lucky Country*, pp. 228–9.
75 Horne, *Time of Hope*, pp. 1–120; Ian Hancock, 'Liberal Governments 1966–72', p. 212.
76 Horne, *Time of Hope*, ch. 3; Ian Hancock, *Gorton*, pp. 223–4, 294–7; Bolton, *Oxford History*, pp. 168–73.
77 Horne, *Time of Hope*, p. 15.
78 ibid., p. 7; Ian Hancock, 'Liberal Governments', pp. 211–12.
79 Horne, *The Lucky Country*, p. 229.
80 Fergus McPherson & Richard Whitington, 'The Australia Party's Campaign' in Mayer (ed.), *Labor to Power: Australia's 1972 Election*.
81 Kemp, *Society and Electoral Behaviour*, pp. 343–4.
82 All quotations in this paragraph are from Freudenberg, *A Certain Grandeur*, pp. 64–6.
83 Horne, *Time of Hope*, pp. 97–8.
84 Malcolm Mackerras, 'The swing' in Mayer (ed.), *Labor to Power*, p. 234.

7 Fraser

1 Kemp, 'A leader and a philosophy' in Mayer (ed.) *Labor to Power*, pp. 51–2.
2 Fraser, 'National Objectives – Social, Economic and Political Goals', p. 24.
3 ibid., p. 25.
4 ibid., p. 27.
5 John Edwards, *Life Wasn't Meant to be Easy: A Political Profile of Malcolm Fraser*, p. 32.

6 Ayres, *Malcolm Fraser: A Biography*, pp. 67–8; CPD H of R, vol. 9, 22 February 1956, pp. 149–52.
7 These precepts are either direct quotations or paraphrases from the ANZAAS speech. 'Life wasn't meant to be easy' is from 'Towards 2000: Challenge to Australia', Fifth Alfred Deakin Lecture, 20 July 1971, p. 2.
8 Handbill, 1975 election material, ML.
9 Fraser in a lunchtime conversation with Robert Manne at La Trobe University, September 2000.
10 Interview with Robin Hughes, in *Malcolm Fraser*, video recording, Film Australia, 1994.
11 Kelly, *The Unmaking of Gough*, pp. 368–9.
12 Mackerras, 'Uniform Swing: Analysis of the 1975 Election', p. 41.
13 Walsh, *Poor Little Rich Country: The Path to the Eighties*, p. 203.
14 Reprinted in Australian Political Science Association, *Australian Politics: A New Ball Game*, p. 2. See also Fahey, *The Balls of Bob Menzies: Australian Political Songs, 1900–1980*, 'Malcolm Fraser, Grazier', p. 282, and 'Once a jolly grazier squatted down in Canberra, Under the shade of the local GG'. The source given for this is the *Macquarie University Radical Songster*, Sydney, 1985.
15 McQueen, 'None dare call it conspiracy', in *Australian Politics: A New Ball Game*, pp. 23–7; reprinted in McQueen, *Gallipoli to Petrov: Arguing with Australian History*, pp. 246–52.
16 Horne, *Death of the Lucky Country*, pp. 75–6.
17 Moorhouse, *Days of Wine and Rage*, p. 101.
18 See Graham Little, 'Whitlam and Whitlamism' in Fabian Papers, *The Whitlam Phenomenon*, pp. 68–71. In a very perceptive essay on the interactions between political and cultural reform Little argues that Whitlamism was a combination of Whitlam's rational, Fabian program of political reform with the expansive cultural radicalism of the time which recognised itself in the insouciance and daring of Whitlam's political style. Fraser drew cultural energy from those who saw the risks in Whitlamism's disregard for the restraints of scarcity and convention.
19 Speech delivered in Brisbane for Citizens for Democracy, 4 March 1977, published in Geoffrey Dutton (ed.), *Republican Australia*, Sun Books, Melbourne, 1972, p. 198.
20 Marr, *Patrick White: A Life*, p. 547.
21 Cited in Brett, *Robert Menzies' Forgotten People*, p. 10.
22 Marr, *Patrick White*, p. 578.
23 The proceedings of this meeting and the aims of Citizens for Democracy are published in Gollan (ed.), *Kerr and the Consequences: The Sydney Town Hall Meeting 20 September 1976*.
24 ibid., p. 33.
25 Inglis, *This is the ABC: The Australian Broadcasting Commission 1932–1983*, pp. 397–9.
26 Walsh, *Poor Little Rich Country*, p. 118.
27 Alan Patience, 'Immigration', pp. 412–15.
28 McKernan, *Beryl Beaurepaire*, chs 5 and 6.
29 Ayres, *Malcolm Fraser*, pp. 353, 430.
30 Ian Hancock, *John Gorton: He Did It His Way*, p. 376.
31 CPD H of R, vol. 104, 27 March 1977, pp. 555–8.

32 See Warhurst (ed.), *Keeping the Bastards Honest: The Australian Democrats First Twenty Years*, chs 2, 3, 4.
33 Bean, ch. 5 in Warhurst (ed.), *Keeping the Bastards Honest*, pp. 77–81.
34 See Windshuttle, *Unemployment*, chs 8 and 9.
35 Figures on inflation and unemployment are taken from Kevin Davis, 'Managing the economy', pp. 72 and 109.
36 CPD H of R, vol. 126, 9 March 1982, p. 713.
37 See table 3 in Kevin Davis, 'Managing the economy', p. 77.
38 Ayres, *Malcolm Fraser*, pp. 428–32.
39 Bob Ellis, *The Things We Did Last Summer: An Election Journal*, p. 115.
40 See the exchanges reprinted in ibid., ch. 11.
41 ibid., pp. 177–9.
42 Kelly, *The End of Certainty*, ch. 2.
43 Kemp, 'Liberalism and conservatism in Australia', in Head & Walter, *Intellectual Movements and Australian Society*, pp. 340–55.
44 Kelly, *The End of Certainty*, pp. 77–8.
45 Fraser, 'National Objective', p. 28.
46 See Graham Little on Malcolm Fraser in *Strong Leaders: Thatcher, Reagan and an Eminent Person*.

8 Neo-liberalism

1 For example Kelly, *The End of Certainty*, Gordon, *A True Believer: Paul Keating*.
2 Mackay, *Reinventing Australia: The Mind and Mood of Australia in the 90s*; Emy, *Remaking Australia: The State, the Market and Australia's Future*; Carroll & Manne (eds), *Shutdown: The Failure of Economic Rationalism and How to Rescue Australia*; Pusey, *Economic Rationalism in Canberra: A Nation Building State Changes Its Mind*; Kelly, *The End of Certainty*.
3 Jaensch, *The Hawke–Keating Hi-jack: The ALP in Transition*; Beilharz, *Transforming Labour: Labour Traditions and the Labor Decade*; Maddox, *The Hawke Government and Labor Tradition*; Andrew Scott, *Running on Empty: The Modern British and Australian Labor Parties*.
4 Whitwell, 'Economic ideas and economic policy: The rise of economic rationalism in Australia', pp. 8–23.
5 Kelly, *End of Certainty*, p. 86.
6 Walsh, *Poor Little Rich Country: The Path to the Eighties*, pp. 40–1; Kelly, *The End of Certainty*, pp. 211–14.
7 There are many articles which rehearse the causes of Australia's trade problem: for example, Ravenhill, 'Australia and the global economy'; Schedvin, 'The Australian economy on the hinge of history'. In 1995–96 Australia's share of world merchandise trade was only 1.1 per cent (Department of Foreign Affairs and Trade, Composition of Trade 1995–6, p. 2).
8 Emy, *Remaking Australia*, ch. 3.
9 Galligan & Capling, *Beyond the Protective State: The Political Economy of Australian Manufacturing Policy*, pp. 156–8.
10 Hood, 'Contemporary public management: a new global paradigm'.
11 Osborne & Gaebler, *Reinventing Government: How the Entrepreneurial Spirit is Transforming the Public Sector*.
12 Considine, 'Market bureaucracy', pp. 76–92.

13 See Carroll & Manne (eds), *Shutdown*, for this sort of reasoning.
14 John Hewson, 1990 Menzies Lecture, in Gregory (ed.), *The Menzies Lectures: 1978–1998*, p. 218.
15 Deborah Brennan, 'Reinventing government: circumventing life' in Farrer & Inglis, *Keeping it Together: State and Civil Society in Australia*, pp. 10–11.
16 W. K. Hancock, *Australia*, p. 143.
17 Yeatman, 'Contract, status and personhood', in Davis et al., *The New Contractualism?*.
18 Kelly, *The End of Certainty*, pp. 250–1.
19 Kemp, 'Liberalism and conservatism', pp. 344–55.
20 For an analysis of the Liberal Party of the 1980s in terms of these two factions see O'Brien, *The Liberals: Factions, Feuds and Fancies*.
21 Henderson, *Menzies' Child*, p. 304.
22 Liberal Party Campaign launch, Wesley Centre, Sydney, 1 March 1993; *Australian*, 2 March 1993.
23 See Brett, 'Representing the unrepresented: One Nation and the formation of the Labor Party', p. 29. These figures are based on a table compiled by Catherine Jones during her PhD research at La Trobe University.
24 Painter, 'Economic policy, market liberalism and the "end of Australian politics"'.
25 Manne, 'How the Liberal Party lost middle Australia'.
26 Ian Ward, 'The changing organisational nature of Australia's political parties', pp. 156–7.
27 Kate Legge, 'Whatever happened to people power?', *Weekend Australian*, 30 April–1 May 1994.
28 See David Kemp, 'Defeated by fear, smear and cynicism', *Australian*, 19 March 1993, p. 11.
29 Henderson, *Menzies' Child*, pp. 303–6.
30 Hyde, 'Liberals must have a heart', *Australian*, 16 March 1993, p. 9.
31 Hewson, 1990 Menzies Lecture in Gregory (ed.), *Menzies' Lectures*, p. 211.
32 As quoted in Robyn Dixon, 'In hindsight, Libs can find a future', *Age*, 3 April 1993, p. 17.

9 John Howard, Race and Nation

1 Bean et al. (eds) *The Politics of Retribution: The 1996 Federal Election*, pp. 3–4.
2 The Redfern Park Speech, 10 December 1992, Sydney, reprinted in Ryan (ed.), *Advancing Australia: The Speeches of Paul Keating*, p. 227.
3 See, for example, excerpts from transcripts in Gordon, *A True Believer: Paul Keating*, pp. 254, 264.
4 For example, the brilliant portrayal of him by Max Gillies as Barry Humphries' Sandy Stone in Rundle & Gillies, *Your Dreaming: Poets, Pontificators and Expatriates*.
5 *Future Directions: It's a Time for Plain Thinking*, Liberal and National Parties, December 1988; for more extended discussion, see Brett, 'Future Directions: New Conservatism's manifesto' and Kelly, *The End of Certainty*, pp. 428–33.
6 *Future Directions*, p. 89.
7 *Sydney Morning Herald*, 5 December 1988.
8 *Future Directions*, p. 89.
9 Kelly, *The End of Certainty*, pp. 420–8.
10 Greg Sheridan, 'Howard's Big Regret', *Weekend Australian*, 7–8 January 1995.

11 'The Liberal Tradition: The Beliefs and Values which guide the Federal Government', 1996 Sir Robert Menzies Lecture, 18 November 1996 in Gregory (ed.), *The Menzies Lectures*, p. 322.
12 Cited in Henderson, *A Howard Government? Inside the Coalition*, p. 29.
13 Andrew Robb, 'The Liberal Party campaign', p. 37. See also John Howard's address to the Queensland Division of the Liberal Party State Council, 22 September 1996, p. 4.
14 Robb, 'The Liberal Party campaign', pp. 36–7.
15 Barry Jones, 'Notes on the Labor defeat', in Jungwirth (ed.), *Labor Essays*, p. 5.
16 Robb, 'The Liberal Party campaign', p. 41.
17 John Howard, 'The Australia I believe in: The values, directions and policy priorities of a coalition government', Liberal Party of Australia, Canberra, 1995.
18 Marilyn Lake, 'Howard's Battle Cry', *Age*, 29 October 1996.
19 This argument is developed in greater detail in Brett, 'Pauline Hanson, John Howard and the politics of grievance'.
20 <www.liberal.org.au/reports/mainstream/>
21 The two-candidate preferred swing was 19 per cent. Based on the Australian Electoral Commission results for the federal division of Oxley.
22 CPD H of R, vol. 208, 10 September 1996, pp. 3860–3.
23 Simms & Warhurst (eds), *Howard's Agenda: The 1998 Election*, p. 8.
24 Bean, 'Nationwide electoral support for One Nation in the 1998 federal election', in Leach et al., *The Rise and Fall of One Nation*, p. 136.
25 John Howard, Address to the Queensland Division of the Liberal Party State Council, 22 September 1996. See also, Shaun Carney, 'Howard's failure to speak his mind', *Age*, 9 November 1996.
26 Reply to Question without notice, 8 October 1996, CPD H of R, vol. 208, 1996, pp. 4857–9. An edited version of this reply was published in the *Australian*, 9 October 1996, under the heading 'Tolerance part of policy'.
27 CPD H of R, vol. 209, 30 October 1996, p. 6159.
28 See, for example, Address at the launch of the National Multicultural Advisory Council Report, 'Australian Multiculturalism for a new century: Towards inclusiveness', Mural Hall, Parliament House, 5 May 1999.
29 Jupp, *From White Australia to Woomera, The Story of Australian Immigration*, ch. 5.
30 Henderson, *A Howard Government?*, p. 27.
31 John Howard, Address to Australia Day Council's Australia Day Luncheon, Darling Harbour, Sydney, 24 January 1997. See also, 'The role of government: A modern Liberal approach', The Menzies Research Centre – 1995 National Lecture Series, 6 June 1995, for a less developed formulation of the same position.
32 Frank Brennan, *The Wik Debate: Its Impact on Aborigines, Pastoralists and Miners*, University of New South Wales Press, Sydney, 1998.
33 Human Rights and Equal Opportunity Commission, *Bringing Them Home: National Inquiry into the Separation of Aboriginal and Torres Strait Islander Children from Their Families*, Commonwealth of Australia, 1997.
34 John Howard, Speech to Reconciliation Convention, 27 May 1997.
35 Markus, *Race: John Howard and the Remaking of Australia*.
36 Liberal Party of Australia, *Future Directions*, p. 96.
37 John Howard, 'Treaty is a recipe for separatism', in Baker (ed.), *A Treaty with the Aborigines*, pp. 6–7.
38 See, for example, Howard's Address to Corroboree 2000 'Towards reconciliation', 27 May 2000.

39 Reynolds, *The Other Side of the Frontier: Aboriginal Resistance to the European Invasion of Australia*.
40 John Howard, Thomas Playford Lecture, Adelaide Town Hall, 5 July 1996; see also the 1996 Sir Robert Menzies Lecture, 'The Liberal Tradition', in Gregory (ed.), *The Menzies Lectures*.
41 Speech to Reconciliation Convention, 27 May 1997.
42 Doorstop interview, Torres Strait Islands Media Association, Thursday Island, 9 July 1997.
43 Editorial, 'Australia's racist past', *Sydney Morning Herald*, 26 November 1996.
44 Russell Ward, *The Australian Legend*. See Michael Roe's excellent discussion of Ward's thesis and the responses to it in Davey & Seal, *The Oxford Companion to Australian Folk Lore*, pp. 34–41.
45 John Hirst, 'The pioneer legend'.
46 Graeme Turner, *Making it National: Nationalism and Australian Popular Culture*, ch. 1.
47 Address to Federation of Ethnic Communities Council National Conference, Brisbane, 20 November 1998.
48 Keynote Address to Australian Council of Social Services National Congress, Adelaide, 5 November 1998.
49 'The Australia I Know' in Constitutional Essays on website of Australians for a Constitutional Monarchy, 11 November 2002, <www.morepublic.com.au>.
50 New Year's Message, 31 December 1999.
51 Fifth Annual Sir Edward 'Weary' Dunlop Asialink Lecture, Melbourne, 11 November 1997.
52 Speech to the Dawn Service, Gallipoli, Turkey, 25 April 2000.
53 Address at the State Funeral of Alec William Campbell, the Cathedral Church of St David, Hobart, 24 May 2002.
54 Workers Online, 137, 24 May 2002 <www.workers.net.au>.
55 John Howard, 'Peerless Bradman an inspiration across time', *Age*, 27 February 2001; see also Sir Donald Bradman Oration, Melbourne, 17 August 2000.
56 'We believe', in Starr, *The Liberal Party of Australia*, p. 198.
57 Volunteer Awards ceremony, Cronulla Leagues Club, Sydney, 14 August 2001.
58 La Nauze, *Walter Murdoch: A Biographical Memoir*, p. 97.
59 Howard's comments, made on 18 May 1997, are cited in Gerard Henderson, 'The Liberals have lost the ABC war', *Age*, 4 June 2002.
60 Inglis, *This is the ABC, The Australian Broadcasting Commission 1932–1983*, ch. 8.
61 Robert Manne, 'The ABC of IPA bias', *Age*, 16 April 2001, commenting on an Institute of Public Affairs seminar on the ABC.
62 Quoted in Paul Kelly, 'When Johnny comes marching home', *Weekend Australian*, 27–28 October 2001.
63 Solomon (ed.), *Howard's Race: Winning the Unwinnable Election*, ch. 7.
64 Address at Federal Liberal Party campaign launch, Sydney, 28 October 2001.
65 Solomon (ed.), *Howard's Race*, pp. 50, 67–8; Marr & Wilkinson, *Dark Victory*.
66 See McCallum's *Girt By Sea: Australia, the Refugees and the Politics of Fear*, and responses in Issue 6.
67 Philip Adams, 'The best of a bad lot', *Weekend Australian*, 16–17 November 2002.
68 See for example, Tony Wright, 'Dog Whistler', *Age*, 8 April 2000.
69 Betts, *The Great Divide: Immigration Politics in Australia*, ch. 4.

70 Bean, 'Nationwide electoral support for One Nation' p. 150.
71 Betts, *The Great Divide*, p. 320.
72 Rundle & Gillies, *Your Dreaming*, Introduction and Conclusion.
73 Gouldner, *The Future of Intellectuals and the Rise of the New Class*; Hannerz, 'Cosmopolitans and locals in world culture'.
74 Merton, *Social Theory and Social Structure*, pp. 387 ff.
75 Address to Federal Liberal Party campaign launch, 28 October 2001.

Conclusion

1 'The Liberal Party', Brookes papers, NLA MS 1924/18/51, p. 4.
2 Marsh, *Beyond the Two Party System: Political Representation, Economic Competitiveness and Australian Politics*, part II.
3 Ian Ward, 'The changing organisational nature of Australia's political parties'.

Bibliography

Many of the sources used for this book were ephemeral – speeches, leaflets and pamphlets. Sometimes these were held in particular named collections, sometimes copies were found in the manuscript collections of individuals. In such cases this information has been given in the endnotes. Sometimes a speech or pamphlet was in the library's general collection, sometimes under the name of a politician, sometimes under the name of the political party. In such cases I have given the name of the library at which I located a copy, and again the information is in the relevant endnote. The speeches of John Howard since he became Prime Minister were all accessed through the Prime Minister's home page <www.pm.gov.au>.

Books, Articles and Theses

Aimer, Peter, *Politics, Power and Persuasion: The Liberals in Victoria*, James Bennett (for the Liberal Party of Australia, Victorian Division), Melbourne, 1974.

Aitkin, Don, 'Countrymindedness – the spread of an idea' in S. L. Goldberg and F. B. Smith (eds), *Australian Cultural History*, 1988.

Aitkin, Don, *Stability and Change in Australian Politics*, Australian National University Press, Canberra [1977], 2nd edn, 1982.

Alford, Robert, *Party and Society: The Anglo-American Democracies*, Rand McNally & Co, Chicago, 1963.

Alomes, Stephen, 'Culture, ethnicity and class in Australia's dominion period, 1900–1939', in Colm Kiernan (ed.), *Australia and Ireland 1788–1988: Bicentenary Essays*.

Alomes, Stephen & Catherine Jones (eds), *Australian Nationalism: A Documentary History*, Angus & Robertson, Sydney, 1991.

Anderson, W. H., 'Liberal lead to an expanding nation', 1956 Federal Presidential Address, Liberal Party Secretariat.

Australian Political Science Association (APSA), *Australian Politics: A New Ball Game*, APSA Monograph 16, May 1976.

Aveling, Marion, A History of the Australian Natives Association: 1871–1900, PhD thesis, Monash University, 1970.

Ayres, Philip, *Malcolm Fraser: A Biography*, William Heinemann, Melbourne, 1987.

Badger, C. R., *The Reverend Charles Strong and the Australian Church*, Abacada Press (on behalf of the Charles Strong Memorial Trust) Melbourne, 1971.

Baker, K. (ed.), *A Treaty with the Aborigines*, Institute for Public Affairs, Policy Issue no. 7, 1988.

Bean, Clive, 'The forgotten cleavage? Religion and politics in Australia', *Canadian Journal of Political Science*, 32 (1999), pp. 551–69.

Bean, Clive, Marian Simms, Scott Bennett & John Warhurst (eds), *The Politics of Retribution: The 1996 Federal Election*, Allen & Unwin, Sydney, 1997.

Beaumont, Joan (ed.), *Australia's War 1914–1918*, Allen & Unwin, Sydney, 1995.

Beilharz, Peter, *Transforming Labor: Labour Traditions and the Labor Decade*, Cambridge University Press, Cambridge, 1994.

Bell, Stephen & Brian Head (eds), *State, Economy and Public Policy in Australia*, Oxford University Press, Melbourne, 1994.

Betts, Katherine, *The Great Divide: Immigration Politics in Australia*, Duffy & Snellgrove, Sydney, 1999.

Blake, Robert, *The Conservative Party from Peel to Churchill*, Eyre & Spottiswood, London, 1970.

Bollen, J. D., *Protestantism and Reform in New South Wales 1890–1910*, Melbourne University Press, Carlton, 1972.

Bolton, Geoffrey, *The Oxford History of Australia*, vol. 5, 1942–1988, Oxford University Press, Melbourne, 1990.

Bongiorno, Frank, 'The origins of Caucus 1856–1901' in John Faulkner & Stuart Macintyre (eds), *True Believers: The Story of the Federal Parliamentary Labor Party*, Allen & Unwin, Sydney, 2001.

Bongiorno, Frank, *The People's Party: Victorian Labor and the Radical Tradition 1875–1914*, Melbourne University Press, Carlton, 1996.

Bourinot, Sir George, *Bourinot's Standing Orders*, rev. edn, McLelland & Stewart Ltd, Toronto, 1963.

Brett, Judith, 'Class, religion and the foundation of the Australian party system: a revisionist interpretation', *Australian Journal of Political Science*, 37 (2002), pp. 39–56.

Brett, Judith, 'Future directions: New Conservatism's manifesto', *Current Affairs Bulletin*, 96 (June 1989), pp. 11–17.

Brett, Judith, 'Pauline Hanson, John Howard and the politics of grievance' in Gray & Winter (eds), *The Resurgence of Racism*, pp. 7–28.

Brett, Judith, 'Representing the unrepresented: One Nation and the formation of the Labor Party' in *Two Nations: The Causes and Effects of the Rise on the One Nation Party in Australia*, Bookman Press, Melbourne, 1998, pp. 26–37.

Brett, Judith, *Robert Menzies' Forgotten People*, Pan Macmillan, Sydney, 1992.

Breward, Ian, *A History of the Australian Churches*, Allen & Unwin, Sydney, 1993.

Brisbane, Katharine (ed.), *Entertaining Australia: An Illustrated History*, Currency Press, Sydney, 1991.

Broome, Richard, *Treasure in Earthen Vessels: Protestant Christianity in New South Wales Society 1900–1914*, University of Queensland Press, St Lucia, Queensland, 1980.

Brown, Nicholas, *Governing Prosperity: Social Change and Social Analysis in Australia in the 1950s*, Cambridge University Press, Cambridge, 1995.

Burchall, G., C. Gordon & P. Miller, *The Foucault Effect: Studies in Governmentality*, Harvester Wheatsheaf, London, 1991.

Burke, Edmund, 'Thoughts on the causes of the present discontents' (1770), in Robert A. Smith (ed.), *Edmund Burke on Revolution*, Harper Torchbooks, Harper & Row, New York.

Carroll, John & Robert Manne (eds), *Shutdown: The Failure of Economic Rationalism and How to Rescue Australia*, Text Publishing, Melbourne, 1992.

Cathcart, Michael, *Defending the National Tuckshop: Australia's Secret Army Intrigues of 1931*, McPhee Gribble/Penguin, Melbourne, 1988.

Childe, Vere Gordon, *How Labour Governs: A Study of Workers' Representation in Australia*, Melbourne University Press, Carlton, 1964 [1923].

Cochrane, Peter, 'How are the Egyptians behaving? Herbert Brookes, British Australian', *Australian Historical Studies*, 30 (1999), pp. 303–18.

Colley, Linda, *Britons: Forging the Nation 1707–1837*, Yale University Press, New Haven, 1992.

Collini, Stefan, *Public Moralists: Political Thought and Intellectual Life in Britain, 1850–1930*, Clarendon Press, Oxford, 1991.

Connell, R. W. & Terry Irving, *Class Structure in Australian History*, Longman Cheshire, Melbourne, 1980.

Considine, Mark, 'Market bureaucracy' in Farrer & Inglis, *Keeping it Together*.

Cook, Alex, *The State Savings Bank of Victoria: Its Place in the History of Victoria*, Macmillan, Victoria, 1934.

Cooksey, P. (ed.), *The Great Depression in Australia*, special issue of *Labour History*, 1970.

Copland, D. B., *Australia in the World Crisis, 1929–1933*, Cambridge University Press, Cambridge, 1934.

Costar, Brian (ed.), *For Better or Worse: The Federal Coalition*, Melbourne University Press, Carlton, 1994.

Craddock, Trevor & Maurice Cavanough, *125 Years: The Story of the SSB of Victoria, 1842–1966*, State Savings Bank of Victoria, Melbourne, 1967.

Cramer, Sir John, *Pioneers, Politics and People: A Political Memoir*, Allen & Unwin, Sydney, 1989.

Crisp, L. F., *The Australian Federal Labour Party 1901–51*, Hale & Iremonger, Sydney, 1978 [1955].

Crisp, L. F., *Australian National Government*, Longman Cheshire, Melbourne, 1965.

Current Affairs Bulletin, 'Hire purchase', 11 May 1959.

Davey, G. B. & G. Seal (eds), *The Oxford Companion to Australian Folklore*, Oxford University Press, Melbourne, 1993.

Davies, A. F., 'Victorian Government and politics' in G. Leeper (ed.), *Introducing Victoria*.

Davis, G., B. Sullivan and A. Yeatman (eds), *The New Contractualism?*, Macmillan, Melbourne, 1997.

Davis, Kevin, 'Managing the economy', in Allan Patience & Brian Head (eds), *From Fraser to Hawke*.

Davison, Graeme, *The Rise and Fall of Marvellous Melbourne*. Melbourne University Press, Carlton, 1978.

Davison, Graeme, Tony Dingle & Seamus O'Hanlon (eds), *The Cream Brick Frontier: Histories of Australian Suburbia*, Monash Publications in History, no. 19, Monash University, Clayton, 1995.

De Toqueville, A., *Democracy in America*, Harper & Row, New York, 1966 [1935].

Drake Brockman, C. (ed.), *Voluntary War Workers' Record*, Australian Comforts Fund, 1918.

Duncan, B., *Crusade or Conspiracy? Catholics and the Anticommunist Struggle in Australia*, University of New South Wales Press, Kensington, NSW, 2001.

Duncan, B., *Crusade or Conspiracy: Catholics and the Anti-communist Struggle in Australia*, University of New South Wales Press, Kensington NSW, 2001.

Duncan, John, *A Centenary of Thrift: A Brief History of the Launceston Bank for Savings*, Launceston, 1935.

Dunn, Margaret, *The Dauntless Bunch: The Story of the YWCA in Australia*, YWCA of Australia, Melbourne, 1991.

Dutton, Geoffrey, *Republican Australia*, Sun Books, Melbourne, 1972.

Duverger, Maurice, *Political Parties: Their Organisation and Activity in the Modern State*, 3rd edn, Methuen, London, 1964.

Eather, Warwick, '"Everywoman! This is your business": the Australian Women's Movement Against Socialisation', *Journal of Interdisciplinary Gender Studies*, 2 (1997), pp. 57–75.

Eather, Warwick, 'The Liberal Party of Australia and the Australian Women's Movement Against Socialisation 1947–1954', *Australian Journal of Politics and History*, 44 (1998), pp. 191–208.

Edwards, Cecil, *Bruce of Melbourne: Man of Two Worlds*, Heinemann, London, 1965.

Edwards, John, *Life Wasn't Meant to be Easy: A Political Profile of Malcolm Fraser*, Mayhem, Sydney, 1977.

Eggleston, F. W., *Reflections of an Australian Liberal*, Cheshire, Melbourne, 1953.

Ellis, Ulrich, *A History of the Australian Country Party*, Melbourne University Press, Carlton, 1963.

Ellis, Ulrich, *The Country Party: A Political and Social History of the Party in New South Wales*, Cheshire, Melbourne, 1958.

Ellis, Bob, *The Things We Did Last Summer: An Election Journal*, Fontana Collins, Sydney, 1983.

Emy, Hugh, *Remaking Australia: The State, the Market and Australia's Future*, Allen & Unwin, Sydney, 1993.

Emy, Hugh, Owen Hughes and Race Mathews (eds), *Whitlam Revisited: Policy Development, Policies & Outcomes*, Pluto Press, Sydney, 1993.

Encel, Sol, *Equality and Authority: A Study of Class, Status and Power in Australia*, Cheshire, Melbourne, 1970.

Fabian Papers, *The Whitlam Phenomenon*, McPhee Gribble/Penguin, Melbourne, 1986.

Fahey, Warren, *The Balls of Bob Menzies: Australian Political Songs, 1900–1980*, Angus & Robertson, Sydney, 1989.

Farrer, A. & J. Inglis, *Keeping it Together: State and Civil Society in Australia*, Pluto, Sydney, 1996.

Faulkner, C. C., *The Commonwealth Bank of Australia: A Brief History of its Establishment, Development and Service to the People of Australia and the British Empire*, Sydney, 1923.

Firth, Stewart & Jeanette Hoorn, 'From Empire Day to Cracker Night' in Peter Spearritt & David Walker, *Australian Popular Culture*, Allen & Unwin, Sydney, 1979.

Fitzhardinge, L. F., *William Morris Hughes: A Political Biography*, vol. 2, Angus & Robertson, Sydney, 1979.

Foley, Meredith, *The Women's Movement in NSW and Victoria, 1918–1938*, PhD thesis, University of Sydney, 1985.

Foucault, Michel, 'Governmentality', in G. Burchall, C. Gordon & P. Miller (eds), *The Foucault Effect*.

Fraser, Malcolm, 'National objectives – social, economic and political goals', presented to the 46th ANZAAS Congress, January 1975, reprinted in *Australian Quarterly*, 47 (March 1975), pp. 24–35.
Freudenberg, Graham, *A Certain Grandeur*, Macmillan, Melbourne, 1977.
Gabay, Al, *The Mystic Life of Alfred Deakin*, Cambridge University Press, Cambridge, 1992.
Galligan, Brian & Ann Capling, *Beyond the Protective State: The Political Economy of Australian Manufacturing Policy*, Cambridge University Press, Cambridge, 1992.
Gilbert, Alan, 'Protestants, Catholics and loyalty: an aspect of the conscription controversy, 1916–17', *Politics*, 4 (1971), pp. 15–25.
Goldberg, S. L. & F. B. Smith (eds), *Australian Cultural History*, Cambridge University Press in association with the Australian Academy of the Humanities, 1988.
Gollan, Myfanwy (ed.), *Kerr and the Consequences: The Sydney Town Hall Meeting 20 September 1976*, Widescope, Camberwell, Victoria, 1977.
Gordon, Michael, *A True Believer: Paul Keating*, University of Queensland Press, St Lucia, Brisbane, 1993.
Gouldner, Alvin, *The Future of Intellectuals and the Rise of the New Class*, Macmillan, London, 1979.
Gray, Geoffrey & Christine Winter (eds), *The Resurgence of Racism: Howard, Hanson and the Race Debate*, Monash Publications in History, no. 24, Monash University, Clayton, 1997.
Greely, Andrew, 'Protestant and Catholic: is the analogical imagination extinct?', *American Sociological Review*, 54 (1989), pp. 485–502.
Green, O. S., *From Orchard to Brick Veneer: Malcolm Street Blackburn and Environs, 1955–1985*, self published, Blackburn, 1987.
Greenwood, Gordon (ed.), *Australia: A Social and Political History*, Angus & Robertson, Sydney, 1955.
Gregory, Alan (ed.), *The Menzies Lectures: 1978–1998*, Sir Robert Menzies Lecture Trust, Melbourne, 1999.
Grenfell Price, A., *The Menace of Inflation*, 2nd edn, F. W. Preece & Sons, Adelaide, 1931 (reprinted 16 March and 28 March).
Gruen, Fred, 'What went wrong? Some personal reflections on economic policies under Labor', *Australian Quarterly*, 48 (1976) pp. 15–32.
Gunn, Heather, For the 'Man on the Land': Rural Women and the Victorian National Party 1917–1996, PhD thesis, La Trobe University, Bundoora, 1996.
Hamilton, Celia, 'Irish-Catholics of New South Wales and the Labor Party, 1890–1910', *Historical Studies*, 8 (1958), pp. 254–67.
Hancock, Ian, *John Gorton: He Did It His Way*, Hodder, Sydney, 2002.
Hancock, Ian, 'Liberal Governments 1966–72' in J. Nethercote (ed.), *Liberalism and the Australian Federation*.
Hancock, Ian, *National and Permanent? The Federal Organisation of the Liberal Party of Australia, 1944–1965*, Melbourne University Press, Carlton, 2000.
Hancock, W. K., *Australia*, Ernest Benn, London, 1930.
Hannerz, Ulf, 'Cosmopolitans and locals in world culture', *Theory, Culture and Society*, 7 (1990), pp. 237–51.
Hart, Philip, J. A. Lyons: A Political Biography, PhD thesis, Australian National University, Canberra 1967.

Hasluck, Alexandra, *Portrait in a Mirror: An Autobiography*, Oxford University Press, Melbourne, 1981.
Hasluck, Paul, *Mucking About: An Autobiography*, University of Western Australia Press, Perth, 1994 [1977].
Hazlehurst, Cameron (ed.), *Australian Conservativism: Essays in Twentieth Century Political History*, Australian National University Press, Canberra, 1979.
Head, Brian, 'Economic crisis and political legitimacy: the 1931 Federal Election', *Journal of Australia Studies*, 3 (June 1978), pp. 14–29.
Head, Brian & James Walter, *Intellectual Movements and Australian Society*, Oxford University Press, Melbourne, 1988.
Henderson, Gerard, *Menzies' Child: The Liberal Party of Australia, 1944–1994*, Allen & Unwin, Sydney, 1994.
Henderson, Gerard, *A Howard Government? Inside the Coalition*, HarperCollins, Sydney, 1995.
Hewitt, Geoff, 'The All for Australia League in Melbourne', *La Trobe Historical Studies*, no. 3, March 1972, La Trobe University, Bundoora, pp. 5–15.
Hilliard, David, 'Church, family and sexuality in Australian in the 1950s', *Australian Historical Studies*, no. 109 (1997), pp. 133–46.
Hilliard, David, 'The religious crisis of the 1960s: the experience of the Australian churches', *Journal of Religious History*, 21 (June 1997), pp. 209–27.
Himmelfarb, Gertrude, *The De-moralisation of Society: From Victorian Virtues to Modern Values*, Choice in Welfare Series, no. 22, Institute of Economic Affairs, Health and Welfare Unit, London, 1995.
Hirst, John, 'The pioneer legend', *Historical Studies*, 18 (1978), pp. 316–37.
Hogan, Michael, *The Sectarian Strand: Religion in Australian History*, Penguin, Ringwood, Vic., 1987.
Hood, C., 'Contemporary public management: a new global paradigm', *Public Policy and Administration*, 10 (1995), pp. 104–17.
Horne, Donald, *Death of the Lucky Country*, Penguin, Ringwood, Vic, 1976.
Horne, Donald, *The Lucky Country: Australia in the Sixties*, rev. edn, Angus & Robertson, Sydney, 1978 [1964].
Horne, Donald, *Time of Hope: Australia 1966–72*, Angus & Robertson, Sydney, 1980.
Hughes, Colin, *Readings in Australian Government*, University of Queensland Press, St Lucia, Brisbane, 1968.
Hughes, Colin & B. D. Graham, *Handbook of Australian Government and Politics, 1890–1964*, Australian National University Press, Canberra, 1968.
Human Rights and Equal Opportunity Commission, *Bringing Them Home: National Inquiry into the Separation of Aboriginal and Torres Strait Islander Children from Their Families*, Commonwealth of Australia, 1997.
Humphries, Barry, *More Please*, Viking, Melbourne, 1992.
Hunt, Harold, *The Story of Rotary in Australia 1921–1971*, Rotary, Melbourne, 1971.
Ingham, S. M., 'Political parties in the Victorian Legislative Assembly, 1880–1900', *Historical Studies*, 4 (1950), pp. 241–56.
Inglis, Ken, *This is the ABC: The Australian Broadcasting Commission 1932–1983*, Melbourne University Press, Carlton, 1983.
Irving, Baiba, The Nationalist Party, 1919–1930: Organisation and Ideology, PhD thesis submitted to University of Sydney, 1972. Copy in Baiba Burzon's papers, Mitchell Library.

Irving, Helen, *To Constitute a Nation: A Cultural History of Australia's Constitution*, Cambridge University Press, Cambridge, 1997.
Jaensch, Dean, *The Hawke–Keating Hi-jack: The ALP in Transition*, Allen & Unwin, Sydney, 1989.
Johnson, Carol, *Governing Change: Keating to Howard*, University of Queensland Press, St Lucia, Brisbane, 2000.
Johnson, Louise C. (ed.), *Suburban Dreaming: An Interdisciplinary Approach to Australian Cities*, Deakin University Press, Geelong, 1994.
Johnson, Paul, *Saving and Spending: The Working Class in Britain, 1870–1939*, Clarendon Press, Oxford, 1985.
Jungwirth, Gary (ed.), *Labor Essays*, Pluto Press, Sydney, 1997.
Jupp, James, *From White Australia to Woomera: The Story of Australian Immigration*, Cambridge University Press, Cambridge, 2002.
Kelly, Paul, *The Unmaking of Gough*, 1976 [rev. edn Allen & Unwin, Sydney, 1994].
Kelly, Paul, *The End of Certainty: Power Politics and Business in Australia*, Allen & Unwin, Sydney, 1992 [2nd edn 1994].
Kemeny, Jim, *The Great Australian Nightmare: A Critique of the Home Ownership Ideology*, Georgian House, Melbourne, 1983.
Kemp, David, *Foundations for Australian Political Analysis: Politics and Authority*, Oxford University Press, Melbourne, 1988.
Kemp, David, 'A leader and a philosophy', in Henry Mayer (ed.), *Labor to Power*.
Kemp, David, 'Liberalism and conservatism in Australia' in Brian Head & James Walter (eds), *Intellectual Movements and Australian Society*.
Kemp, David, 'Political parties and Australian culture', *Quadrant*, 21 (December 1977), pp. 3–13.
Kemp, David, *Society and Electoral Behaviour in Australia: A Study of Three Decades*, University of Queensland Press, St Lucia, Brisbane, 1978.
Kiernan, Colm, 'Home rule for Ireland and the formation of the Australian Labor Party 1883–91', *Australian Journal of Politics and History*, 38 (1992), pp. 1–11.
Kiernan, Colm (ed.), *Australia and Ireland 1788–1988: Bicentenary Essays*, Gill & Macmillan, Dublin, 1986.
Kingston, Beverley, *The Oxford History of Australia*, vol. 3, 1860–1900, Oxford University Press, Melbourne, 1988.
Kymlicka, Will & Wayne Norman, 'Return of the citizen: a survey of recent work on citizenship theory', *Ethics*, 104 (1994), pp. 352–81.
La Nauze, J. A., *Alfred Deakin: A Biography*, vols 1 and 2, Melbourne University Press, Carlton, 1965.
La Nauze, John, *Walter Murdoch: A Biographical Memoir*, Melbourne University Press, Carlton, 1977.
Lake, Marilyn, *Getting Equal: The History of Australian Feminism*, Allen & Unwin, Sydney, 1999.
Lake, Marilyn, 'The republic, the federation and the intrusion of the political', *Vox Republicae*, special issue of *Journal of Australian Studies*, 47 (1996), pp. 5–15.
Leach, Michael, Geoffrey Stokes & Ian Ward, *The Rise and Fall of One Nation*, University of Queensland Press, St Lucia, Brisbane, 2000.
Lee, Andrew, Nothing to Offer but Fear? Non-Labor Federal Election Electioneering in Australiana 1914–1954, PhD thesis, Australian National University, Canberra, 1997.

Leeper, G. W. (ed), *Introducing Victoria*, Melbourne University Press, Carlton, 1955.
Little, Graham, *Strong Leaders: Thatcher, Reagan and an Eminent Person*, Oxford University Press, Melbourne, 1988.
Little, Graham, 'Whitlam and Whitlamism' in Fabian Papers, *The Whitlam Phenomenon*, pp. 68–71.
Lloyd, Clem, The formation and development of the United Australia Party: 1929–1937, PhD thesis, Australian National University, Canberra, 1984.
Lloyd, Clem, 'The rise and fall of the United Australia Party', in J. R. Nethercote (ed.), *Liberalism and the Australian Federation*.
Loveday, Peter, 'Antipolitical political thought', in P. Cooksey (ed.), *The Great Depression and Australia*.
Loveday, P., A. W. Martin & R. S. Parker (eds), *The Emergence of the Australian Party System*, Hale & Iremonger, Sydney, 1977.
Low, Vernon Stanley, *The Philosophy of Hire Purchase*, Modern Printing Co., Melbourne, (1961?).
Lyons, Enid, *So We Take Comfort*, Heinemann, London, 1963.
Lyons, Mark, Aspects of Sectarianism in NSW, PhD thesis, Australian National University, Canberra, 1972.
McCallum, Mungo, *Girt by Sea: Australia, the Refugees and the Politics of Fear*, Quarterly Essay, Issue 5, Black Ink Press, Melbourne, 2000.
McCalman, Janet, *Journeyings: The Biography of a Middle-Class Generation, 1920–1990*, Melbourne University Press, Carlton, 1993.
McConville, Chris, *Croppies, Celts and Catholics: The Irish in Australia*, Edward Arnold, Melbourne, 1987.
MacDonagh, Oliver, 'Emigration from Ireland to Australia: an overview' in Colm Kiernan (ed.), *Australia and Ireland 1788–1988: Bicentenary Essays*.
MacDonagh, Oliver, 'The Irish in Victoria 1851–91: a demographic essay', in T. D. Williams (ed.), *Historical Studies*, papers read before the Irish Conference of Historians VIII, Gill & Macmillan, Dublin, 1971.
Macintyre, Clem, *Political Australia: A Handbook of Facts*, Oxford University Press, Melbourne, 1991.
Macintyre, Stuart, *Colonial Liberalism: The Lost World of Three Victorian Visionaries*, Oxford University Press, Melbourne, 1991.
Macintyre, Stuart, *Oxford History of Australia*, vol. 4, 1901–1942, Oxford University Press, Melbourne, 1986.
McIntyre, A. J. & J. J. McIntyre, *Country Towns of Victoria: A Social Survey*, Melbourne University Press, Carlton, 1944.
Mackay, Hugh, *Reinventing Australia: The Mind and Mood of Australia in the 90s*, Angus & Robertson, Sydney, 1993.
McKernan, Michael, *Australian Churches at War: Attitudes and Activities of the Major Churches 1914–1918*, Catholic Theological Faculty and Australian War Memorial, Sydney and Canberra, 1980.
McKernan, Michael, *The Australian People and the Great War*, Nelson, Melbourne, 1980.
McKernan, Michael, *Beryl Beaurepaire*, University of Queensland Press, St Lucia, Brisbane, 1999.
Mackerras, Malcolm, 'Uniform swing: analysis of the 1975 election', in Australian Political Science Association, *Australian Politics, A New Ball Game*.

McKibbin, Ross, *Classes and Cultures in England, 1918–1951*, Oxford University Press, Oxford, 1998.
McKibbin, Ross, *The Ideologies of Class: Social Relations in Britain 1880–1950*, Clarendon Press, Oxford, 1990.
McMullin, Ross, *The Light on the Hill: The Australian Labor Party, 1891–1991*, Oxford University Press, Melbourne, 1991.
McQueen, Humphrey, *Gallipoli to Petrov: Arguing with Australian History*, Allen & Unwin, Sydney, 1984.
Maddox, Graham, *The Hawke Government and Labor Tradition*, Penguin, Ringwood, Victoria, 1989.
Maddox, Marion, *For God and Country: Religious Dynamics in Australian Federal Politics*, Department of the Parliamentary Library, Commonwealth of Australia, 2001.
Manne, Robert, 'How the Liberal Party lost Middle Australia' in Costar (ed.), *For Better or Worse*.
Markus, Andrew, *Race: John Howard and the Remaking of Australia*, Allen & Unwin, Sydney, 2001.
Marr, David, *The High Price of Heaven*, Allen & Unwin, Sydney, 1999.
Marr, David, *Patrick White: A Life*, Random House, Sydney, 1991.
Marsh, Ian, *Beyond the Two Party System: Political Representation, Economic Competitiveness and Australian Politics*, Cambridge University Press, Cambridge, 1995.
Martin, Alan, *Robert Menzies: A Life*, vols I and II, Melbourne University Press, Carlton, 1993 and 1999.
Maskell, Roy E., *The Hire Purchase and Instalment Habit: Trends in Australia, New Zealand, Great Britain and the United States of America*, Law Book Company, Sydney, 1964.
Matthews, Trevor, 'The All for Australia League' in Cooksey (ed.), *The Great Depression*.
May, A. L., *The Battle for the Banks*, Sydney University Press, Sydney, 1968.
Mayer, Henry (ed.), *Catholics and the Free Society*, Cheshire, Melbourne, 1961.
Mayer, Henry, *Labor to Power: Australia's 1972 Election*, Angus & Robertson, Sydney, 1973.
Mayer, Henry, 'Parties of initiative and resistance', in H. Mayer (ed.), *Australian Politics: A Reader*, F. W. Cheshire, Melbourne, 1966.
Menzies, Robert, *Afternoon Light: Some Memories of Men and Events*, Cassell, Melbourne, 1967.
Menzies, Robert, *The Forgotten People and Other Studies in Democracy*, Angus & Robertson, Sydney, 1943.
Merton, Robert, *Social Theory and Social Structure*, Glencoe Free Press, Glencoe, Illinois, 1957.
Moore, Andrew, *The Right Road? A History of Right Wing Politics in Australia*, Oxford University Press, Melbourne, 1995.
Moorhouse, Frank, *Days of Wine and Rage*, Penguin, Ringwood, Victoria, 1980.
Morris, R. J., 'Clubs, societies and associations' in F. M. L. Thompson (ed.), *The Cambridge Social History of Britain, 1750–1950*, vol. 3.
'M.P.', *The Young Man's Parliamentary Guide*, pocket edn, Macmillan Canada, 1919.
Murdoch, Walter, *The Australian Citizen: An Elementary Account of Civic Rights and Duties*, Whitcombe & Tombs, Melbourne, 1912.

Murdoch, Walter, *Collected Essays*, Angus & Robertson, Sydney, 1938.
Murphy, D. J. 'Religion, race and conscription in World War I', *Australian Journal of Politics and History*, 20 (1974), pp. 155–63.
Murphy, John, *Imagining the Fifties: Private Sentiment and Political Culture in Menzies' Australia*, University of New South Wales Press, Sydney, 2000.
Murray, Robert, *The Split: Australian Labor in the Fifties*, Cheshire, Melbourne, 1984.
Murray, R. & K. White, *A Bank for the People: A History of the State Savings Bank of Victoria*, Horgreen Publishing Co., Melbourne, 1992.
Needham, Lilias, *Charles Hawker: Soldier – Pastoralist – Statesman*, Griffin Press, Adelaide, 1969.
Nethercote, J. R. (ed.), *Liberalism and the Australian Federation*, Federation Press, Annandale, NSW, 2001.
Norton, Philip (ed.), *The Conservative Party*, Prentice Hall/Harvester Wheatsheaf, London, 1996.
O'Brien, Connor Cruise, *Parnell and His Party, 1880–90*, Oxford University Press, Oxford, 1957.
O'Brien, Patrick, *The Liberals, Faction, Feuds & Fancies*, Penguin, Ringwood, Victoria, 1985.
O'Farrell, Patrick, *The Catholic Church and Community in Australia*, Nelson, Melbourne, 1977.
O'Farrell, Patrick, *The Catholic Church in Australia: A Short History, 1788–1967*, Nelson, Melbourne, 1968.
O'Farrell, Patrick, 'The history of the New South Wales labour movement, 1880–1910: a religious interpretation', *Journal of Religious History*, 2 (1962), pp. 133–51.
O'Farrell, Patrick, *The Irish in Australia*, University of New South Wales Press, Sydney, 1987.
Osborne, D. & T. Gaebler, *Reinventing Government: How the Entrepreneurial Spirit is Transforming the Public Sector*, Plume, New York, 1993.
Ostrogorski, M., *Democracy and the Organisation of Political Parties*, 2 vols, Macmillan, London, 1902.
Painter, Martin, 'Economic policy, market liberalism and the "End of Australian Politics"', *Australian Journal of Political Science*, 31 (1996), pp. 287–99.
Patience, Alan, 'Immigration', in Patience & Head (eds), *From Fraser to Hawke*.
Patience, Alan & Brian Head (eds), *From Fraser to Hawke*, Longman Cheshire, Melbourne, 1989.
Pearce, George, *Carpenter to Cabinet*, Hutchinson, Melbourne, 1951.
Potts, David, A study of three nationalists in the Bruce–Page government of 1923–1929, MA thesis, University of Melbourne, Parkville, 1972.
Puplick, Christopher, *Is the Party Over? The Future of the Liberals*, Text, Melbourne, 1994.
Puregger, Marjorie, *Mr Chairman: A Guide to Meeting Procedure, Ceremonial Procedure and Forms of Address*, 5th edn, University of Queensland Press, St Lucia, Brisbane, 1986 [1962].
Pusey, Michael, *Economic Rationalism in Canberra: A Nation Building State Changes its Mind*, Cambridge University Press, Cambridge, 1995.
Putnam, Robert, *Bowling Alone: The Collapse and Revival of American Community*, Simon & Schuster, New York, 2000.
Radi, Heather & Peter Spearritt, *Jack Lang*, Hale & Iremonger, Sydney, 1977.

Ravenhill, John, 'Australia and the global economy' in Bell & Head (eds), *State, Economy and Public Policy*.
Reynolds, Henry, *The Other Side of the Frontier: Aboriginal Resistance to the European Invasion of Australia*, History Department, James Cook University, Townsville, 1981.
Richmond, Keith R., 'Reaction to radicalism: non-labour movements 1920–1929', *Journal of Australian Studies*, 5 (1979), pp. 50–63.
Rickard, John, *Class and Politics: New South Wales, Victoria and the Early Commonwealth 1890–1910*, Australian National University Press, Canberra, 1976.
Rickard, John, *A Family Romance: The Deakins at Home*, Melbourne University Press, Carlton, 1996.
Rickard, John, 'The middle class: what is to be done?', *Historical Studies*, 19 (1981), pp. 446–53.
Rivett, Rohan, *Australian Citizen: Herbert Brookes, 1867–1963*, Melbourne University Press, Carlton, 1965.
Robb, Andrew, 'The Liberal Campaign' in Bean et al., *The Politics of Retribution*.
Robert, General Henry, *Robert's Rules of Order* (1876), pbk edn, Spire Books, 1967.
Robson, J. M. (ed.), *Collected Works of John Stuart Mill*, vol. 19, University of Toronto Press, Toronto, 1977.
Robson, L. L., *The First AIF: A Study of its Recruitment, 1914–1918*, Melbourne University Press, Carlton, 1970.
Roe, Michael, 'The Australian legend', in Davey & Seal (eds), *Oxford Companion to Australian Folklore*.
Rowse, Tim, 'The middle class – an untidy prominence', *Thesis Eleven*, 25 (1990), pp. 147–61.
Runce, Neil, *The Economics of Instalment Credit*, Australian Studies in Economics, University of London Press, London, 1969.
Rundle, Guy & Max Gillies, *Your Dreaming: Poets, Pontificators and Expatriates*, Pluto Press, Sydney, 2002.
Ryan, Mark (ed.), *Advancing Australia: The Speeches of Paul Keating*, Big Picture Publications, Sydney, 1995.
Rydon, Joan, *The Federal Legislature: The Australian Commonwealth Parliament 1901–1980*. Oxford University Press, Melbourne, 1986.
Sawer, Geoffrey, *Australian Federal Politics and Law 1901–1929*, Melbourne University Press, Carlton, 1956.
Sawer, Geoffrey, *Australian Federal Politics and Law, 1929–1949*, Melbourne University Press, Carlton, 1963.
Schedvin, C. B., *Australia and the Great Depression: A Study of Economic Development and Policy in the 1920s and 1930s*, Sydney University Press, Sydney, 1970.
Schedvin, C. B., 'The Australian economy on the hinge of history', *Australian Economic Review*, 1st quarter, 1987, pp. 20–30.
Schedvin, C. B., 'The long and short of the Great Depression' in Cooksey (ed.), *The Great Depression in Australia*.
Schneider, Russell, *War Without Blood: Malcolm Fraser in Power*, Angus & Robertson, Sydney, 1980.
Scott, Andrew, *Running on Empty: The Modern British and Australian Labor Parties*, Pluto Press, Sydney, 2000.

Scott, Ernest, *Australia During the War*, the Official History of Australia in the War of 1914–1918, vol. 11, Robert O'Neill (ed.), University of Queensland Press, St Lucia, Brisbane, and Australian War Memorial, Canberra, 1989.

Simms, Marian & John Warhurst (eds), *Howard's Agenda: The 1998 Election*, University of Queensland Press, St Lucia, Brisbane, 2000.

Singleton, Gwynneth (ed.), *The Howard Government: Australian Commonwealth Administration, 1996–1998*, University of New South Wales Press, Sydney, 2000.

Smith, Robert A. (ed.), *Edmund Burke on Revolution*, Harper Torchbooks, Harper & Row, New York, 1968.

Snedden, Billy & M. Bernie Schedvin, *Billy Snedden: An Unlikely Liberal*, Macmillan, Melbourne, 1990.

Solomon, David (ed.), *Howard's Race: Winning the Unwinnable Election*, HarperCollins, Sydney, 2002.

Spann, R. N., 'The Catholic vote in Australia', in Henry Mayer (ed.), *Catholics and the Free Society*.

Spearritt, Peter, *Sydney's Century: A History*, University of New South Wales Press, Sydney, 2000.

Starr, Graeme, *The Liberal Party of Australia: A Documentary History*, Drummond/Heinemann, Melbourne, 1980.

Thompson, F. M. L. (ed.), *The Cambridge Social History of Britain, 1750–1950*, vol. 3, Cambridge University Press, Cambridge, 1990.

Tiver, Peter, *The Liberal Party: Principles and Performance*, Jacaranda Press, Milton, Qld, 1978.

Tracy, David, *The Analogical Imagination*, Seabuty, New York, 1982.

Turner, Graeme, *Making it National: Nationalism and Australian Popular Culture*, Allen & Unwin, Sydney, 1994.

Turner, Henry Gyles, *The First Decade of the Australian Commonwealth: A Chronicle of Contemporary Politics 1901–1910*, Mason, Firth & McCutcheon, Melbourne, 1911.

van Vree, Wilbert, *Meetings, Manners and Civilisation: The Development of Modern Meeting Behaviour*, Leicester University Press, London, 1999.

Vincent, John, *The Formation of the Liberal Party 1857–1868*, Constable, London, 1966.

Wahrman, D., *Imagining the Middle Class: The Political Representation of Class in Britain, 1780–1840*, Cambridge University Press, Cambridge, 1995.

Walsh, Maximilian, *Poor Little Rich Country: The Path to the Eighties*, Penguin, Ringwood, Victoria, 1979.

Ward, Ian, 'The changing organisational nature of Australia's political parties', *Journal of Commonwealth and Comparative Politics*, 29 (1991), pp. 153–74.

Ward, Russel, *The Australian Legend*, Oxford University Press, Melbourne, 1958.

Warhurst, John, 'Catholics, Communism and the Australian party system: a study of the Menzies years', *Politics*, 14 (November 1979), pp. 222–42.

Warhurst, John (ed.), *Keeping the Bastards Honest: The Australian Democrats First Twenty Years*, Allen & Unwin, Sydney, 1997.

Watson, Don, *Recollections of a Bleeding Heart*, Knopf, Sydney, 2002.

Watt, E. D., Western separation: the history of the Secession Movement in Western Australia, 1918–1935, MA thesis, University of Western Australia, Perth, 1957.

Webb, Leicester, 'The Australian party system' in Colin Hughes (ed.), *Readings in Australian Government*.

Whitlam, Gough, *The Whitlam Governments: 1972–1975*, Viking, Ringwood, Victoria, 1985.
Whitwell, Greg, 'Economic affairs' in Hugh Emy et al., *Whitlam Revisited*.
Whitwell, Greg, 'Economic ideas and economic policy, the rise of economic rationalism in Australia', *Australian Economic History Review*, 33 (1993), pp. 8–23.
Willard, M., *History of the White Australia Policy*, Melbourne University Press, Carlton, 1974 [1923].
Windshuttle, Keith, *Unemployment*, Penguin Books, Ringwood, Victoria, 1979.
Yeatman, Anna, 'Contract, status and personhood', in Davis, Sullivan and Yeatman (eds), *The New Contractualism*.

Rare periodicals

Australian National Review, ML
Fighting Line, ML
The Liberal, SLV
Popular Politics, SLV
United Australia Review, ML
The Vigilant, SLV
The Woman, SLV

Manuscript collections

Australian Women's National League, SLV MS 8713
Herbert Brookes, NLA MS 1924
Congregational Union, SLV MS 9239
J. Hume Cook, NLA MS 601
Elizabeth Couchman, NLA MS 2752
Alfred Deakin, NLA MS 1540
Dominion League of Western Australia, Battye Library, WA 431A
John Latham NLA MS 1009
Enid Lyons, NLA MS 4852
Joseph Lyons, NLA MS 4851
Robert Menzies, NLA MS 4936
George Meudell, SLV MS 9558
Archdale Parkhill, NLA MS 4742

Index

Abbott, Tony, 132
Aborigines, 126, 146, 158; see also indigenous issues
Adams, Philip, 207, 209
Adelaide Citizens' League, 102
affluence, 125
   post war, 135, 138, 150, 173, 178, 190
Aitkin, Don, 36, 39, 77
Albiston, Walter, 51
All for Australia Leagues, 102, 103, 104, 112, 113
alliances, 23, 114, 146
Alston, Richard, 132
anarchy, 69–75
Anderson, W. H., 5
Anstey, Frank, 20
Anzac legend, 75; see also Campbell, Alec; Gallipoli
arbitration, 21, 77, 84
aristocracy, 11, 79, 121
arts, 143, 155–6, 157
Asia, 125–6, 142, 146, 186
Australia Council for the Arts, 146
Australia Day, 47
Australia Party, 144, 159
Australian Broadcasting Corporation (ABC), 157, 207
Australian Communist Party, 73, 128–9
Australian Defensive League, 52
Australian Labor Party (ALP), 3, 4, 33, 48, 115, 117, 167
   1983 – 1996, 186
   1996 – 2003, 167, 215
   and the 'Australian legend', 203–4
   and Catholics, 35–40, 44, 52–6, 130, 132
   Federal Caucus, 18, 24, 25, 48, 94
   Federal Executive, 26
   and Liberal Protectionists, 20–1, 22–7
   loyalty of support, 5, 119
   membership, 181, 215
   Menzies on, 13–14
   and the middle class, 73, 144, 146–9, 152, 154, 156, 186–9, 203
   and party identification, 36, 188, 213
   as party of anarchy, 69–75
   organisation of, 16–18, 23, 24–7
   voting pledge, 17–18, 24, 26, 27, 40–1, 43, 46, 145
   reform of, 144–7
   refugee policy, 208
   Split, 128–30
   strengths of, 28–30
   transformation of, 167
   see also conscription; neo–liberalism; working class
'Australian Legend', 203–6
Australian Liberalism, 40, 119, 201, 205, 206
Australian Liberals, 48, 55, 69, 177
   beliefs of, 2, 9, 40, 139, 173, 213–14
   defining of, 1–7
   organisation of, 16, 27, 31–4
   philosophy of, 56, 178
   problems for, 215–17
   see also Deakin, Alfred; Liberal Party of Australia
Australian Women's Movement Against Socialisation, 118
Australian Women's National League (AWNL), 26, 28, 60, 67, 117

Bagot, Captain E. D. A., 102
Baldwin, Stanley, 79
Bank of England, 96, 97
banking, 91–2
banks, 86, 97, 98, 110, 163, 178
   attempted nationalisation, of 34, 43, 63, 91, 118
Barnett, Mark, 137
Barton, Gordon, 144, 159
Beazley, Kim, 208–9
Benson, Irving, 44

Betts, Katherine, 209–10
Black, George, 17
Blackburn Declaration, 73
Blainey, Geoffrey, 186
Bolshevik Revolution, 70, 73
Bolshevism, 72, 73, 82
bonds:
    of honour, 94–100
    war, 86–94
Boyd, Robin, 125
Bradman, Sir Donald, 205
Brennan, Frank, 101
Breward, Ian, 130
Britain, 2–3, 14–15, 68, 81, 93–4, 96; *see also* British Empire; World War I
British Commonwealth, 126
British Conservative Party, 2–3, 79–80
British Empire, 45, 47, 52, 63, 76, 78, 82, 126
    as protection, 21, 45, 76
British Labour Party, 2–3, 79
British Liberal Party, 3, 15, 25–6, 41, 42, 79
Brookes, Herbert, 28, 29, 43, 51–2, 63, 74
Broome, Richard, 38
Brown, Nicholas, 138
Bruce, Stanley Melbourne, 2, 71, 76–85, 109, 114, 162
Bruce–Page government, 80
Burke, Edmund, 3–4, 14–15, 149
business, 86, 107, 206
    and the ALP, 170
    and bonds, 89, 98, 99
    and the Liberals, 6, 159, 162
    small, 77, 135, 184, 188, 194
        and GST, 206, 209
    and the UAP, 113, 118

Calwell, Arthur, 141, 142, 145
Campbell, Alec, 204–5
Campbell, Eric, 105
Campbell Report, 163, 168
capital, 6, 76, 90, 110, 170
Carruthers, Joe, 28
Cashmore, Jennifer, 9
Catholic Social Studies Movement; *see* Movement
Catholics, 11, 45, 51, 72, 128
    and the ALP, 35–40, 44, 52–6, 129–30, 132
    and liberal parties, 35, 55, 119, 130, 132
    and party identification, 36–40, 49
    Protestant views of, 44, 46–7, 49–52
    as working class, 36–9, 130
    and WW I, 44–52

caucus, 25–6, 43
Chaney, Fred, 177, 184
character, 10, 69, 93, 108, 123, 133, 138
    Australian, 203, 204, 211
    and public order, 65
Chifley, Ben, 9, 63, 118, 129
Childe, V. G., 18
China, 143
Chipp, Don, 159–60
choice, 118, 163, 174, 177, 178
Citizens for Democracy, 156
Citizens' Leagues, 102–3, 104
citizenship, 54, 57, 121, 123, 128, 130, 175
    and the common good, 132–4
    and indigenous Australians, 197, 199–200, 202
    and individuals, 127, 214
    language of, 205, 211, 213
    and meetings, 65–9
    and the middle class, 11, 59, 60, 172–3
    order and anarchy, 69
    and organised selfishness, 139–40
    training in, 91
    and working class, 57–64
Clark, G. D., 41
Clark, Manning, 155, 156
class, 5, 20, 209
    and 1975 election, 153–4
    and the ALP, 15, 186, 188, 190
    in England, 78, 79
    and the Liberals, 15
    and the Nationalists, 84
    and political identity, 189–91
    see also middle class; working class
class conflict, 9, 11, 58, 85, 190, 215
class relations, 2, 4, 6–7, 13, 94, 122–3, 213–14
Cold War, 30, 117, 118, 119, 157
Colley, Linda, 45, 59
Collini, Stefan, 93
commonsense, 31, 107, 140, 175, 201, 209
    and the economy, 91, 179, 181, 192
    financial, 94, 106, 108, 111, 140
    and the Liberals, 31, 32, 34, 51, 176, 182
    and the Nationalists, 70
Commonwealth Bank, 88, 92, 96, 97
Commonwealth Liberal Party, 5, 23, 24–5, 26, 27, 28, 213
communism, 72–4, 82, 105, 118, 128, 161, 162
Communist Party; *see* Australian Communist Party
community, moral, 7, 210–11, 215, 216

competition, 162–3, 171–2, 174, 175–6, 179, 206
conscription, 50, 53, 75
 referenda, 48–50, 52, 61, 70, 71, 76
 and Vietnam War, 133, 142, 145
conservatism, 1–3, 19, 20, 22–3, 78–80, 145, 159, 201
 and Howard, 185, 206
 and Lyons, 105
 and Menzies, 154
Constitutional Clubs, 102
constitutional reform, 156–7
constitutionalism, 66, 78, 82
Consultative Council (NSW), 113
consumption, 100, 110, 135, 138, 150, 178, 206
Cook, Alex, 92
Cook, Hume, 20
Cook, Joseph, 17, 18, 24, 30, 48, 70
Copland, 106
cosmopolitans, 210–11, 217
Cotton, John, 41
Couchman, Elizabeth, 117
Country Party, 6, 76–7, 102, 112, 114, 115, 117, 164; *see also* National Party of Australia
Cramer, John, 35, 54, 119
credit, 97, 135–7, 178, 179
 expansion of, 96, 108, 109, 111
 and 'sound finance', 96, 110
Crisp, L. F., 6
Crossroads, 32
cultural elites, 157, 196, 206–7
Curtin, John, 114, 115

Dash, Captain G. M., 87, 88
Davies, Alan, 116
Davison, Barbara, 124
Davison, Graeme, 121, 124
De Toqueville, Alex, 64, 65
Deakin, Alfred, 1, 19, 30, 40, 41–3
 and the ALP, 70
 and Commonwealth Liberal Party, 28, 213
 and Fusion, 1, 20–7; *see also* Fusion Party
 and political organisation, 27–8
Deakinite Settlement, 21, 170
debt, 22, 81, 92, 94, 96, 97
 foreign, 81, 168
 hire-purchase, 136, 137
 personal, 135, 138
 repudiation of, 87, 94, 107, 108, 109
 war, 81, 96, 99
democracy, 15, 26, 41, 65, 69, 83, 152

Democratic Labor Party (DLP), 129, 130, 142
Democrats, Australian, 159–60
Dennis, C. J., 95
depression, 63, 74, 93–7, 100, 106, 108, 118
 1890s, 75, 122
deregulation, 163–4, 171, 176, 178
Disraeli, Benjamin, 26
Downer, Alexander, 32, 33, 166, 183, 184
drinking, 36, 132
Dunlop, Edward 'Weary', 204
duty 11, 61, 101, 134, 177
 and war bonds, 88–9, 98

economic rationalism, 160, 168–72, 174, 175, 176
economy, 77, 87–90, 167, 173
 in 1900s, 21, 76; in 1920s, 80, 81, 96; in 1930s, 107; in 1940s, 116; in 1950s, 129, 138; in 1970s, 32, 148–9; in 1980s, 149, 160–1, 162–4, 168–72, 179
 reform of, 163–5, 179–82, 183
 see also Fraser, Malcolm; Howard, John; Keynesianism; savings; thrift
education, 93, 122, 141, 145, 172, 209–10
 and the ALP, 70, 119
Edwards, John, 150, 153
Eggleston, Frederic, 34, 70, 77, 139, 214
elections, 18, 34, 166–7, 213
 1891, 16; 1894, 18; 1901, 19; 1903, 19; 1910, 5, 19, 20, 25, 26, 29, 35, 52, 213; 1911, 15; 1914, 31, 48; 1917, 48–9; 1919, 72, 76, 78; 1922, 86; 1925, 82; 1928, 84; 1929, 31, 84, 112; 1934, 113; 1937, 113; 1940, 114; 1943, 31, 115; 1946, 26, 117; 1949, 34, 35, 119, 123, 130; 1954, 119, 129; 1955, 119, 130; 1966, 142, 145; 1972, 31, 146, 147; 1975, 31, 152–6; 1977, 161; 1980, 161; 1983, 32, 149, 161, 164; 1990, 166, 179; 1993, 32, 166, 179, 181–2; 1996, 183, 188, 191; 1998, 183, 193; 2002, 183, 208, 215
Elizabeth II, 126; *see also* monarchy
Ellis, Ulrich, 103
Empire Day, 45, 47
employer groups, 153, 176
environment, 143, 146, 158
Evatt, Herbert Vere (Bert), 119, 129, 144
exports, 76, 81, 96, 164, 169–71

Fadden, Arthur, 115
family, 138, 184–5, 186, 194, 200, 215

254

farmers, 76–7, 161
Federal Liberal League, 28
Federal Parliamentary Labor Party; *see* Australian Labor Party (ALP)
federalism, 140
Fightback!, 32, 179
Fighting Line, 72, 73
finance, 78, 149
  'sound', 93–6, 108, 110, 128, 135, 138; *see also* Lyons, Joseph
financial crisis of 1930–31, 63, 108, 118
Fisher, Andrew, 43, 48, 87
foreign ownership, 143
foreign policy, 143, 145, 157
'Forgotten People, The', 7, 8, 28, 120, 155, 180, 185, 188
Fraser, Malcolm, 148, 149, 202, 203, 207
  and the economy, 149, 150–1
  and elections: 1975, 152–6; 1983, 32; 1993, 182
  in government, 31–2, 157–65
  opposition to, 156–7
  philosophy of, 149–50
free trade, 1, 17, 21
Free Traders, 18, 19, 20, 21
freedom, 13, 27, 163, 175, 177
  British, 45, 47
  of judgement, 27, 42–3, 128
  religious, 40–1, 43
Freemasons, 51
Fusion Party, 19, 40–4
  loyalty and WWI, 44–52
  meaning of, 20–7
Future Directions, 33, 184–6, 200

Gabay, Al, 42
Gaden, John, 157
Gallipoli, 75, 196, 204
gambling, 36, 132
Gibson, Sir Robert, 96
Gilbert, Alan, 37, 47
Gillies, Max, 209
globalisation, 148, 171, 203, 210, 211, 217
goods and services tax (GST), 32, 179, 182, 209
Gorton, John, 142, 143, 155, 158, 203
government, 18–19, 191
  good, 70, 76, 147
  and character, 10, 139
  and Fraser, 32, 152, 162, 165
  spending, 77, 97, 163, 167, 170
  and Fraser, 149, 150–1, 157, 158, 161, 163

Grasby, Al, 158
Greens, 216
Group, The, 104, 107
Groupers, 128, 130
Gullet, Henry, 105

Hamilton, Celia, 36
Hancock, Ian, 142
Hancock, W. K., 2, 174
Hanson, Pauline, 103, 168, 191, 209; *see also* One Nation Party
Hardy, Charles, 103
Harradine, Brian, 198
Hart, Philip, 113
Hasluck, Alexandra, 118–19
Hasluck, Paul, 119
Hawke, Bob, 161–2, 166, 179, 189
Hawker, Charles, 105
Hayden, Bill, 161
health, 145
Heathershaw, J. T., 97
Henley, Thomas, 47
Hewson, John, 32–3, 166, 173, 179–82, 183, 184
Hilliard, David, 131
Himmelfarb, Gertrude, 10
Hindle, John, 41, 46
hire purchase, 135–8, 139
history, 183, 201–2, 203, 205
Hogan, Michael, 45, 46
Holt, Harold, 30, 141–2, 143
home ownership, 8, 93, 120–5, 138, 190
homes, 86, 120
honour, 87, 91, 94–6, 98, 100, 209
Hood, Alex, 157
Horne, Donald, 125, 138, 141–4, 146, 147, 154–5, 156, 159
Howard government, 132, 172, 191, 208–9, 216
Howard, John, 32, 157, 166–7, 176, 180, 183, 206
  and the 'Australian legend', 203, 204–6
  and the battlers, 188, 189
  and class identity, 190
  creativity as leader, 127, 182, 184
  election successes, 183
  and *Future Directions*, 184–6
  and history, 202–3
  and indigenous issues, 197–202
  and the intellectual and cultural elite, 206–7, 209
  on liberalism, 1
  on multiculturalism, 195–6

255

Howard, John (cont.)
   and the national interest, 186–7, 191
   nationalism of, 211–12, 216
   and Pauline Hanson, 192, 193–4
   on race and immigration, 186, 194, 209
Hughes, Billy, 1, 75, 76, 78, 84, 114, 115
   and conscription, 48–50, 53, 71
human rights, 134, 210, 216
Humphries, Barry, 106, 156, 209
Hyde, John, 32, 182

identity:
   class, 209
   national, 8, 183, 195–6
   politics of, 56, 186
   social, 9, 132, 185, 186, 195
immigration, 81, 127, 142, 143, 186, 192, 194, 209
imperialism, 44, 45, 202
incentives, 80, 163, 175–6
income, 91, 92–3, 110, 176
   national, 8, 106, 169–70
independence, 177, 178, 190
   and party membership, 11, 13, 15, 25, 27, 40–1
   and religion, 42–4, 57
indigenous issues, 53, 147, 183–4, 186, 196–7, 214, 215
   and Hanson, 192–4
   and Howard, 185, 186, 197–202
   see also Aborigines
individualism, 117, 177–9, 184, 189, 194, 196, 215
   and organisations, 26, 28
individuality, 13, 27, 28
individuals, 127, 176, 190, 194–5, 200, 214–15
   and citizenship, 63–4, 127, 175, 214
   and class, 9, 11, 122
   and independence, 11, 13
   and interests, 69, 139, 167, 179
   and national identity, 8
   and organisations, 30
   in religions, 43, 55–6, 57
   and rights of groups, 134
   and self-interest, 175
industrial action, 16, 17, 75
Industrial Groups; *see* Groupers
industrial relations, 81–2, 84, 85, 170, 176, 206
inflation, 96, 108–12, 148, 150, 151, 160–1, 168
intellectuals, 153–7, 183, 206, 207, 211

intelligentsia; *see* intellectuals
interdependence, 90, 107, 216, 217
interests, 6–7, 69, 190, 206
   and the ALP, 187, 188
   and citizenship, 139
   and class, 10, 11, 20, 21, 39, 58, 85, 214
   economic, 213
   and the Liberals, 187
   national, 3–4, 14, 74, 140, 167, 173
      and the ALP, 11, 146, 189
      and Bruce, 80, 85
      Howard on, 186–7
      and the Liberals, 53, 54, 56, 187, 191
      and the Nationalists, 49, 74, 80, 83
   sectional, 4, 52–56, 146, 187
   special, 174
   vested, 34, 159, 173, 181, 187, 188
      and the ALP, 187
      and the Country Party, 77
      and the Liberals, 22, 70
investment, 81, 89, 96, 110, 126, 160, 169
Irish settlers, 36–7, 43, 45, 51

James, William, 93
Johnson, Paul, 92
Jones, Barry, 188

Keating, Paul, 166, 168, 179, 181, 183–4, 189, 196, 202
Kelly, Paul, 168
Kemp, David, 36, 144, 149–50
Kennett government, 172
Kerr, Sir John, 152, 154, 156
Keynesianism, 117, 135, 148, 150–1, 162, 163, 181
   and the household economy, 112, 139, 173
knowledge, 65, 140, 141, 202, 210, 211, 212
Kyabram movement, 21

La Nauze, John, 58
Labor Electoral League, 17–18
labour, 1, 16, 21, 90, 110, 170
   deregulation, 171, 176, 185
   and parties, 4, 16–17, 18, 29, 122, 189, 203
   see also Australian Labor Party (ALP); working class
labour movement, 9, 17, 29, 48, 67, 129, 187, 188
Lake, Marilyn, 7, 60
Lang, Jack, 94, 97, 101, 103, 111
Lang Labor Party, 101, 104

Latham, John, 52, 80, 81, 85, 98, 104, 112
leadership, 30–3, 149, 166, 167, 182, 204, 215
and the middle class, 10, 66, 67–8
trade union, 150, 153
legitimacy, 53, 69, 70, 71, 74, 148, 149, 154
Liberal Party of Australia, 1, 128, 166
formation of (1944–45), 13, 117–19
membership, 181, 215
organisation of, 31–3
philosophy of, 31, 127, 149, 176, 184
policy reform in, 141–3, 146–7
support for, 6–7, 119–20
see also Australian Liberals; Menzies, Robert
Liberal Protectionists, 18, 19, 20–7
Liberal, The 5, 7, 27, 28, 29, 30, 43, 51
liberalism, 1, 5, 6, 29, 40, 54–56, 200–1, 215
British, 42
economic, 182, 184, 185, 206
Little, Graham, 155
loan conversion campaign, 94–100, 103
locals, 210–11, 212
Loveday, Peter, 102
loyalty, 2, 57, 126, 129
imperial, 36, 44–52
national, 71–2, 213
party, 5, 25, 27, 56, 101, 129
Lynch, Philip, 132
Lyne, Sir William, 20
Lyons, Enid, 104, 106, 112, 136
Lyons, J. B., 136
Lyons, Joseph, 2, 102, 109, 111, 209
and debt repudiation, 87, 94–5
and loan conversion, 97–101
popularity of, 104, 105
resignation from Labor Party, 101, 102, 108, 111
and the UAP, 1, 80, 104–5, 113–4, 115

Mabo decision, 183, 184, 197
MacDonagh, Oliver, 37, 38
Macintyre, Stuart, 8
Maddox, Marion, 132
management, 171–2, 174, 175
Mannix, Daniel, 43, 49, 52, 63, 128
Markus, Andrew, 199
Marxism, 154, 189
May, A. L., 63
McCalman, Janet, 7, 10
McCormack, John, 50
McEwan, John, 141, 164

McKernan, Michael, 62
McKibbin, Ross, 93–4
McMahon, William, 143
McPhee, Ian, 177, 184
Melbourne Agreement, 97
Menzies, James, 22
Menzies, Robert, 120, 184, 189, 203
and bonds, 98
and Burke, 14
and Catholics, 35
and class relations, 8, 122, 142
and communism, 129
on conservatism, 2
cultural values of, 125–8
and debt repudiation, 107
and formation of the Liberal Party, 13–14, 116–17, 118
and individuality, 28
as leader, 30
on liberalism, 1
and the middle class, 125, 141
and political organisation, 30
and the UAP, 114–15
Merton, Robert, 210
middle class, 7–11, 34, 122, 139–44; *see also* party identification
Mill, John Stuart, 10–11, 142
Mitchell, Jean, 91
monarchy, 2, 126, 177, 203
money, 86, 89, 90–1, 94
morality, 10, 66, 68, 73, 91, 108, 160
and religion, 59, 131
Moran, Cardinal, 46
Moran, H., 38
Movement, the, 128
multiculturalism, 53, 158, 185–6, 192, 194–6, 209
Munro-Ferguson, Sir Ronald, 49
Murdoch, Walter, 58–9, 60, 64, 207
Murphy, John, 119, 124

nation, 120, 123, 139, 177, 186, 215, 216–17
and class differences, 213
and the economy, 87–90
nation-building, 61, 78, 80, 92, 133, 196
nation state, 200, 211
National Citizens' Reform, 22
National Competition Policy, 172
National Farmers' Federation, 164
National Party of Australia, 167, 171
National Union (Victoria), 113, 114, 117
nationalisation, 150; *see also* banks

nationalism, 71, 75, 97, 116, 156, 192
    and the ALP, 196, 203
    assimilationist, 185–6, 200
    British, 45, 79
    and Howard, 184, 194, 196, 206, 211–12, 216
Nationalist Party, 48, 69–76, 95, 104, 112
    and Bruce, 78, 80
    and non-party political organisations, 33, 104
    and 'Safety First', 80, 83, 86
native title, 183–4, 197–8, 209
neo-liberalism, 162, 167–8, 170, 172, 181–2
    and deregulation, 163
    and Fraser, 31–2, 149, 164
    and Hewson, 166
    and Howard, 1
    and human behaviour, 173, 192
    and the Liberal Party, 176
New Guard, 105
'new public management', 171–2, 174, 175
New South Wales Labor Party, 39
New South Wales Protestant Federation, 51
Niemeyer, Sir Otto, 96–7
non-party political organisations, 102–4, 116

obligation, 67, 177, 215, 217
    and liberalism, 195, 200
    and nation, 98, 99, 175, 211, 213, 216
    see also citizenship
occupation, 8, 37, 38
O'Farrell, Patrick, 39, 53, 54
One Nation Party, 168, 193, 209; *see also* Hanson, Pauline

Page, Earle, 76, 114
Painter, Martyn, 181
Papua New Guinea (PNG), 143
Parkhill, Archdale, 28, 112
parliamentarians, 14
    affiliations of, 36–7, 128, 132, 180–1
parties, 3–5, 13, 14–16, 217
party identification, 7, 9, 36, 181, 213, 215
    and class/religion, 36–9, 188, 207
patriotism, 62, 99, 100, 102, 119, 135
    and Britain, 45, 127
    and Catholics, 47, 48
    and war bonds, 87–90, 98
Patterson, J. B., 69
Peacock, Andrew, 32, 166, 179, 186
Pearce, George, 80, 110
People's Liberal Party, 51

People's Party (Queensland), 115
People's Party (Victoria), 28
petit bourgeois, 190–1
Petrov, Vladimir, 129
political organisation, 3, 13–19, 27–34, 60
population, 8–9, 81, 127, 169, 214
    Catholics in, 37, 45, 47
populism, 191
prejudice, 4, 37, 44, 55, 56, 197
Preston Stanley Vaughan, Millicent; *see* Vaughan, Millicent Preston Stanley
Price, Grenfell, 109
primary commodities, 76, 77, 81, 169–70
privatisation, 167, 170, 191
production, 80, 84, 90, 138
property, 73, 75, 77, 79, 92, 138
    intellectual, 164
    and party affiliation, 86
protection, 22, 24, 171, 192
    industry, 164, 167
    tariff, 17, 21, 81, 169–70
Protectionists; *see* Liberal Protectionists
protest movements, 63, 145–6, 157
Protestantism, 11, 39–41, 50–2, 214
    and Australian Liberals, 35, 36, 44, 52
    British, 41, 45, 55
    and citizenship, 57, 128
    decline of, 128–32
public choice theory, 173
public order, 65, 66, 67, 69–75, 85
public service, 164, 171–2, 173–5
    Commonwealth, 24, 31, 61, 140–141, 145
Puplick, Chris, 177
puritanism, 93
Putnam, Robert, 133

race, 45, 126–7, 177, 186, 209
racism, 158, 192, 193–5, 199, 202
Rattigan, Alf, 164
recession, 135, 160, 179, 180, 182
reconciliation, 198, 199, 201, 209
referenda:
    Aboriginal policy (1967), 142, 197, 198; banning of CP (1950), 129; Commonwealth powers (1944), 145; conscription (1916), 48; conscription (1917), 49; prices and rent control (1948), 118; republic (1999), 126; WA secessionist (1933), 104
refugee policy, 208–9, 216
Reid, George, 1, 18, 20, 21–3, 70, 72
religion, 37, 39, 41, 42–3, 55, 132; *see also* Catholics; parliamentarians; Protestantism

republicanism, 45, 75, 126, 156, 184, 203
repudiation; *see* debt
resources, 122, 143, 160, 170
Reynolds, Henry, 202
rhetoric, 180, 181–2, 184, 206
Ricketson, Staniforth, 98, 107
rights, 133–4, 175, 177, 211, 213, 215
   and citizenship, 58, 64
   individual, 139, 176, 216
   and liberalism, 200
   see also indigenous issues
Rivett, Rohan, 52, 63
Robb, Andrew, 187, 188
Robert Menzies' Forgotten People, 7, 120
Roman Catholic Church; *see* Catholics
Rundle, Guy, 209
Russia, 72–3, 118
Ryan, T.J., 49
Rydon, Joan, 39

sacrifice, 60, 61, 107, 205
   financial, 98, 151
   in war, 61, 88, 89
'Safety First', 70, 80, 86
Santamaria, B. A., 128, 129
savings, 86–92, 100, 135, 188
   and class, 92–4
   and inflation, 110–11
   and investment, 96
   and longterm prosperity, 139
   and war, 106
Schedvin, Boris, 97, 100
schools, 43, 53, 54, 91, 130, 133
Scott, Ernest, 62–3, 90
Scott, Rose, 60
Scullin government, 69, 96, 104
Scullin, James, 37, 85, 94, 97, 100–1, 108, 111
secessionist movements, 103–4
sectarianism, 35, 43, 45–55, 57, 69, 72, 129, 130
Seidler, Harry, 154
self–interest, 4, 60, 86, 173–5, 178
   subordination of, 57, 63, 65, 66, 132
self–reliance, 149, 176, 177, 190, 205
selfishness, 52, 53, 60, 139, 167, 179
service, 60–3, 69, 74, 88, 204
   ethics of, 11, 173, 174, 177
   obligations of, 59, 133
Services and Citizens Party, 10
Sinn Fein, 49, 71
Snedden, Billy Mackie, 158, 159
social capital, 65
social contract theory, 175

social democracy, 150, 163, 175, 179
social justice, 22, 132, 160, 163
socialism, 22, 72, 73, 77, 117, 118, 129, 150
'Sound Finance'; *see* finance
Soviet Union, 72–3, 118
Spann, R. N., 37, 38
stagflation, 135, 148
standard of living, 138, 139
State Savings Bank of New South Wales, 91
State Savings Bank of Victoria, 92
states, 53, 84, 103, 145, 157
   and national government, 116, 140, 143
   rights, 33, 116, 143, 145, 158
stereotypes, 37, 79, 153
strikes, 16, 53, 75, 81–3, 122, 153, 154, 160
shearers', 16, 153

Tampa, 208
tariffs, 84, 161, 164, 167, 170
Tate, Frank, 62
taxation, 32, 77, 110, 117, 140, 163, 182, 191
Taylor, Una, 124
Telstra, 191
terrorism, 208
Theodore, Ted, 87, 94, 100, 101, 108, 109, 111, 112
think–tanks, 32, 163, 164, 176, 177
thrift, 62, 87, 89–92, 106, 138, 188
trade, 18, 21, 77, 81, 168, 181; *see also* exports
trade unions, 16, 53, 77, 82, 146
   and the ALP, 144, 145, 154, 159, 190, 215
   and Bruce, 81, 85
   Catholics in, 128
   and communism, 128
   and conscription, 48
   and Fraser, 150, 151, 153, 157, 160
   and the middle class, 122

unemployment, 84, 138, 148, 150, 192
   and depression, 96, 97, 105
   and Fraser, 151, 160–1
Union Jack, 46, 71, 73, 95
United Australia Party (UAP), 1, 33, 69, 80, 104–5, 112–15
United States, 65
urban citizens' movements, 103

values, 9–10, 33, 77, 126, 127
Vaughan, Millicent Preston Stanley, 118
Victorian Protestant Federation, 51
Vietnam War, 74, 131, 142, 143
Vigilant, The, 43, 52, 54

Vincent, John, 41, 42
virtue, 9–11, 59, 87, 91, 139, 190
   Protestant, 35, 40, 57
voluntary associations, 64–5, 69
volunteers, 205, 206

Walsh, Max, 157
war bonds, 86–94
Ward, Russel, 203
Warner, Sir Arthur, 138
welfare, 134, 159, 162, 191
welfare state, 31, 140, 163, 171, 174
Western Australia, 103–4
Westminster system, 19, 31, 74
White Army, 105
White Australia, 21, 24, 45, 78, 146, 158, 192, 194
White, Patrick, 155–6
Whitlam governments, 31, 142, 147, 148, 151, 197
   and 1975 election, 152–6

Whitlam, Frederick, 144
Whitlam, Gough, 144–7, 152–6
Wik decision, 197, 198
Woman, The, 26, 29, 100
women, 59–60, 61–2, 66, 91, 107, 133
   and public order, 75, 83, 109
   and war bonds, 89, 90
women's movement, 134, 145, 158
Women's Reform League, 73
work, 184, 188–9, 190, 194
working class, 11, 36–9, 57–64, 67, 79, 92–4, 122, 130
   and the ALP, 4, 145, 213
   see also labour
World War I, 44, 61–3, 74–5, 81
   financing of, 87–90
World War II, 114, 115, 132

Yeatman, Anna, 175
Young Women's Christian Association (YWCA), 59, 133

For EU product safety concerns, contact us at Calle de José Abascal, 56–1°, 28003 Madrid, Spain or eugpsr@cambridge.org.

www.ingramcontent.com/pod-product-compliance
Lightning Source LLC
LaVergne TN
LVHW040614250326
834688LV00035B/555